SITA'S VOICE

SITA'S VOICE

in the Assamese *Rāmāyaṇa*

Selected Verses from the Rāmāyaṇa *of Mādhava Kandalī and the* Uttarakāṇḍa *of Śaṅkaradeva*

Translated and edited with an introduction by

Tilottoma Misra

ZUBAAN
128 B Shahpur Jat, 1st floor
New Delhi 110 049
Email: contact@zubaanbooks.com
Website: www.zubaanbooks.com

First published by Zubaan Publishers Pvt. Ltd 2024

10 9 8 7 6 5 4 3 2 1

ISBN: 978 93 90514 18 2 (paperback)
ISBN: 978 93 90514 27 4 (ebook)

Zubaan is an independent feminist publishing house based in New Delhi with a strong academic and general list. It was set up as an imprint of India's first feminist publishing house, Kali for Women, and carries forward Kali's tradition of publishing world quality books to high editorial and production standards. *Zubaan* means tongue, voice, language, speech in Hindustani. Zubaan publishes in the areas of the humanities, social sciences, fiction, general non-fiction, as well as books for children and young adults under its Young Zubaan imprint.

Typeset in Gentium Book Basic 11/13 by Nithya V
Printed and bound at Chaman Enterprises

Bālmīki racilā śāstra gadya padya chande
tāhāka bicāra āmi kariyā pravande
aponāra buddhi artha ji mata bujhilon
saṅkṣepa kariyā tāka pada biracilon
samasta rasaka kone janibāka pāre
pakṣī saba urai jena pakhā anusāre

Mādhava Kandalī, *Kiṣkindhākāṇḍa, 26:73–78*

[Vālmīki composed his śāstra *in poetic verse and prose. I have carefully studied that work and tried to compose these verses according to my own understanding of his work. Who can ever comprehend each and every sentiment of the poet? A bird can fly only as far as his wings will permit.]*

Karajore buddhaloka, bolo kṣemiyoka mora
āmāra ajogya iṭo karmma
Padata duṣaṇa pāi, nindibeka nujuvāi,
mahanta janara kṣamā dharmma

Śaṅkaradeva, *Uttarakāṇḍa*, 19:5

[I humbly seek the forgiveness of the wise for having taken up a task of which I am not capable. Forgiveness being the sacred dharma *of holy men, I hope they will not find fault with my verse and censure me.]*

CONTENTS

PREFACE

The *Rāmāyaṇa* tradition that has existed in Assam from around the fourteenth century or possibly even earlier has not received the same kind of scholarly attention as other South Asian traditions centred round the epic. In recent decades, several studies have focused specifically on the possibility of re-reading or questioning the tradition from diverse perspectives. These studies, however, contain very few references to the *Rāmāyaṇa* or 'Ramakatha' tradition in north-eastern India. It is in this context that I have written and translated this work on the *Rāmāyaṇa* of Mādhava Kandalī and the *Uttarakāṇḍa* by Śaṅkaradeva. My attempt in this present work has been to bring into focus the socio-political, religious and gender contexts that might have existed in north-east India in the fourteenth and fifteenth centuries and that might have inspired the vernacular poets to represent the characters and events in the epic in a certain manner.

The idea initially was to write a paper on the unique portrayal of Sītā in the Assamese *Rāmāyaṇa* of Mādhava Kandalī, Śaṅkaradeva, and Mādhavadeva, which differs in very significant ways from the way the character has been depicted in the Vālmīki text. This endeavour, which might have served as an introduction to both scholars and lay readers alike, however, ran into the difficulty of finding an authentic English translation of the five *kāṇḍas* of the *Rāmāyaṇa* of Mādhava Kandalī and the *Uttarakāṇḍa* by Śaṅkaradeva. The next step, if I wished to continue with this idea of writing about Sītā, was to attempt a translation of some selected verses from the text. In this endeavour, I realised once again that translating an Indian epic into English single-handedly, even a vernacular version of the Sanskrit text, was a daunting task. All the more so if the language used in the text belonged to an ancient variation/strand of a literary language that bears very little resemblance to the spoken languages of Assam in modern times. A large number of words used by the poets, which might have been once an intrinsic part of the spoken language of the common people, do not find any place in existing lexicons of the Assamese language. This fact added to the challenges of translation. Fully aware of the limitations of the present work, I can only hope that future scholars will take up the task of offering a more complete translation as well as an interpretation of the innumerable insights that lie embedded in it.

I would like to express my deep gratitude to Rahul Govind, who first inspired me to enter the world of the Indian *kavyas* and *mahakavyas*. Had it not been for the conversations I had with him on numerous occasions, I would never have thought it possible to shoulder a task like this. I am also grateful to my daughter Sanghamitra for helping me get access to books and journals at different stages of my work and for her patience in helping me deal with the multiple problems in the typescript of the manuscript. To both Rahul and Sanghamitra, I offer my thanks for reading the whole manuscript and providing valuable suggestions at every stage of my work. Perhaps the quality of my work would have improved significantly had I been able to incorporate in it all their suggestions. So, I alone am responsible for all the defects that remain. I owe my thanks to Dr Lilavati Saikia Bora for her generous help and suggestions in reading the text of Mādhava Kandalī. I acknowledge with gratitude the help I have received from the librarian and staff of the Gauhati University Library, Department of Historical and Antiquarian Studies, Guwahati, the Indian Institute of Advance Study, Shimla, and the Nehru Memorial Museum and Library, New Delhi.

I am grateful to Debdutta Sanyal for her painstaking work in inserting the necessary diacritical marks in my manuscript and for preparing the note on transliteration. To Udayon I am grateful for his constant support and encouragement during the long period of gestation that this work required. For their love and for being always there for me, I thank Arindam and Jaya. I also owe my thanks to my little granddaughter Anasuya, who listened eagerly to my tales from the epics and asked many questions that always set me thinking. Lastly, I take this opportunity to express my special thanks to Urvashi Butalia for her continuing faith in my work and for her helpful editorial comments and suggestions.

INTRODUCTION

Rāma, Rāma-*kathā* and the *Rāmāyaṇa* in the Assamese Tradition

The figure of Rāma has seldom attracted Assamese Vaiṣnava devotees as much as that of Kṛṣṇa. Rāma has been considered an incarnation of Viṣṇu, while Kṛṣṇa has been worshipped as Viṣṇu himself. Significantly, there is also no known religious sect in Assam that claims to be "exclusively Ramaite".[1] While there are many references to Kṛṣṇa in the copper-plate inscriptions found in Assam that date back to the early seventh century, there is hardly any mention of Rāma in the early literary records of the region. Biswanarayan Shastri has observed that, while a large number of temples dedicated to Rāma or Māruti exist all over India, there is no evidence of the existence of such a temple intact or in ruins, in Assam. According to him, even in the architecture of ancient Assam, there is no known

1 Satyendranath Sarma, *Epics and Puranas in Early Assamese Literature*, Baniprakash, Guwahati, 1972, p. 15.

evidence of the Rāma legend being represented anywhere.[2] The *Rāmāyaṇa* of Mādhava Kandalī, therefore, as well as the two *kāṇḍas* prefixed and appended to it by Mādhavadeva and Śaṅkaradeva,[3] have never held "that exalted position in popular estimation which the *Rāmacarita-mānasa* of Tulsidas has been occupying for the last few centuries in north India."[4] Rāma and Sītā seldom attained the stature of divinity in the imagination of the Assamese people, although the heroic and miraculous elements in the *Rāmāyaṇa* and 'Rāma-kathā' have continued to be a lively ingredient of folk drama and musical performances of the *ojā-pāli*.[5] It is understandable, therefore, that for the common people of this region the Assamese *Rāmāyaṇa* is hardly the religious text that the *Bhāgavata-purāṇa* is. But Śaṅkaradeva made an effort, in his own rendition of the *Uttarakāṇḍa* as well as in the interpolated verses in Mādhava Kandalī's text ascribed to him and to his disciple Mādhavadeva, to portray Rāma as the ultimate godhead, the soul of all living beings, as in other vernacular versions

---

2 Biswanarayan Shastri, "The *Rāmāyaṇa* in Assamese Literature", in V. Raghavan ed., *The Ramayana Tradition in Asia,* Sahitya Akademi, New Delhi, (1980), 2009 reprint, p. 583.

3 See pages 6-7 for biographical notes on Mādhava Kandalī and Śaṅkaradeva. Mādhavadeva (1489-1586) who was often referred to as '*prana bandhava*' (soul mate) [Neog, p. 110] by Śaṅkaradeva, was the principal disciple of the saint. He was a sensitive poet, a musician, and a scholar besides being the most diligent organiser of the Vaiṣṇava institutions set up to disseminate the religious teachings of Śaṅkaradeva.

4 Satyendranath Sarma, 1972, p. 15. Tulsidas's *Rāmacaritamānas* has been called the "Bible of northern India" by some western scholars (see John Mandeville Macfie, *The Ramayana of Tulsidas or the Bible of Northern India*, T&T Clark, Edinburgh, 1930).

5 The robust tradition of *ojāpāli* was and is still widely popular in rural Assam. This tradition has been traced back to the period between the fifteenth and sixteenth centuries CE and it evolved as a very vigorous form that was used both by the Vaiṣṇava preachers as well as by worshippers of Śiva and the mother goddesses.

of the *Rāmāyaṇa* text.[6] In his actual rendering of the character of Rāma in the *Uttarakāṇḍa*, however, there is no attempt to tone down the apparent weaknesses in the character of the hero. Readers are often bewildered by the critical portrayal of this divine being, which comes through not only in Sītā's severe indictment of his unjust behaviour towards her but also in the poet's own narration of the story.

In the first half of the fourteenth century CE, Mādhava Kandalī, also known as Kavirāja Kandalī, composed his *Saptakāṇḍa Rāmāyaṇa* in the literary vernacular of Assam. In one of the several colophonic verses that intersperse the text, the poet states that he has rendered the *Rāmāyaṇa* of Vālmīki into the "language of man" at the request of the Barāhi king Mahāmāṇikya, who was ruling over central Assam around that time. Śaṅkaradeva pays unstinting compliments to his predecessor Mādhava Kandalī for being "faultless" (*apramādī*) poet whose style cannot be matched by any later poet, including himself.[7] Mādhava Kandalī's *Rāmāyaṇa* has been considered one of the earliest vernacular renderings of the epic into verse in northern India. It predates Kṛttibāsa's Bengali *Rāmāyaṇa* (fifteenth century CE), Tulsidāsa's *Rāmacaritamānasa* (sixteenth century CE), and the Oriya *Jagamohana Rāmāyaṇa* of Balarāma Dāsa (sixteenth century CE). Mādhava Kandalī claims in a colophonic verse at the end of his *Laṅkākāṇḍa*

---

6 In the devotional verses that conclude his *Uttarakāṇḍa*, Śaṅkaradeva says, "*Rāma mor iṣṭa deva, Rāmakehe kara sevā, gati mor Rāmar caraṇa / Rāma dharma, Rāme karmma, Rāmase bāndhava marma, jāni lailu Rāmara caraṇa śaraṇ.*" ["My only god is Rāma. He is the fountain of all my actions and my devotion. He is my only friend and hence I seek salvation at his feet"].

7 "My predecessor Mādhava Kandalī, who is a poet without a flaw, rendered the story of Rāma into verse. In comparison, my effort is as futile as that of a rabbit aspiring to produce the dung of an elephant." (*Uttarakāṇḍa*, 19:6).

that he had rendered his "seven-*kāṇḍa*" *Rāmāyaṇa* in verse;[8] but the *Ādikāṇḍa* and the *Uttarakāṇḍa*, even if they had been part of the original work, are absent from the copies of the manuscripts that have been in circulation since the neo-Vaiṣṇava period, which began in the fifteenth century with the advent of Śaṅkaradeva and his disciples, who initiated a vigorous movement for the dissemination of the *ekaśaraṇa nāma-dharma*. One can therefore only conjecture about the existence or non-existence of these *kāṇḍas* in the original Mādhava Kandalī text. But, as stated in the *Kathā Guru Carita*, Śaṅkaradeva and his disciple Mādhavadeva had decided to complete the vernacular *Rāmāyaṇa* of Mādhava Kandalī by supplementing the initial and concluding books that were missing in the available text. There are various scholarly opinions that suggest differing views on the original size of the Vālmīki *Rāmāyaṇa*. According to one, the *Saptakāṇḍa Rāmāyaṇa* which is now accepted as the original Sanskrit *Rāmāyaṇa*, has been in circulation probably from around the second or third century CE. Satyendranath Sarma, however, is among those who have a different view. According to him, the *Ādikāṇḍa* and the *Uttarakāṇḍa* were not integral parts of the original Vālmīki text but were later additions to it. To prove this point, he has argued that the concluding verses of the *Yuddhakāṇḍa* in the Vālmīki text indicate that the poet meant these to be the concluding verses of the epic, because it is the prevailing tradition to conclude an epic with the *phalasruti* (punchline). The Narada narrative in the *Ādikāṇḍa* also does not refer to the events in the Uttarakāṇḍa. The *Ādikāṇḍa* and *Uttarakāṇḍa* contain many episodes related to the birth of Hanumāna, Vāli-Sugrīva, and several *asuras*, including stories related to the birth of Rāvaṇa. Also, several episodes unrelated to the main story of Rāma-Sītā, including the killing of Śambuka by Rāma,

---

8 *"sapta kāṇḍa Rāmāyaṇa padabandhe nibandhila..."*

have been ascribed to later brahmanical interpolations. According to Sarma, the *Adikāṇḍa* and *Uttarakāṇḍa* have been added to the Vālmīki text in order to bestow divinity on Rāma, whereas in the central five *kāṇḍas* of the Vālmīki text, Rāma has been depicted more as an ideal male than as a god. These and other arguments, according to Sarma, based on the study of the structure and verse form of the Sanskrit *Rāmāyaṇa,* point towards the fact that there had been in existence an older tradition of accepting the *Rāmāyaṇa* only with five *kāṇḍas.*[9] However, referring to the critical edition of the *Rāmāyana,*[10] which includes many of the passages suspected to be later interpolations, Sheldon Pollock, in his discussion of the divinity of Rāma, rejects the views of western scholars like A.W. von Schlegel and Christian Lassen, who have questioned the authenticity of those portions of the epic which bestow divinity on Rāma. Pollock states emphatically that Rāma's divinity has always been an "integral and authentic feature of the poem" and that, in the whole history of indigenous scholarship on the epic, never has any doubt been cast on this status of the hero, and "never, for example, was the suspicion ever voiced that those portions of the epic explicitly positing Rāma's status as an incarnation of Viṣṇu were deliberate, and unassimilable, sectarian interpolations."[11]

---

9 Satyendranath Sarma, *Ramayanar Itibritta*, Dibrugarh University, 1984, pp. 7-9.

10 *The Vālmīki Rāmāyaṇa: Critical Edition.* (1960-1975). 7 vols. Baroda: Oriental Institute. General editors: G.H. Bhatt and U.P. Shah.

11 Sheldon Pollock, Introduction to *The Rāmāyaṇa of Vālmīki* , *Volume III: Aranyakanda*, Motilal Banarasidass, Delhi, 2007, p. 15.

The *Kathā Guru Carita*[12] assigns a miraculous authority to the task undertaken by Śaṅkaradeva to complete the work of Mādhava Kandalī, who was said to have appeared to Śaṅkaradeva in a dream, appealing to him to save his *Rāmāyaṇa* from the hands of plagiarists. This might be a reference to endeavours made by Ananta Kandalī, a sixteenth-century Assamese Vaiṣṇava poet and a contemporary of Śaṅkaradeva, to re-write Mādhava Kandalī's *Rāmāyaṇa* with appropriate *bhakti* content inserted into it because the earlier text was found to be lacking in the devotional element. Śaṅkaradeva, however, decided to keep the Mādhava Kandalī text intact, introducing the *bhakti* element only at the beginnings and ends of verses, "like the floral motifs in the fringes" of woven garments.[13] In his version of the *Uttarakāṇḍa*, therefore, Śaṅkaradeva seeks to retain the style and mode of versification of Mādhava Kandalī's text, though Rāma's

---

12 *Kathā Guru Carita,* edited by Upendrachandra Lekharu, was the first printed version of a manuscript obtained from Barpeta Satra by Banikanta Kakati. This edition contains a Foreword by Banikanta Kakati and Birinchi Kumar Barua, Guwahati, 1952 [reprint edition, Dattabarua, Guwahati, 2006, p. 119]. Maheswar Neog subsequently edited and published it again in 1980 as *Guru-carita-kathā.* According to Neog, "The author of this voluminous work does not subscribe his name to the work; nor is its place of writing mentioned. But from circumstantial evidences it has been considered as having been written in the Barjaha-satra, Nowgong, in the early decades of the eighteenth century" (Maheswar Neog, *Early History of the Vaisnava Faith and Movement in Assam*, 1998 (third edition), p. 20). Banikanta Kakati and Birinchi Kumar Barua in their Foreword to the first edition have said, "of all the biographies of the Vaisnavite saints of Assam hitherto discovered the *Kathā Guru Carita* appears not only to be the most voluminous and complete but very trustworthy and authoritative as it was compiled within the sacred precincts of a Satra."

13 According to the *Katha Guru Carita,* Śaṅkaradeva told his disciple Mādhavadeva that there was an attempt by Ananta Kandalī to obliterate the "*śāstra*" composed in verse by Mādhavadeva's namesake. So he entrusted Mādhavadeva with the beginning while he himself composed the concluding part, thus retaining the whole intact but embellishing it with appropriate "advice" (*upadeśa).* Earlier, there was no *upadeśa* in the text, only benedictions ("*sādhu, sādhu*"). See *Kathā Guru Carita,* edited by Upendra Chandra Lekharu, p. 119.

divinity is extolled here as in all *bhakti* texts.[14] It is important to mention that, although Śaṅkaradeva celebrates the unquestioned greatness of his predecessor, his *Uttarakāṇḍa* bears evidence of his own creative genius, not only in his handling of the vernacular with great competence, but also in his depiction of the last part of the epic, especially in the characterisation of Rāma and Sītā, for which he was not dependent on his predecessor Mādhava Kandalī. It is precisely because of the innovations in the handling of the story, characterisation, and elevation of the common speech into a nuanced poetic medium that Śaṅkaradeva's *Uttarakāṇḍa* deserves to stand on its own as a discrete text.

The Assamese *Rāmāyaṇa* of Mādhava Kandalī is not simply a pale precis of a standard Rāmāyaṇa narrative nor a literal translation of the Vālmīki text, but a broadly faithful version of it, with several abridgements, embellishments, and omissions. The fourteenth-century Assamese poet, it has been claimed, catered to popular taste in making the alterations.[15] In one of his characteristic signature passages, Mādhava Kandalī makes the authorial statement that his composition is based on his own understanding of the Vālmīki text and that he has taken the liberty to summarise certain portions in order to cater to the taste of the common readers/listeners. The poet, therefore, gives the disclaimer that his is a worldly story, not a divine revelation, thus releasing his text from any religious

---

14 It would be pertinent to mention here that *bhakti* needs to be differentiated into at least three categories in the Assamese *Rāmāyaṇa*: the devotional elements already present in the Mādhava Kandalī text, the *bhakti* that was sought to be introduced by the Vaiṣṇava poet Ananta Kandalī, and the *bhakti* elements that were introduced by Śaṅkaradeva and Mādhavadeva, which were obviously meant to give a devotional substance to the text without interfering with its original unique character as a vernacular text with a difference.

15 See Satyendranath Sarma, *Ramayanar Itibritta*, Dibrugarh University, 1984, p. 259, 264, 289; Basanta Kumar Dev Goswami, *A Critical Study of the Ramayana Tradition of Assam*, Punthi Pustak, Calcutta, 1994, p. 172.

associations.[16] In the light of such confessions, it would be interesting to study how, in the hands of the Assamese *Rāmāyaṇa* poets writing between the fourteenth and sixteenth centuries, the character of Sītā attains new dimensions in conformity with the prevailing cultures of eastern India around that period.

Mādhava Kandalī's *Rāmāyaṇa,* as available today in five parts, is steeped in the *bhakti-rasa,* especially in the introductory and concluding verses of some of the chapters. Scholars have conjectured, however on the basis of information provided in the *Kathā Guru Carita,* that the two Vaiṣṇava poets, Śaṅkaradeva and Mādhavadeva, introduced the *bhakti* elements into the text of Mādhava Kandalī because it was found to be deficient in that regard. Significantly, though, the interpolations by the later Vaiṣṇava poets do not affect the main text, in which Rāma, Lakṣmaṇa, and Sītā are portrayed as human beings whose human frailties make them more appealing to the audience, as in Vālmīki's text. The insertion of the bhakti elements increased the importance of the work as a *bhakti* text, but at the same time the whole enterprise required a revision and editing of the original work, which endowed the text with features that were probably absent in the original work.[17] However, despite such attempts to transform the text into a *bhakti* text, the Assamese *Rāmāyaṇa* of Mādhava Kandalī, Śaṅkaradeva, and Mādhavadeva can still be read as a significant regional version of the epic in which the central characters bear the stamp of the poets' understanding of the contemporary local context.

---

16 "This composition is not in the language of the gods but in that of the common man" ("*deva vāṇī nuhi iṭo loukika se kathā*"). *Saptakāṇḍa Rāmāyaṇa*, by Mādhava Kandalī, *Kiṣkindhākāṇḍa*, Chapter 26.

17 See M. Neog, "Assamese Literature before Śaṅkaradeva", in Banikanta. Kakati edited, *Aspects of Early Assamese Literature*, Gauhati University, 1953, p. 28.

According to Ramcharan Thakuria, who has collated four of the *kāṇḍas* of Mādhava Kandalī's text, no attempt had previously been made to collate or write a complete history of all the available manuscripts.[18] The oldest available manuscript is from the latter half of the sixteenth century. No complete list of all the manuscripts has ever been prepared. Hence, the number of extant manuscripts remains uncertain. Thakuria refers to as many as 42 versions of the different *kāṇḍas*, which he has come across in Hemchandra Goswami's *Descriptive Catalogue of Assamese Manuscripts* and in the handwritten catalogues preserved in the library of the Department of Historical and Antiquarian Studies and the Kamrup Anusandhan Samity at Guwahati, the Barpeta Satra, the Chamaria Satra, and the Haigriva Madhava temple at Hajo, and the library of Gauhati University. Of these, only one manuscript was found to be complete, with five *kāṇḍas* composed by Mādhava Kandalī—Ayodhyā, Araṇya, Kiṣkindhā, Sundara, and Laṅkā—and the Ādi and Uttara *kāṇḍas* composed by Mādhavadeva and Śaṅkaradeva respectively. All the printed editions of the text of Mādhava Kandalī's *Rāmāyaṇa* are based on this manuscript, which is available in the Department of Historical and Antiquarian Studies, Guwahati.[19] Though there are two available copies of the manuscript of Śaṅkaradeva's *Uttarakāṇḍa*, both of which are in the possession of the Kamarupa Anusandhan Samity, Hemchandra Goswami, in his *Descriptive Catalogue of Assamese Manuscripts*, gives the details of only one, which bears the date *Śaka* 1740. The other one,

18 Ramcharan Thakuria, *The Rāmāyaṇa of Mādhava Kandalī: A Text-critical and Historical Study of Four Kāṇḍas of Rāmāyaṇa, viz., Ayodhyā, Araṇya, Kiṣkindhā, and Sundara Kāṇḍas*, unpublished thesis, Gauhati University, 1983, chapter 2.

19 The available printed editions of the text are: (1) *Sampurna Asamiya Sat-kanda Ramayana*, edited by Madhavchandra Bardalai, Barpeta, 1899; (2) *Asamiya Sat-kanda Ramayana*, ed. by Prasannalal Chaudhury, Barpeta, 1941; (3) *Sapta-kanda Ramayana*, ed. by Harinarayan Datta Barua, Nalbari, 1952; (4) *Kaviraja Madhavakandali Virachita Ramayana*, ed. by Kanakchandra Sarma, Bebejia, 1941 (reprinted Lawyers' Book Stall, Guwahati, 2008).

according to him is named *Lakṣmaṇa-Barjan.*[20] The present translations of verses from Mādhava Kandalī's *Rāmāyaṇa* and Śaṅkaradeva's *Uttarakāṇḍa* are based on the printed version of the text edited by Kanakchandra Sarma.

Orthographical Problems in the Texts

Śaṅkaradeva referred to Mādhava Kandalī as an "unerring" poet of the earlier times (*"pūrba kavi apramādī"*). The available manuscripts, none of which bear the signature of the poet himself but belong to a later date, show several variations in the spellings of words. Many of the errors in spelling may have been because of the ignorance or carelessness of the scribes. A more plausible explanation for the supposed "errors" has been given by Maheswar Neog in his preface to the *Orunodoi.* Rejecting the views of some of the Christian missionaries, who, having undertaken the project of standardizing the language, dismissed the old Assamese language as lacking any standard and consisting of "slovenly modes of pronunciation and capricious varieties of spelling", Neog says that diligent textual criticism can indicate some specific methods in the so-called slovenly spellings.[21] A study of the ancient Assamese scripts found in rock inscriptions and copper plates may lead to the conclusion that the old Assamese writings must have had a special history and standard of their own, which was followed in the works of the writers like Mādhava Kandalī. Words borrowed from one language by another, according to Neog, usually conform to the

---

20 Hemchandra Goswami, *Descriptive Catalogue of Assamese Manuscripts*, University of Calcutta, 1930, pp. 149–150

21 *The Orunodoi 1846-1854 (monthly magazine devoted to religion, science and general intelligence)*, edited by Dr. Nathan Brown, compiled and re-edited by Maheswar Neog, Publication Board Assam, Guwahati, 1983, Preface, p. 125.

norms of spelling and pronunciation of the new language. So, Sanskrit words, when they reached Assam after passing through various stages of Magadhi and Prakrit, attained a specific *tadbhava* form in Assam. It would be wrong, therefore, to try and "correct" the spellings of such words and write them as in the original Sanskrit. The available printed texts of Mādhava Kandalī's *Rāmāyaṇa* and Śaṅkaradeva's *Uttarakāṇḍa* have, however, not adhered to this principle but have used a more modern system of orthography. Despite orthographical variations in the manuscripts of the texts, most scholars have agreed that "the peculiar Assamese pronunciations" which are entirely different from the modern Bangla or Hindi pronunciation of such words, have been "consistently maintained" in all the old Assamese texts, including those of Hema Sarasvatī and Mādhava Kandalī.[22]

The Life and Works of Mādhava Kandalī and Śaṅkaradeva

Considering the significance of Mādhava Kandalī's vernacular rendering of Vālmīki's *Rāmāyaṇa* as early as the middle of the fourteenth century, surprisingly little is known about the poet and his times except for the scanty material available in a few colophonic verses in the text and an uncorroborated reference in the *Kathā Guru Carita*. There is little material to fall back upon in order to construct a story about the life and works of this poet. The *Kathā Guru Carita* mentions a Mādhava Kandalī who was the guru of a Brahmin pundit named Raghavācārya. Raghavācārya was said to have visited the *ṭol* where Śaṅkaradeva studied, which leads us merely to the conjecture that Mādhava

22 Kaliram Medhi's Preface to Hema Saraswati's *Prahlāda Carita*, cited in Ramcharan Thakuria, p. lxxii.

Kandalī might have belonged to the same region in central Assam where Śaṅkaradeva was born.[23] But one cannot be sure if this Mādhava Kandalī was the same as the *Rāmāyaṇa* poet to whom Śaṅkaradeva reverentially refers as his unparalleled predecessor. Most scholars agree that Mādhava Kandalī or Kavirāja Kandalī, probably lived in the present-day Nagaon district of Assam, because there was a *moujā* in that district where some families bearing the name Kandalī were known to have resided.[24] As stated in the *Laṅkākāṇḍa* of his *Rāmāyaṇa,* he rendered the verses of the *Rāmāyaṇa* into local speech at the request of his patron, the Barāhi king Mahāmāṇikya. Mādhava Kandalī has also been credited with another composition, named *Devajit*. According to Hemchandra Goswami,[25] only one manuscript copy of this text is available, which bears the date 1885 CE. The 744 available verses of this manuscript describe the battle between Arjuna and Indra, during which Kṛṣṇa acted as Arjuna's charioteer and guide. In a colophon, the poet, calling himself Mādhava Kandalī, claims that the story has been taken from the *Padma-purāṇa*. Though the poem bears ample evidence of being influenced by Vaiṣṇava ideals, scholars are doubtful whether the author is the Mādhava Kandalī of the Assamese *Rāmāyaṇa* or some other later and inferior poet bearing that same name.[26]

---

23 Upendra Chandra Lekharu ed., *Kathā Guru Carita*, p. 20.

24 Satyendranath Sarma, *Ramayanar Itibritta*, p. 253.

25 Hemchandra Goswami, *Descriptive Catalogue of Assamese Manuscripts*, pp. 44–45.

26 Satyendranath Sarma, *Asamiya Sahityer Samikshatmak Itibritta*, p. 83.

The life and works of Śaṅkaradeva (1449-1568)[27] have been recorded, thanks to the efforts of his numerous disciples, in many *caritas* or hagiographies. Among these may be mentioned *Śrī-guru-varṇanā* of Aniruddha Dāsa, Bhūṣaṇa Dvija's *Mahāpuruṣa Śaṅkaradeva*, Daityāri Ṭhākur's *Śaṅkaradeva-Mādhavadeva Jīvana-carita*, Rāmacarana Ṭhākur's *Śaṅkara-carita*, Ramānanda Dvija's *Guru-carita.* The *Bardowā-guru-carita* and *Kathā-guru-carita* of anonymous authorship are also considered valuable sources of information on the lives and works of Śaṅkaradeva and Mādhavadeva. From all these sources, Śaṅkaradeva's genealogy as well as the approximate dates of various events and activities in his life can be constructed successfully. Śaṅkaradeva himself has traced his genealogy in the colophonic verses of his *Uttarakāṇḍa* as well as in certain verses of his *Amṛta-manthana, Ajāmilopākhyāna,* and the tenth book of the Bhagawata. From all these accounts, it can be surmised that the saint belonged to a family of Kāyastha Bāra Bhuñās who were powerful feudal chiefs in Assam and who ruled over territories adjacent to the kingdoms of the Cuṭīyās and the Kachārīs before the Ahoms established their rule in all these areas. The *caritas* have referred to the migration of the Bāra Bhuñās, the ancestors of Śaṅkaradeva, from Kanaujapārā to the kingdom of Gauḍeśvara and thence to Kāmarūpa during

27 Though scholars have mostly agreed upon *Śaka* 1490 (1568 CE) as the date on which the saint died, there are diverse opinions about the date of his birth. Edward Gait would suggest a later date, thirty or forty years after 1449 CE, as the more probable date of his birth. However, almost all the *caritas* or the lives of the saints have allowed him "a duration of life covering roughly 120 years, the full span attributed to a *mahapurusha.*" (see Maheswar Neog, *Early History of the Vaisnava Movement*, p. 98.). Recent scholarship on the subject, however, tends to favour the date suggested by Aniruddha Dasa (1651-1717) as a more plausible date of Śaṅkaradeva's birth. According to this view, Śaṅkaradeva was born in 1463 CE and lived for 105 years. (For details of this academic debate, refer to Baniprasanna Misra's *Srimanta Śaṅkaradeva and His Times: Some Further Historical Problems*, Tezpur University, 2016, pp. 3–15.)

the reign of the Koch king Durlabhanārāyaṇa. It was Durlabhanārāyaṇa who requested Canḍīdāsa, the great-great-grandfather of Śaṅkaradeva, to settle at Bardowa in central Assam. This region, situated on the southern bank of the Brahmaputra, was a fertile area and the Bāra Bhuñās family ruling over the region was the target of constant raids by the neighbouring Kachārī rulers. In his *Uttarakāṇḍa*, Śaṅkaradeva describes his ancestral land with pride and happiness: "Situated favourably on the banks of the Louhitya was the village of Bardowa, which had an abundance of fish and crops. Rajādharā, the lotus of the Kāyastha clan, was the master of this village."[28] Śaṅkaradeva, who was the great-grandson of Rajādharā, was born in a village named Alipukhuri near Bardowa. His father was Kusumbara and his mother Satyasandhyā. Both his parents died early and the boy was brought up by his grandmother Khersuti with affection and care. He was educated at the Sanskrit *ṭol* of the Brahmin teacher Mahendra Kandalī, where he studied the Vedas, the Upaniṣadas, the epics, the Saṃhitās, the tantras, and the *kāvyas*, besides grammar and the lexicon. After the completion of his school education, he was said to have taken up his responsibilities as a leader of the Bāra Bhuñā clan and also fulfilled his duties as a householder. At the age of thirty-two, Śaṅkaradeva left home on his first pilgrimage. According to the *Kathā-guru-carita*, he visited almost all the important pilgrimage centres in northern and southern India connected with Kṛṣṇa and Rāma worship. He finally settled down for a considerably long sojourn in Jagannath Puri, where he came into contact with different shades of Vaiṣṇava thought and got initiated into the *Bhāgavata-purāṇa*, which became central to his religious preaching later. After about twelve years of pilgrimage, Śaṅkaradeva returned home to Bardowa and

---

28 Śaṅkaradeva,'Uttarakāṇḍa', *adhyāya* 19.

began disseminating his religious teachings in innovative ways through music, dance, and dramatic performances.

However, Śaṅkaradeva was compelled to leave the Bāra Bhuñā territory and migrate to the northern bank of the Brahmaputra because of increasing hostility from the Kachārīs in the neighbourhood. He moved with his kinsmen and the disciples to places like Singari, Gangmau, Rauta, Ghiladhari, and finally settled in Dhuwahat. It was here that he first met Mādhavadeva, "a scholar, poet, and fine singer",[29] who became his greatest and most gifted disciple. This was the period when Śaṅkaradeva established himself as the foremost Vaiṣṇava preacher in Assam and a large number of followers joined him and became a part of the new Vaiṣṇava fraternity. However, his growing fame attracted the attention of the Ahom ruler, who considered his religion a threat to the *śākta* worship conducted by Brahmin priests, which had been patronised by the Ahoms until then. In the face of the persecution unleashed by the Ahom king, Śaṅkaradeva was compelled to migrate once again, this time to the Koch kingdom of Kāmarūpa. He changed his residence several times in the region near Barpeta and finally settled down at Patbausi, where, except for a brief pilgrimage to Puri, he spent most of his time until his death in 1568 CE. While in the Koch kingdom, Śaṅkaradeva once again faced the hostility of the Brahman priests in the royal court of Naranārāyaṇa. Apprehending that the growing popularity of Śaṅkaradeva's teachings amongst the masses would pose a threat to their own vocation, they sought the intervention of the king to restrain the activities of the saint and his disciples in the kingdom. However, Śaṅkaradeva was fortunate to receive the protection of the king's powerful brother Cilārāya, and he was given a safe passage to the royal court, where

---

29 Maheswar Neog, *Vaisnava Faith and Movement in Assam*, p. 110.

he impressed the king with his knowledge, scholarship, and his spiritual mission. Naranārāyaṇa offered him friendship and protection for the rest of his stay in the Koch kingdom. [30]

Śaṅkaradeva's life and work prove beyond doubt his versatile genius and multi-faceted personality. He was a preacher who established *ekaśaraṇa nāmadharma* that evolved into a vigorous social movement, inspiring an inclusive humane attitude towards religion and dispelling the stranglehold of brahmanical despotism that kept the religious texts out of reach of the common people. The process of rendering Sanskrit texts into the local language that had started about a hundred years previously reached its full maturity during the time of Śaṅkaradeva. Śaṅkaradeva was, however, not only a translator of the epics and *purāṇas* but also displayed considerable creative genius in adapting the texts to suit local needs, and he achieved this by borrowing elements from various folk traditions and introducing them into his religious drama, dance, music, and songs. Śaṅkaradeva rendered several *skandhas* of the *Bhāgavata-purāṇa* into Assamese as well as a large number of tales drawn from it. The *Kīrtana-ghoṣa*, considered the poet's magnum opus, was written by him over various phases in his life and completed while he was in the Koch kingdom. The *Guṇamālā*, which contains the essence of the *Bhāgavata-purāṇa* in 378 "nimble six-syllable

---

30 It may be mentioned that the Koch kings, like the Kachārī rulers, were *śākta* worshippers, according to historical records. The ancient reigning deity of Kāmatāpura, the capital of the Koch kingdom, was the goddess Kāmateśvarī. There are also stories about the disappearance/destruction of the temple of goddess Kāmākhyā in Kāmarūpa at some point and its being re-built by the Koch king Naranārāyan (see Khan Choudhury Amanatulla Ahmed, *Kochbeharar Itihas*, p. 127–128). According to some of the *caritas*, King Naranārāyaṇa, after he had met Śaṅkaradeva, had requested the Vaiṣṇava guru to initiate him into the Vaiṣṇava religion preached by him. But Śaṅkaradeva either declined to do so or passed away before he could decide (see Maheswar Neog, *Early History of the Vaisnava Faith and Movement in Assam*, p. 120).

rhyming quadruplets,"[31] was completed in the Koch capital and presented to Naranārāyaṇa at his request. This work is considered to be one of the greatest achievements of Śaṅkaradeva. He is said to have composed a large number of Vaiṣṇava hymns (*bargīta*) set to classical *rāgas*, though only about thirty-four of them have survived. He wrote several *aṅkīya-nāṭas* and enacted them before rural audiences at different locations. The best known amongst them, which are still widely popular in Assam, are *Patnīprasāda, Pārijāta-haraṇa-nāṭa, Kālīdamana yātrā, Rukmiṇī-haraṇa-nāṭa, Keligopāla-nāṭa,* and *Rāmavijaya-nāṭa. Kurukṣetra*, a dramatic rendering of chapters 82-85 of the tenth book of the *Bhāgavata-purāṇa*, is said to be a later composition of the saint, but it does not bear his characteristic signature lines anywhere in the text. The *Uttarakāṇḍa* of the *Rāmāyaṇa* rendered by Śaṅkaradeva into the literary language of Assam, which had attained a great deal of maturity since the time of Mādhava Kandalī, is in many ways different from his other translations or adaptations because, despite all the verses in praise of the divine self of Rāma that have been generously introduced into the text , Śaṅkaradeva's critical assessment of Rāma's personality, which expresses itselfthrough the apparent mood of devotion, sets this text apart from all his other works as a composition that rises above a mere verbatim translation of the Sanskrit text.

The figure of Kṛṣṇa occupies the central position in five of Śaṅkaradeva's plays: *Patnīprasāda, Rukmiṇī-haraṇa, Pārijāta-haraṇa, Keli-gopāla,* and *Kālī-damana*. It is only in *Rāma-vijaya*, the very last amongst his dramatic compositions, that Rāma is portrayed as the central character. The hero in all the plays of Śaṅkaradeva possesses divine attributes—he is dignified and patient (*dhīra*) and sometimes indulges

31 Maheswar Neog, p. 183.

in softer moments of dalliance (*lalita*) when he is in the company of the female characters or his playmates. Śaṅkaradeva wrote very few *bargītas* in which Rāma is the central object of the devotee's attention. According to his biographers, Śaṅkaradeva had confessed that, whenever he tried to narrate the story of Rāma, he unconsciously started relating the story of Kṛṣṇa, thereby acknowledging his total devotion to the latter.[32] However, one of the most popular hymns (*śuna śuna re sura bairī pramāṇā*), composed by him in the *Āśovārī rāga*, recreates the scene of the battle between the forces of Rāma and Rāvaṇa with the help of powerful images. The brisk staccato rhythm of the eighteen lines of verse conveying the sights and sounds of the battlefield makes it one of the most memorable compositions of Śaṅkaradeva.

The *Ādikāṇḍa* of Mādhavadeva and the *Uttarakāṇḍa* of Śaṅkaradeva, which complete the Assamese *Rāmāyaṇa* of Mādhava Kandalī, are significant components of the neo-Vaishnavite *bhakti* literature of Assam. In the *Uttarakāṇḍa* of Vālmīki, only about one-third of the book deals with the Rāma-Sītā story. The first part of the book (about thirty-five chapters) is devoted mainly to the genealogies of the *rākṣasas* and of the monkey-hero Hanumanta.[33] In the *Uttarakāṇḍa,* Śaṅkaradeva has largely avoided all the portions that have no direct link with the Rāma-Sītā story, though he has skilfully brought in some portions of Rāvaṇa's past life, especially his encounter with Sahasrārjuna, Vāli, and Balirāya (*Adhyāya* 13), through the recital of Lava and Kuśa. There is also another significant omission in Śaṅkaradeva's text: there is no mention here of the story of Rāma killing the *śudra* Śambuka for

32 Maheswar Neog, *Early History of the Vaishnava Faith and Movement in Assam*, p. 194.

33 Satyendranath Sarma, *Epics and Puranas in Early Assamese Literature*, p. 33.

committing the transgression of performing a vedic sacrifice, which is included in the Vālmīki text.[34]After killing Śambuka, Rāma earns the praise of all the gods and Brahmins for setting his kingdom free from the grave sin committed by the *śudra,* who was posing a challenge to the existing caste structure. This story has been cited by numerous scholars as one of the questionable actions of Rāma that cannot be easily justified as an instance of *dharma* or morally correct behaviour. In some of the later versions of the epic, this controversial episode has been retold in order to infuse it with some moral justification and absolve Rāma of any blame for the deed. For instance, where the Vālmīki text gives the offending *śudra* no chance to save himself from Rāma's sword, the *Ānanda Rāmāyaṇa* of the fourteenth or fifteenth century CE tries to introduce "elements of Rāma's divinity and Śambuka's *bhakti*" into the tale, which provides sufficient justification for the deed to reassure the devotees of Rāma about the righteousness of his behaviour.[35] Śaṅkaradeva, who was a Vaiṣṇava but a *kāyastha* and had to encounter the fierce hostility of the Brahmin priests for his effort to establish a path of devotion based on a more egalitarian mode of worship, could not have whitewashed the story of Rāma and Śambuka to make it acceptable to his disciples. Interestingly, Śaṅkaradeva omits not only this story from his text but also the whole section in the Vālmīki text that deals with the story of Nārada advising Rāma to defend the concept of an ideal Rāmarājya in which the traditional hierarchical order of society is to be maintained.[36]

---

34 *Vālmīki Rāmāyaṇa*, 'Uttarakāṇḍa', in *Śrīmad Vālmīkīya Rāmāyana*, Volume 2, (with Hindi translation), Gita Press, Gorakhpur, 47th reprint, Sarga 76.

35 Vidyut Aklujkar, "Crying Dogs and Laughing Trees in Rama's Kingdom: Self-reflexivity in *Ananda Ramayana*", in Paula Richman ed., *Questioning Ramayana*, p. 96.

36 'Uttarakāṇḍa' in *Śrīmad Vālmīkīya Rāmāyaṇa, Sarga* 73-75.

It is because of this decision to re-tell the tragic end of the Rāma-Sītā story in his own way that Śaṅkaradeva calls his version '*Uttarakāṇḍara kathāsāra*', or the essence of the *Uttarakāṇḍa*. After briefly summing up the story of the *Rāmāyaṇa* up until the fire ordeal of Sītā, Śaṅkaradeva takes up the story from the forty-fifth chapter of the original Vālmīki version. But he briefly summarises or skips over many of the episodes that he does not consider relevant to the main Rāma-Sītā story. The narrative acquires a richness and emotional depth from the moment it begins to concentrate on the portrayal of the two central characters, Rāma and Sītā. According to William L. Smith, the reason Śaṅkaradeva skips over the whole of the first thirty-six *sargas* is that the poet wished to highlight the intensity of the tragedy that was to unfold in the *Uttarakāṇḍa.*[37]

It may be pertinent to mention here the philosophical base of most of Śaṅkaradeva's writings. The *Bhāgavata-purāṇa* and the *Bhagavad-gītā* begin with the *biṣāda yoga* (the spiritual exercise drawn from the realization of the existential sorrow that permeates the human world). Śaṅkaradeva was intensely aware of this basic condition of human existence and he belived that the path of escape (*mokṣa*) from this was through total devotion (*bhakti*) to the Primary Cause that moves this universe. Without attaining the philosophical state of mind that prepares a person to encounter all adversities, even the wise may commit fatal errors that lead them to their inevitable destiny.[38] Śaṅkaradeva in his *Uttarakāṇḍa* may have prepared the audience at the very beginning of the book for the disaster that would befall Rāma and Sītā subsequently. In *Adhyāya* 15 of his text, he skilfully allows the twins to briefly summarise

---

37 See William L. Smith, "The Wrath of Sītā: Śaṅkaradeva's Uttarakāṇḍa", www.atributetoŚaṅkaradeva.org, downloaded on 10.6.2017.

38 For a more detailed discussion of this see Bapchandra Mahanta, *Aitihasik Patabhumit Mahapurush Śaṅkaradeva*, Guwahati, 1987, pp. 226–229.

the dialogue between Rāma and Agastya so that the more important part of the story, the tragic banishment of Sītā, may receive the central focus: "*ehimāne thaila Rāma Agasti saṃbāda, gāibe lailā Jānakīra nirbbāsa biṣāda*" ("summing up thus briefly the dialogue between Rāma and Agastya, they began to sing the sad story of Jānakī's exile.").

Sītā in the *Rāmāyaṇa* of Vālmīki and in the Vernacular Versions of Mādhava Kandalī and Śaṅkaradeva

Sītā speaks in her own voice on about ten occasions in the seven books of Vālmīki's *Rāmāyaṇa*. In the *Ayodhyākāṇḍa,* we hear her voice for the first time when she expresses her shock at seeing Rāma return dejected from his father's palace on the day appointed for his coronation.[39] Rāma tells his wife about his exile and then prepares her for the long years of separation from him. He advises her to submit herself totally to the rules of *pātivratya* during his absence—observing appropriate vows and fasts, worshipping the household gods, and doing her duty towards his parents and all the other elders in the family. He even seeks to caution her against possible moral transgressions in her behaviour towards his brothers: that she should accept Bharata as her master during his absence but look upon him and his other brothers as her own siblings. The oblique insinuation hinted at in this injunction is not lost upon the sensitive Sītā, as her response to this speech reveals. For the first time in the epic, Sītā speaks up in a spirited manner, rejecting his argument about the true duties of a wife. Remonstrating with her husband, who tries to frighten her by listing all the possible dangers that life in the forest entails, she says that she will be able to withstand it all in the protective care of her brave husband. When Rāma

---

39 *Rāmāyaṇa of Vālmīki, Vol. II, Ayodhyākāṇḍa*, Sarga 23, trans. by Sheldon Pollock, New York University Press, 2008 [all future references to *Rāmāyaṇa Book Two* are from this edition].

stands his ground even after these arguments, Sītā fires her final salvo at him: she had been made to believe at the time of her marriage that Rāma wields great power, but, now it seems that he is no more than a woman with the body of a man. Why else is he so eager, "like a procurer", to hand his wife over to the care of other men?[40] Thus, in Vālmīki's text, Sītā's moral and intellectual powers are emphasised as much as her physical beauty.

Though Vālmīki represents Sītā as the embodiment of *pātivratya,* we see another dimension of her character as she leaves the palace in Ayodhya and enters the forest with Rāma and Lakṣmaṇa. The forest, unlike a city, is the place where life is not bound by the strict rules and discipline of family and social life. It is a space where the individual, free from all social or family responsibilities, can be totally in communion with herself. In Vālmīki's *Rāmāyaṇa*, Rāma appears to be bound by his kingly responsibilities even in the forest. When the Brāhmaṇas living in their *āśramas* on the outskirts of the forest appeal to Rāma for protection from the *rākṣasas* inhabiting the forest region, Rāma at once makes it his mission. He kills 14,000 *rākṣasas* and assures the sages that he considers it his royal responsibility to protect them. "I come as king, night-stalker, to end the life of evildoers and all who wish the world ill,"[41] he warns the *rākṣasa* Khara before he destroys him. Not only the *rākṣasas* but also other denizens of the forest become targets of the *kṣatriya* brothers' weapons. Vālmīki describes the first acts of transgression committed by the brothers as they cross the Ganga on their way to the forest: "On the further bank the brothers killed four large animals—a boar, an antelope,

---

40 Ibid: 27.

41 *The Rāmāyaṇa of Vālmīki*, Vol. III, *Araṇyakāṇḍa*, Sarga 28:10, trans. by Sheldon Pollock, (Princeton, 1984), Motilal Banarasidass, Delhi, 2007 [all future references to 'Araṇyakāṇḍa' of Vālmīki are from this edition].

and a great black buck."[42] Rāma's first words to Lakṣmaṇa as they prepare to settle down in the peaceful Chitrakuta region are: "Bring the flesh of a black antelope, and we shall offer a sacrifice to our hut."[43] Rāma is therefore quite aware of the transgressions that he will be committing in the forest. When the sage Sutīkṣṇa invites Rāma to stay in his *āśrama*, Rāma replies, "Most illustrious sage, I might chance to slay the herds of animals congregated here with one of my sharp-edged arrows that flash like lightning bolts. You would be implicated in it, and what worse misfortune than that?"[44] Sītā's character, on the other hand, merges smoothly with the forest's soul as soon as she bids farewell to the city. In fact, she even wishes for her husband to also be influenced by life in the forest to abandon the *kṣatriya* code and "renounce the kingship altogether" even after he completes his period of exile (III, 8.25). She observes silently the propensity for violence in her husband and Lakṣmaṇa and speaks out at last on the eve of their final departure for the forests of Daṇḍakāraṇya. As she hands over the weapons to the two brothers, she reflects philosophically on the dangers of "unprovoked violence". Of the three evils that a man can commit deliberately—telling lies, having sexual intercourse with another man's wife, indulging in unprovoked violence—Sītā considers the third to be the worst (III, 8.1). Absolving her husband of the possibility of committing the first two transgressions, she says, "But the third one, violence—the taking of life without provocation and recklessly—to this you may be prone." Elaborating on the dangers of this vice, she says, "You and your brother are going to the forest, bow and arrow in hand, and I fear that the sight of any forest-dweller might cause you to shoot your arrows. For, in this world, a bow to a *kshatriya*

42 *The Rāmāyaṇa of Vālmīki*, Vol. II, *Ayodhyākāṇḍa*, Sarga 46:75.

43 Ibid, 50:15.

44 *The Rāmāyaṇa of Vālmīki, Araṇyakāṇḍa*, 6:20.

is kindling to a fire: if it comes too close, his blazing power flares up wildly."

It is evident from this speech that Sītā includes the *rākṣasas* among the "forest-dwellers" and forbids Rāma from killing them without cause: "[I am] reminding you—not teaching you—that on no account should you take up your bow and, unprovoked, turn your thoughts to killing the *rākṣasas* of Dandaka. My mighty husband, I disapprove of your killing creatures that have done no wrong" (8.20). Sītā, like Vasanti, the goddess of the woods in Bhavabhuti's *Uttara-ramacharita,*[45] is the benevolent spirit of the forest who reminds Rāma about the sanctity of the woods. Her concern for the denizens of the forest, whether sages, *rākṣasas,* or wildlife, makes her conscious of the incongruity of wielding arms in the forest: "Mighty *kshatriyas*, finding themselves in the forests inhabited by men who practice self-restraint, need bows only for protecting those in distress. How incongruous they are, weapons and the forest, the *kshatriya* order and the practice of asceticism—it is all so at odds. We must respect the customs of the place. Wicked thoughts, my noble husband, can come from handling weapons. When you are back in Ayodhya, you may follow the *kshatriya* code again" (8.20). When Rāma argues that it is necessary for him to wield arms in order to protect the ascetics, Sītā narrates a story to illustrate her point that constant proximity to weapons of violence has an adverse effect on the human personality.

Sītā's counsel to her husband in this scene reflects one of the central themes of the *Rāmāyaṇa*—that the killing of the innocent can lead to a chain reaction of violence on a massive scale, resulting in universal suffering and destruction. The killing of Shravanakumar by Daśaratha,

45 Bhavabhuti's *Uttararamacarita*, trans by P.V. Kane and C.N. Joshi, Motilal Banarasidass, Delhi, 1962.

albeit by mistake, set in motion the whole story of destruction and separation that is at the heart of the epic. In fact, the very origin of the verse form (*śloka*) invented by Vālmīki for his *kāvya* springs from his sorrow (*śoka*) when he saw the heartrending lamentation of a bird for its mate, killed cruelly by a hunter's arrow. Sītā's advice to Rāma on the eve of their entry into Daṇḍakāraṇya is, therefore, reflective of a wisdom that seeks to protect the wilderness from the rapacious intentions of armed men from the city who have no respect for a way of life that is different from their own.

Sītā, in Vālmīki's *Rāmāyaṇa*, retains her firm belief in the need to shun unprovoked violence even after her harrowing experience in Rāvaṇa's custody. When Hanumāna, in his excessive devotion to Sītā and Rāma, wishes to inflict terrible punishment on the *rākṣasa* women who had been guarding her and tormenting her psychologically, Sītā speaks once again about the need for the victor to restrain himself from being unnecessarily vindictive. Restraining Hanumāna's urge to thrash the *rākṣasīs*, Sītā pleads on behalf of the hapless women who were mere slaves acting on Rāvaṇa's orders. Then, citing a verse from a *purāṇa* that describes a boar telling a tiger that no one can take upon himself the iniquity of the perpetrator of vicious deeds, she says to Hanumāna, "A noble person must act compassionately whether people are wicked, virtuous or even if deserving of death. For, leaping monkey, no one is entirely innocent. One should not harm the *rākṣasas*, who can take on any form at will and take pleasure in injuring people, even when they do evil."[46]

---

46 *The Rāmāyaṇa of Vālmīki, Yuddhakāṇḍa*, sarga 101, pp. 36–37, trans. and annotated by Robert P. Goldman, Sally J. Sutherland Goldman, and Baren A. van Nooten, Motilal Banarsidass, Delhi, 2010.

Some scholars believe that the four principal characters in the epic—Rāma, Lakṣmaṇa, Sītā, and Bharata—have been portrayed by Vālmīki as characters who display a "moral stasis" and "do not grow or change in the course of the narrative, or develop through inner struggle in the presence of moral choice."[47] But on occasions such as the two cited above, Sītā is shown to have transcended the traditional role of the *pativratā* who is not expected to articulate her opinions in public without the permission of her husband. Vālmīki, therefore, does not portray her merely as an embodiment of a certain set of patriarchal values, with no possibility of acquiring an agency of her own. In the delineation of her character, the poet allows ample space for questioning certain values associated with the concepts of hierarchical power. Sītā's voice of resistance may not always be clearly heard in the Vālmīki text, but it is audible above the din of battles and struggle for power as a contrapuntal strain.

In the Assamese *Rāmāyaṇa* text, especially the *Uttarakāṇḍa* ascribed to Śaṅkaradeva, Sītā speaks at length. In the final scene, she declares forcefully her decision to reject Rāma's proposal to take her back after making her go through another test by fire. Sītā's last speech, in which she vents her anger against Rāma, contains strong words of condemnation that would not have found a place in the Vālmīki text, where Sītā is portrayed as a woman who rarely uses words that might have been considered inappropriate given her social position as a *pativrata* wife well-versed in the rules of *streedharma*. It is intriguing that the Assamese Vaiṣṇava poet chose to put those strong words in the mouth of Sītā in his vernacular version of the Sanskrit text despite the fact that his stated intention was

47 Sheldon Pollock, Introduction to *The Rāmāyaṇa of Vālmīki, Ayodhyākāṇḍa*, p. 49.

to instil *bhakti-rasa* into the text composed by Mādhava Kandalī. It remains a mystery therefore why Śaṅkaradeva depicted the character of Sītā in such a way as to almost make her a representative of the feminist voice of protest against a patriarchal order in which the woman's part was scripted to be meek and subservient to the masculine will. In Śaṅkaradeva's *Uttarakāṇḍa,* Sītā does not hesitate to refer to Rāma as 'Yamkal'—the very incarnation of the lord of Death. This portrayal of Sītā is unusual for a composition by a leading Vaiṣṇava writer and preacher in whose religious structure women were generally excluded.

In Mādhava Kandalī's *Rāmāyaṇa,* Sītā is represented as a woman with extraordinary physical beauty. She is aware of her physical charm and the power she can wield over her husband because of this. For instance, in the scene where Rāma returns home after his aborted coronation ceremony, he laments the turn of events that compels him to bid farewell to Sītā, who is endowed with such extraordinary physical attributes. The poet, through Rāma's lips, goes into ecstatic detail describing the exotic beauty in each of her limbs (*Ayodhyākāṇḍa,* 12:1–19). When Rāma finally concludes with the words, "I would tie a rock around my neck and drown myself in the ocean rather than deprive myself of the pleasure of your company," Sītā too responds in a similar tone, reminding her beloved of all the pleasures he had derived from her body: "Like a bumble-bee, you, my beloved, had been enjoying the pleasures of my body which is tender as a *campaka* bud... Why do you now wish to leave me? Which part of my body appears defective to you now?" (*Ayodhyākāṇḍa,* 12: 24–29). Significantly, in the Vālmīki *Rāmāyaṇa* there is no such reference to Rāma's lamentations at the thought of leaving his wife behind. He does not dwell upon the beauty of Sītā, nor does he mention that he would miss her company while in exile.

Sītā's aggressive behaviour towards Lakṣmana in the episode of the golden deer is, in Mādhava Kandalī's version of the *Rāmāyaṇa,* expressed not only through the use of the choicest abusive language (she calls him a caṇḍāla, *pāpiṣṭha, durācārī*) surpassing the use of such verbal abuses by Vālmīki's Sītā, but also through her uncontrolled physical gestures, which generally characterise rustic behavior: "she pulls her tresses and beats her chest with clenched fists" (*Araṇyakāṇḍa,* 12:28–37). However, these gestures may also signify the adoption of a dramatic idiom with which the audience would have been familiar. Perhaps in keeping with the portrayal of Sītā with all the attributes of an ordinary woman, Mādhava Kandalī omits the whole section in Vālmīki's *Araṇyakāṇḍa* on Sītā's sensible and intelligent discourse on the need to shun unprovoked violence in the forest. However, there could be another more plausible reason for the omission of this crucial discourse. The Assamese poet might have realised that the so-called "brahmanical perception" of the relationship between the state and the forest in ancient India[48] would have been quite alien to the culture represented by Kandalī's royal patron and the audience, consisting of the indigenous communities of the north-eastern region.

Mādhava Kandalī's Sītā, despite her earthy attributes, has been endowed with suitable dignity in situations where she asserts her difference from an ordinary woman who is fickle and runs after trivial pleasures. When the distraught Kauśalyā asks her to be always attentive to her husband Rāma, she replies, "Do not consider me to be an ordinary woman, mother," and then goes on to talk about the virtues of the *pātivratya* dharma.[49] These words find

48 For a detailed discussion of this view see B. D. Chattopadhyaya, "The State Perception of the 'Forest' and the 'Forest' as State in Early India", in *The Concept of Bharatavarsha and Other Essays*, Permanent Black, Ranikhet, 2017, p. 60.

49 Mādhava Kandalī, *Ayodhyākāṇḍa,* 15:30.

an echo in her speech at the end of the *Laṅkākāṇḍa*, when she replies to Rāma's unjust accusation.[50] Though Sītā's memorable words to Rāma in the Vālmīki *Rāmāyaṇa* on the need to shun unnecessary violence towards the denizens of the forest have not been retained in the text of Mādhava Kandalī, her sensible views on the topic, which differ radically from those of other heroes of the epic, comes out forcefully when she remonstrates with Hanumanta in the *Laṅkākāṇḍa*. When Hanumanta, in his eagerness to take revenge on the *rākṣasa* women who had tormented Sītā during her sojourn in the *aśoka* garden of Rāvaṇa, Sītā intervenes with these words: "My brother Hanumanta, why are you so angry with these women? The *rākṣasa* women are all slaves of Rāvaṇa, they have no independent agency. Had they dared to defy Rāvaṇa's orders and desisted from threatening me, Rāvaṇa could have put me to sword that instant and no one in this universe could have saved me. These women now can do me no harm but are themselves frightened to death. They have fallen at my feet and have begged for mercy. Who has the power to kill or save anyone? The sins we have committed in our previous lives will determine whether we will live or die."[51] Thus, Sītā's intellectual and moral qualities find sufficient focus in the Assamese text too.

Sītā's views on the subordinate status of women do not come through very forcefully in the Vālmīki text. In the fifth book of Vālmīki's *Rāmāyaṇa*, Sītā cries out in a moment of despair: "How pathetic is this human state! How wretched to be under the power of another! Although I wish to, I cannot end my life."[52] The word used for subjection here is

---

50 Mādhava Kandalī, *Laṅkākāṇḍa*, 50:55.

51 Mādhava Kandalī, *Laṅkākāṇḍa*, 49:27-30.

52 *The Rāmāyaṇa of Vālmīki*, Vol. V: *Sundarakāṇḍa*: 23:20, trans. by Robert P. Goldman and Sally J.S. Goldman, Motilal Banarasidass, Delhi, 2007.

paravaśyatama. Sally Goldman has suggested that Sītā may be referring here either to her forced subjection to Rāvaṇa or to her position as an obedient wife who must seek her husband's permission even to die. It might also indicate Sītā's realisation that anyone who is subject to another lacks the liberty either to live or die.[53] The ambiguity inherent in the Vālmīki text, which may be subject to multiple interpretations, including the feminist one, has however been dispensed with in the Mādhava Kandalī text. Sītā in the Assamese version repeats at least three times the line "*strī jāti parādhīn, nahe svatantarī*" ("women are a subjugated race, they are never independent"),[54] thus using the term "*parādhīn*" in a generalised sense, attributing it to all women, irrespective of their status. The certitude expressed in Mādhava Kandalī's version may have been inspired by Manu's views on the woman's subordinate status. But when Sītā speaks the words, which refer to a universal condition of women lacking freedom within the patriarchal structure, they seem to spring from her deep realisation about the similarity between her own predicament during her confinement in the *aśoka* grove and the condition of the oppressed *rākṣasa* women who were compelled by Rāvaṇa, their master, to torment her. Her words seem to convey her gradual realisation that, for her, there is actually no release from subjugation, whether in Rāvaṇa's garden or in Rāma's kingdom.

In the Assamese *Rāmāyaṇa*, Mādhava Kandalī adheres more or less faithfully to the Vālmīki version of the Sītā–Rāvaṇa and Sītā-Hanumāna encounters in the *Sundarakāṇḍa*. The emotionally charged, turbulent scene between Rāma

---

53 See Sally Goldman, "The Voice of Sītā in Vālmīki's Sundarakāṇḍa" in Paula Richman ed., *Questioning Rāmāyaṇa*, p. 233.

54 Mādhava Kandalī, *Sundarakāṇḍa*, 17:130; *Laṅkākāṇḍa*, 49:27, 50:56.

and Sītā that leads up to the first fire ordeal of Sītā has also been represented in the Assamese version without significant alterations. But Mādhava Kandalī makes Sītā speak a few extra words that sum up her views on a broken relationship between a man and a woman. The irreversible nature of the split that has taken place between Rāma and her because of his lack of faith in her love and devotion to him is indicated by Sītā's remarks: "Relationships, once torn apart, like iron that is broken, cannot be remoulded." ("*bhāgi gailā lohā āur gaḍhana najāy*"). Sītā's next comment is a bitter generalisation about the insensitivity of all men: "*Nirdday puruśjāti kino nidārun*" ("Men are cruel and bereft of mercy").[55] It springs from the realisation that the idyllic relationship between the lovers that had been described so tenderly in the *Araṇyakāṇḍa* has finally come to an end. Significantly, in the Vālmīki text, though Sītā speaks most forcefully during the encounter with Rāma after the end of the battle, the finality and pathos of the broken relationship has not been emphasised as poignantly as in the Mādhava Kandalī version.

It would be interesting to study how Śaṅkaradeva's portrayal of Sītā in the *Uttarakāṇḍa* resembles or differs from his portrayal of women characters in his other works, especially in his religious plays (*aṅkīya-nāṭas*). In keeping with the tradition of Sanskrit drama, the heroine in *aṅkīya-nāṭa* is portrayed only in relation to the hero. She is not endowed with the volition and choice to express her own feelings in relation to the world. In fact, none of the characters have the scope to develop as independent individuals within the limited space provided for dialogues in the plays. Maheswar Neog observes that "the heroine comes into prominence only with the element of love-story

55 In Mādhava Kandalī, *Laṅkākāṇḍa*, 50:62-63.

in the *Rukmiṇī-harana* and the *Rāma-vijaya.*"[56] Rukmiṇī or Sītā in these *aṅkīya-nāṭas* appears as the typical *nāyikā*, a maiden endowed with superb feminine qualities who hears about the superhuman attributes of the hero and craves his company. Sometimes, the heroine is a jealous and quarrelsome lady who compels her beloved to submit to her petty demands, as in the case of Satyabhāmā in *Pārijāta-haraṇa*. In fact, it is only in *Pārijāta-haraṇa* amongst all the *aṅkīya-nāṭas* that at least three women characters—Rukmiṇī, Satyabhāmā, and Śacī—have been endowed with significant articulation, which enables them to stand out as individualized women characters. But the individuation of the female characters in all these texts does not deviate from the practice of depicting them with the typical attributes of *nāyikās*. Scholars are of the opinion that *Pārijāta-haraṇa* together with *Rāma-vijaya* belong to the last phase in the poetic career of Śaṅkaradeva and they display a great deal of maturity.[57] *Rāma-vijaya (Śrī-rāma-vijaya-nāṭaka)*, which was composed and produced around 1568 CE at the request of Śukladhvaja (aka Cilārāya), the brother of the Koch king Naranārāyaṇa, was based on the *Bālakāṇḍa* of the *Rāmāyaṇa*. Sītā in this play is portrayed at the very beginning as a young girl, distressed and haunted by memories of an earlier life in which she had killed herself by jumping into the pyre in the hope of being married to Rāma in her present life. Thus, her *pativratā* self and her destiny—to suffer the ordeal by fire in her present life—seem to be preordained in the play. Sītā in this play is no different from Rukmiṇī in *Rukmiṇī-haraṇa*. She is the exceedingly beautiful woman burning with the uncontrollable desire to become the chosen consort of the hero, who is the incarnation of the supreme god.

---

56 Maheswar Neog, *Early History of Vaisnava Faith in Assam*, Lawyers' Book Stall, Guwahati, 1998 [1965], p. 254.

57 Ibid, p. 203.

Unlike in all of the above texts, the image of Sītā in Śaṅkaradeva's *Uttarakāṇḍa* is radically different from that of the *nāyikās* in the *aṅkīya-nāṭa* where the women generally conform to the *svabhāva* conventionally ascribed to them in Sanskrit literature. In Vālmīki's *Rāmāyaṇa*, as has been pointed out by Sally Sutherland Goldman, the fundamental assumption is that "Sītā does not fall prey to her imputed *svabhāva*" and, even in the most adverse circumstances, she defies "the culturally normative attitudes" expected from women.[58] It is in the light of such an assessment of Sītā's character in the *Rāmāyaṇa* that we may discuss Śaṅkaradeva's handling of the character in his *Uttarakāṇḍa*.

In his poetic rendering of the *Uttarakāṇḍa*, Śaṅkaradeva gives ample scope to Sītā to voice her anger and disillusionment at Rāma's inhuman behaviour towards her. Coming from the pen of a Vaiṣṇava saint-poet, this bitter condemnation of Rāma by his *pativratā* wife seems to be incongruous with the perception of all devotees of Rāma that he is the paragon of virtue. But scholarly exegetes working on the *Rāmāyaṇa* have repeatedly pointed to the manner in which, from the time of Vālmīki onwards, this 'idealized model of humanity has been problematized"[59] in the *Rāmāyaṇa* tradition. Various solutions have been offered in the Indian literary tradition to the bewildering problems raised by Rāma's character. In keeping with the practice of contributing creatively to the *ur-text* of Vālmīki, the Assamese poets have added new emotional

58 Sally J. Sutherland Goldman, "The Voice of Sītā in Vālmīki's Sundarakāṇḍa", in Paula Richman ed., *Questioning Rāmāyaṇas: A South Asian Tradition* (2000), OUP, 2012 reprint, p. 225.

59 See David Shulman, "Fire and Flood: Testing of Sītā in Kampan's *Iramavataram*", in Paula Richman ed., *Many Rāmāyaṇas: The Diversity of a Narrative Tradition in South Asia* (1991), OUP, 2013 reprint, p. 89.

and philosophical dimensions to it, thereby enriching a vibrant tradition.

The silence of Sītā in Vālmīki's *Uttarakāṇḍa* has been broken by Śaṅkaradeva, who allows her to respond with scathing bitterness to the messengers of Rāma when they come to take her back to Ayodhya to face another public test of her chastity. Sītā speaks out in words loaded with bitter irony and cynicism: "Why do you come here to torment me again, to make me remember the agony that I have suffered? If I have any desire left to go back to Ayodhya and enjoy all the comforts of the royal palace, to look upon Rāghava once again in joy, there never would be a woman more bereft of shame than me."[60] Sītā's righteous anger reaches an extreme point when she gives voice to her new perception of her husband's character: "I have no regrets that I am suffering because of my own past deeds (*karma*). My relationship with Rāma came to an end when he rejected me because of the false accusations of some evil men. Now he is sending for me so that he can put me to death once again, since I did not die earlier in the forest. I know in my heart of hearts now that my husband is Death-incarnate for me" (*"jano mor mane Rāma svamī yamkāl"*).[61] The words are so powerful in their ultimate condemnation of misogynistic patriarchal values that they have reverberated through the centuries in Assamese oral folk culture. It may also be conjectured that the Assamese Vaiṣṇava poet might have put into Sītā's mouth words that were already current in the folk expression of the region, using the worst possible term (*yamkāl*) to describe a cruel husband.

60 Śaṅkaradeva, *'Uttarakāṇḍa' 17:50-53.*

61 Ibid, 58-60.

One may pertinently raise questions here about whether the essentially patriarchal norms of womanhood depicted in the Sanskrit epics and *kāvyas*, subjected to questioning in the Assamese versions and whether this questioning substantially differed from the examples found in the numerous variations of the oral and written Rāma stories in other regional languages? An exploration of some of these embedded issues in the Assamese versions of Mādhava Kandalī and Śaṅkaradeva may illuminate the richness of the multiple variants of the Rāma-story present in the whole of South and South-east Asia.

In the Vālmīki text (*sarga* 95:7–12),[62] there is no mention of the episode in which Śatrughna, Vibhīṣaṇa, Suṣeṇa, and Māruti are sent by Rāma to plead with Sītā and bring her back. Sītā's long discourse on the final breach that has occurred in her relationship with her husband finds no mention in the Vālmīki text. Sītā speaks only three *ślokas* in Vālmīki's *Uttarakāṇḍa* before she departs from the world. In the Assamese text, the poet makes her articulate her justified anger against her husband in fifteen couplets while she is in Vālmīki's *āśrama* and seventy-nine couplets and eighteen *dularī* verses when she stands once more before her husband at the sacrificial ground.

Śaṅkaradeva's depiction of the scene of Sītā's final farewell is dramatic as well as powerful in its emotional content. The poet recreates the scene in accordance with the classical dramatic tradition. It must be remembered that Śaṅkaradeva had invented the form of the *aṅkīya-nāṭa,* which is a uniquely creative combination of devotional music, dance, and dramatic dialogue, and that the Assamese saint-poet was also one of the earliest poets to dramatize scenes from the *Rāmāyaṇa.* The emotionally surcharged

62 *Śrīmad Vālmīkīya Rāmāyaṇa*, Vol. 2.

scene of Sītā's final bow to the world is prepared by the poet with a preceding *chabi* section that acts as an interlude. In this, the poet digresses into a brief sketch of his own family history, followed by a modest apology for his endeavour to compose the verses of the *Uttarakāṇḍa* of his great predecessor Mādhava Kandalī. In the next *pada* section, Sītā makes her dramatic entry. Clad in the garment of an ascetic, her body thin and emaciated by the fasts and vows she has undertaken, she walks behind her guardian Vālmīki with eyes downcast, not acknowledging the gazes and comments of the people gathered by the wayside. Unlike Vālmīki's text, in which there is a brief mention of the sages, courtiers, *rākṣasas*, monkeys, and men from all the castes who have assembled at the sacrificial ground to witness the trial of Sītā, the Assamese poet paints a vivid and dramatic picture of the common folk, especially the women, who have come out to the street in large numbers to witness Sītā's sorrow and to sympathize with her. Rāma offers his respects to Vālmīki and the sage reciprocates by performing the ritual of giving Rāma his formal blessings. All this while, Sītā stands aside, eyes downcast in shame and anger. Then Vālmīki makes the public pronouncement that Sītā is pure and the twins who call her mother are actually Rāma's sons. Vālmīki swears by his forefathers and his own ascetic vows that, to the best of his knowledge, Sītā has always remained faithful to her husband Rāma. Rāma's laconic reply is addressed to the sage alone: that, in deference to the assurance given by Vālmīki, he is prepared to take back Sītā, provided the court agrees. At this, Sītā casts fiery glances at her husband, who hangs down his head in shame (21:6–7). It seems that her anger has the power to reduce her husband to ashes and bring about a mighty catastrophe. Sītā remains silent for a while and then, in a gesture that repudiates all patriarchal norms, she speaks directly to the audience. Turning her back on her husband, Sītā says, "This audience may blame me for my words because everyone knows Rāma to be my master and my husband. I followed my husband to exile because being a woman, I have no independent life of my own and I am devoted to him completely" ("*ekeśvarī nārī mai noho svatantarī*"). Significantly, this reiteration of the reality of a woman's position is an echo of a similar line in Mādhava Kandalī's text, indicating that the line is etched in Śaṅkaradeva's memory because of its tragic implication. Repeating once again the final words of condemnation that she had uttered earlier, Sītā says, "The whole world sings the praise of this Rāma, but for me, Rāma is my *yamkāl.* A man who can be so unjust and cruel towards his wife is worse than a *rākṣasa.*" Addressing her husband directly, Sītā says, "*Rākṣasatodhik iṭo tomar kumoti*" ("Your evil designs are more cruel than those of the *rākṣasas*"). Then, in a final act of denunciation, her voice attains universal dimensions as she bravely says, "If after all this I agree to live with you again as your wife, then there never will be a woman more shameless than me." Her last words to her husband, "I do not wish to see this Rāghava's face ever again,"[63] are replete with bitter scorn and disillusionment, something that can never be expected from Vālmīki's Sītā.

Could this be Śaṅkaradeva's unique interpretation of the complex relationships and the difficult philosophical and moral dimensions of the human condition presented in the Vālmīki text? Was the Vaiṣṇava saint overpowered by his creative self in this one instance, compelled to allow his human sympathies for the oppressed to overcome all other considerations? The individuation of Sītā in a manner that empowers her to address her husband, the audience, and the gods boldly and to speak her mind on the nature of human relationships is evidence of the

63 Śaṅkaradeva, 'Uttarakāṇḍa', Section 21:15-53.

literary sensitivities of the author superseding his other self, which would portray Rāma as an incarnation of the infallible supreme being. But, as if to compensate for the complete imaginative empathy with the suffering woman that enables the poet to make his Sītā speak with a tongue of fire, Śaṅkaradeva immediately changes the mood of the narrative by taking recourse to the lighter metrical form of the *dularī* (as opposed to the sombre fourteen-syllabic *pada* couplets in which the greater part of the *kāvya* has been composed by Mādhava Kandalī, Śaṅkaradeva, and Mādhavadeva) in order to depict a surprising change of temper in Sītā. Sītā bids a tearful farewell to her sons and seeks forgiveness from Rāma for having spoken those angry words in a moment of grief. True to the ideals of the *pativratā*, she blames her own fate for having been deprived of the chance to serve her husband faithfully all her life. Thus, *bhakti-rasa* remains ultimately vindicated in this vernacular version of the epic.

Sītā's last speech and her dramatic farewell to the world have inspired diverse poets through the centuries to represent the scene with greater cathartic effect. In Śaṅkaradeva's composition, Sītā emerges as a powerful tragic heroine who towers over all the other characters in the scene of her farewell. She seems to escape beyond all human laws (of kings/Rāma) into the fold of nature. Even Rāma's divinity appears pale in comparison with the brilliant tragic heights achieved by Sītā in this scene. Śaṅkaradeva's handling of this episode in the Assamese *Rāmāyaṇa*, obviously differs from that in the Vālmīki text. It is because of the existence of variations such as these that attention has been focused in recent *Rāmāyaṇa* scholarship on the immense possibilities of re-reading the *Rāmāyaṇa* texts in the regional languages. These texts speak volumes about the different worldviews and cultural variations of the regions from which they emerge.

In the concluding part of Vālmīki's *Uttarakāṇḍa*, when Rāma enters heaven with all his brothers and attains the divine form of Viṣṇu, Sītā is not mentioned by the poet as one of those who finds a place amongst the celestials in heaven. There is only a passing reference to "the wide-eyed Māyā" (110:11) who was once Rāma's spouse. Though Brahmā did console Rāma earlier, after Sītā's final departure from the world, assuring him that he would again meet her in heaven, the concluding verses of the epic do not celebrate the union of Rāma and Sītā in the divine abode of eternal happiness. Amongst those who have attained divine forms and welcome Rāma to their midst in heaven are the *ṛṣis, gandharvas, apsarās, Garuḍa, nāgas, yakṣas, daityas, dānavas* and *rākṣasas*; but Sītā is conspicuous by her absence. Thus, the ultimate rejection of Sītā by Rāma has received poetic confirmation from Vālmīki in the final book of the epic.[64] Śaṅkaradeva's *Uttarakāṇḍa,* too (adhyāya 32–33) celebrates ecstatically the entry of every species of creature from the world that has attained Rāma's blessings into the glorious region of *Santanak,* which has been set apart for them by Rāma's grace; but Sītā is not mentioned anywhere as one of the Rāma-*bhaktas* who deserves to attain this final bliss.

While discussing the dramatic nature of the presentation of Sītā in Śaṅkaradeva's *Uttarakāṇḍa,* one may also refer to the influence of the tradition of performative art on the Assamese *Rāmāyaṇa.* It may be iterated here that the vernacular rendition was primarily meant for recitation before an audience consisting of royalty and common men and women from all castes, especially those who were unacquainted with the Sanskrit language and texts written in that language of the gods. The stanzaic varieties and the use of metres such as *dularī, chhabi,* and *jumudi*, besides the

64 'Uttarakāṇḍa' in *Śrīmad Vālmīkīya Rāmāyaṇa*, Vol. 2, (with Hindi translation), Gita Press, Gorakhpur, 47th reprint, sarga 110:14.

epic *pada* metre, indicate that these verses were primarily intended for public performance. Significantly, various minstrel traditions like that of the *ojāpāli* were widely prevalent in Assam even prior to the neo-Vaisnavite period and it could be a safe conjecture that Śaṅkaradeva would have utilized such a vibrant tradition in order to disseminate his Vaiṣṇava teachings amongst the masses.[65]

Gender relations in Indian history have been the focus, though not always adequately so, of some recent historical scholarship, which has reinstated women as independent beings, with their own agency, and not as mere "adjuncts"[66] to a patriarchal structure. Other than a few exceptions,[67] there continues to be, however, an absence in historical works of sufficient engagement with the gender question in vernacular texts of the *bhakti* tradition, especially those emerging from lesser-known traditions. In the context of historiography of medieval Assam, there are some extant works that mention the quotidian life of women—including their participation in trade, commerce, weaving, and agricultural activities—as an aspect of the larger socio-

65 The Assamese *Gīti-Rāmāyaṇa* of Durgābara Kāyastha, composed around the first half of the sixteenth century, was meant primarily for *ojāpāli* performances in which song, dance, and traditional music form the principal elements. This popular version of the *Rāmāyaṇa* differed considerably from the Vālmīki text in several ways and was closer to the vernacular version of the *Rāmāyaṇa* of Mādhava Kandalī. It can be conjectured that Śaṅkaradeva may have been familiar with the dramatic qualities of the Durgabari composition, which was widely performed by traditional *ojāpāli* performers of Kāmarūpa and Darrang. Even today this Durgabari composition forms the basis of a vibrant tradition of *ojāpāli* popular in western Assam [see Satyendranath Sarma, *Epics and Puranas in Early Assamese Literature*, pp.40-45].

66 B.D. Chattopadhyaya, "General Editor's Preface", in Kumkum Roy ed., *Women in Early Indian Societies*, Manohar, Delhi, 1999.

67 For instance, in Kumkum Roy ed., *Women in Early Indian Societies.*

economic history of the region.[68] These recent studies have gleaned information from the medieval lives of Assamese saints to discuss the powerful and assertive speech of women from this community, often referred to pejoratively in "respectable" parley as "the voice of the marketplace." Though there are hardly any representations of such a voice in Assamese writings of the colonial times, one can find a few instances of the forceful voice of the ordinary woman from the trading community in some nineteenth-century literary texts.[69] In Assamese Vaiṣṇava literature of the neo-Vaisnavite period represented by Śaṅkaradeva and his followers, however, such articulate female voices are hard to come across. In Śaṅkaradeva's *ek-sarania-namdharma,* there was a largely inclusive effort to reach out to the masses across gender, caste, race, and religious categories, yet it is difficult to find in the scholarly studies of the twentieth century any specific references to the role of women within the organized structure of the Assamese Vaiṣṇava movement. This silence is understandable because women were generally excluded from the *sattra* institutions set up by the disciples of Śaṅkaradeva. In such a scenario, it can only be speculated that the portrayal of Sītā in Śaṅkaradeva's *Uttarakāṇḍa* could have been inspired by the poet's own observation of women in society and his inherent respect for the wisdom and views of women in his own family. Śaṅkaradeva lost his parents at an early age.

68 For instance, see Jahnabi Gogoi Nath, "Women, Religion and Society in Assam: Reflections from a Medieval Biographical Work", in Proceedings of the Indian History Congress , 2009-2010, Vol. 70 (2009-2010), pp. 329-337, Indian History Congress.

69 In Gunabhiram Barua's *Ramnabami-Natak*, the author depicts such a character, who is defiant and outspoken even in the presence of her social superiors. Inside the sacred space of a *namghar,* where the traditional religious authority presides, she boldly gives evidence against a corrupt official [see *Ramnabami-Natak: The Story of Ram and Nabami*, trans. and ed., by Tilottoma Misra, Oxford University Press, 2007, p.58].

His mother Satyasandha was said to have burnt herself in the funeral pyre of her husband Kusumavara[70] (one of the few cases of *sati* found in the medieval records of Assam). He was brought up by his grandmother Khersuti, who supervised his early education and instilled in him the desire to acquire a scholarly bent of mind.[71] It was she who decided to send him to the *ṭol* of a Brahmin teacher Mahendra Kandalī, although Śaṅkaradeva's family belonged to the Kāyastha caste. Śaṅkaradeva apparently led a happy family life despite his devotional commitments. He married Suryavati at the age of twenty-one and was grief-stricken at her early death. Their daughter Manu was brought up by Śaṅkaradeva and he bore all the responsibilities of raising her until she was married. It was only after this that Śaṅkaradeva decided to go on a long pilgrimage to Puri and other holy places in north India.[72] On his return, he married Kalindi at the age of forty-eight and once again led a peaceful and contented family life until his death. So, biographers have not recorded any misogynistic tendencies in Śaṅkaradeva's attitude towards women in his family, unlike some of the later leaders of the neo-Vaisnavite movement.[73] Significantly, in the Vaiṣṇava hagiographic literature of Assam, there are occasional references to widows from non-Brahmin castes contributing to the upbringing of sons and grandsons who later became important religious figures in the neo-Vaiṣṇava movement of Assam. One such woman was Bajrangi Ai, the widowed mother of a boy who later became

70 See Maheswar Neog, *Early History of Vaisnava Faith and Movement in Assam*, p. 101.

71 Ibid, p. 102.

72 Maheswar Neog, p. 103

73 Jahnabi Gogoi, citing an incident narrated in the *Guru Carit Katha*, refers to the misogynistic attitude of Harihar Ata, one of the foremost disciples of Mādhavadeva, who demanded of his wife slave-like submission to his will and denied her the respect due to her as the wife of a holy man [see Gogoi, p. 331].

the revered Gopal Ata or Gopaldev (of Bhavanipur and Kaljar *satra*). According to the hagiographical accounts, Bajrangi, after the death of her husband, supported her family by selling wares at a *haat* or marketplace in Nazira, near the Ahom capital.[74]

Except for the scanty material provided by the *Kathā Guru Carita* and other hagiographical texts, there is hardly any reliable mention of the central role played by women in the social or economic life of the communities in medieval Assam. The hagiographical literature on the lives of the Vaiṣṇava saints afford some glimpses into the lives of ordinary women from the labouring or trading classes who worked for the sustenance of the exclusive religious communities of the Vaiṣṇava *satras*, in which women had no active role to play.[75] The *Kathā Guru Carita* records the contribution of women from diverse social classes to the day-to-day life in the Vaiṣṇava monasteries. While studying the representation of these women in the *Kathā Guru Carita*, some women historians have noted the marked difference between the social attitudes of women from the Brahmin and Kāyastha castes and those from the so-called 'lower' castes. The former were mostly the mothers, wives, or daughters of the Vaiṣṇava *bhaktas* and the latter were ordinary women who represented the trading community (the *pohari*) or the women employed in agricultural activities, cattle rearing, poultry farming, or in spinning and weaving. Jahnabi Gogoi Nath has observed that, while the women from the former group appeared to be willing followers of *patibrata* dharma who accepted all the stringent rules of chastity and subservience to patriarchal authority imposed upon them, the women from the lower classes, who were actively involved in economic activities

74 See Jahnabi Gogoi Nath, p. 332.

75 For details see Jahnabi Gogoi Nath, pp. 331–332.

that enabled them to move about freely in the marketplace, were remarkably independent and uninhibited in their speech and social attitudes.[76]

Sītā's powerful voice in the Assamese *Rāmāyaṇa* and the sheer earthiness of her speech, which sometimes appears quite contrary to the measured speech of Sītā in the Vālmīki text, can therefore perhaps be accounted for by the pervasive influence of the local culture of the indigenous communities inhabiting the region of the Brahmaputra valley and its surroundings. This can perhaps also explain the absence of some of the repressive features of Brahmanical Hindu culture from the lives of the women of the poorer classes in the northeastern region.[77] The positive aspects of such a culture and its impact on the social life of the communities would not have impressed some of the proponents of nationalist patriarchy who sought to uphold a glorified picture of womanhood in ancient India. Some of these historians have tried to adopt a casteist and communal framework in order to explain the "deterioration of the status of women" in subsequent times. Altekar,[78] for instance, has attributed the "deterioration" to the events that set in after the Aryan subjugation of the indigenous population of the Gangetic valley and the subsequent incorporation of the "semi-servile" population into the "fourth *sudra* caste". The intermarriages that took place between the "Aryans" and the dark-skinned women from the indigenous communities who had no knowledge of the Sanskrit language or of Hinduism, according to

76 Jahnabi Gogoi Nath, p. 333.

77 Jahnabi Gogoi, pp. 333–334. See also Tilottoma Misra, "Marriage, Conjugal Norms and the Reformist Agenda in Nineteenth century Assam", in *Man and Society: A Journal of North East Studies*, Vol. 1, No. 1, Spring 2004, ICSSR-NERC, Shillong.

78 A.S. Altekar, "The Position of Women in Hindu Civilization: Retrospect and Prospect"[1938], in Kumkum Roy ed., *Women in Early Indian Societies*, p.55.

Altekar, adversely affected the speech and bearing of the "Aryan" women, leading to "natural repercussions" on their social status. Uma Chakravarti, in her critique of this Altekarian paradigm, comments, "The possibility that the *sudra* woman, whom he regards as a threat, could have contributed to a more dynamic and active kind of womanhood for Hindu society would not even occur to Altekar because his focus is on Aryan women...and in his racist view *sudra* women counted for nothing."[79]

Vernacularization of Literary Culture

The earliest known Sanskrit *kāvya* texts or the vernacular texts that appeared towards the middle of the last millennium were written in languages that had acquired a distinctly cosmopolitan character. Sanskrit itself, which for long had been considered as the "language of the gods", is believed to have become suitable for the great epics and *kāvyas* only after it had acquired a more cosmopolitan character.[80] One can only speculate about why, at a certain point in history, writers who were themselves steeped in Sanskrit learning began to choose local vernaculars rather than the more cosmopolitan literary language in which most of the texts they had studied as a part of their academic curriculum were written. It might have been because of the patronage received from royal personages who were receptive to the emerging literatures in the local languages or because of the demands of a new cultural politics that necessitated the use of the vernacular to

79 Uma Chakravarti, "Beyond the Altekarian Paradigm: Towards a New Understanding of Gender Relations in Early Indian History", in Kumkum Roy ed., *Women in Early Indian Societies*, p.77.

80 For a more detailed discussion on this, *see* Sheldon Pollock, *The Language of the Gods in the World of Men: Sanskrit, Culture and Power in Premodern India*, University of California Press, Berkeley, 2006, chapters 1-5.

disseminate more egalitarian, often subversive, ideas amongst the excluded or marginalized sections of the populace. But whatever may have been the reason, it is certain that the poets who, because of the prevalent social inequalities, had been excluded for centuries from the privilege of expressing themselves, committed what was considered to have been the "transgression" of seizing a local language as a tool with which to express themselves boldly, thereby often incurring the wrath of the Brahmin pundits. It would not be wrong therefore to associate a spirit of rebellion with the newly emerging vernacular culture which could have had a subversive role to play in speaking for the subalterns through a language that could be comprehended by the non-literate masses.

The new class of bilingual poets that emerged in Assam around the fourteenth century CE represented an initiative to not only democratize literary culture but also give the local vernacular a more elevated literary form. As mentioned repeatedly by Mādhava Kandalī, Śaṅkaradeva, and Ananta Kandalī in their rendering of the Sanskrit verses of the *Rāmāyaṇa* into the local language, the poets sought to make their verses aesthetically appealing by embellishing them suitably. The new literary vernacular, in their hands, attained a cosmopolitan character and the dignity required to become a suitable vehicle for a vibrant form of dramatic literature in Assam.

Creating a literary language out of a spoken language was itself a task that could have taken several centuries in most regions of the country. Also, there had always been a long period of silence between the transition from the unscripted oral stage to that of acquiring literariness and the appearance of written texts in the vernacular languages. The emergence of vernacular literature in Assam also showed no significant deviation from this general pattern.

Though "a distinctively Assamese script" is known to have been used for the first time for documentary purposes in the inscription of the Kanai Boroshi Bowa rock near Guwahati, dating back to Śaka 1127 (1205 CE),[81] the language of the inscriptions remained Sanskrit for almost four hundred years, until the Ahoms began to use the language that came to be known as Asamiya in their official communications. It is only in the Chamadhara Rampart rock inscription of Śaka 1538 (1616 CE) of the Ahom king Susengpha Pratāpasiṃha that we have an instance of the use of "a distinctively Assamese language".[82] Commenting on the use of Sanskrit in the rock and copperplate inscriptions of ancient and medieval Assam, Maheswar Neog has pointed out the skilful handling of Sanskrit grammar and metre in some of the inscriptions.[83] Neog as well as Dimbeswar Sarma have emphasized the literary flourishes in some of the Sanskrit inscriptions of the rulers of Assam from the thirteenth century onwards. Many of them are replete with poetic descriptions of the beauty of the land and the qualities of the donor of a land grant.[84] Sarma goes to the extent of conjecturing that the literary qualities present in the Nidhanpur Plates of King Bhāskaravarman, who was an ally of Harṣavardhana of Thanesar and who had ruled over Kāmarūpa in the first half of the seventh century, bear resemblance to that of some of the verses of the poet Bāṇabhaṭṭa, though the latter began to produce his

81 A sort of "proto-Assamese script" *(kuṭila-lipi)* had also been used in the Ambari rock inscription of Samudrapāla (1232 CE) and in the Gachtal inscription near Nagaon which is believed to belong to Śaka 1284 (1232 CE) (see Maheswar Neog, *Prachya Shasanavali,* Assam Publication Board, Guwahati, 1974, Introduction, p.128).

82 Maheswar Neog, *Prachya Shasanavali,* Introduction, p.144.

83 "The epigraphs stand testimony to the study of Sanskrit through the centuries in Assam.", Neog, 1974, Introduction, p.138.

84 Dimbeswar Sarma (ed.,) *Kāmarūpaśāsanāvalī,* Publication Board, Assam, Guwahati, 1981, pp.160–168.

literary verses at a date later than that of the Nidhanpur plates.[85] The use of a variety of Sanskrit metres, figures of speech and rhetorical devices like *āryajāti*, *anuṣṭubh śloka*, and *sabdālaṃkāras* like *anuprāsa* and *yamaka*, *virodha* and *utprekṣa*, in the Tezpur Plates of king Vanamāladeva has also received scholarly attention. Pandit Padmanath Vidyavinoda has even discovered in these plates the use of *śleṣas*, a highly sophisticated poetic device that was widely used in ancient Sanskrit poetry.[86]

While studying the process by which a local spoken language reached a stage in which literary compositions became possible in that language, Dimbeswar Sarma has noted that the Sanskrit used in the ancient copper-plate or stone inscriptions of Assam was marked by certain features that seem to point towards the fact that, at some point, the classical language acquired and accommodated within itself some local features that brought it closer to the spoken language of the region. Although some of the peculiar orthographical features that have been observed in the language used in the inscriptions may have arisen because of errors committed by scribes not familiar with the language, the recurrence of some of these "errors" in different inscriptions points to the possibility that, from as early as the eleventh century CE, the influence of local dialects had begun to creep into the Sanskrit that was being used in the inscriptions of Assam. A detailed analysis of such local influences on the Sanskrit that was being used in the copper-plate grants of Ratnapāla and Indrapāla (both kings of the Pāla dynasty, which ruled over Kāmarūpa around the eleventh century CE) reveals the peculiar

85 Dimbeswar Sarma, p.160: "The description of Durjaya, the capital of Kāmarūpa, in the first copperplates grant of Ratnapāla, a king of the 11th century A.D is reminiscent of the description of the *āśrama* of Jāvāli (in Kane ed. *Kādambarī*) by Bāṇabhaṭṭa".

86 Dimbeswar Sarma, pp.163–164.

usage of certain words that are still common in modern Assamese.[87] Sarma points out especially the specificities in the language of the Sualkuchi Grant of Ratnapāla, which bear "striking resemblance" to modern Assamese words.[88] From such instances, Sarma draws the inference that, though it is commonly believed that the literary language of Assam that emerged during the pre-Vaiṣṇava and the Vaiṣṇava periods was a blend of Brajabuli and Maithili, there was also the possibility of another parallel strain developing from an earlier period that might have acted independently in shaping the literary language of Assam. The refutation of the theory of the linear development of languages—from Sanskrit to Prakrit and Magadhi Prakrit and then to the language of the *Caryāpadas* and to Brajabuli and the modern vernaculars. Instead, what is being suggested here is a theory of the simultaneous existence of Sanskrit and other local languages side by side and the possibility of Sanskrit being influenced by the local languages as much as the latter derived models from Sanskrit. Sarma's observations are based on his analysis of the significantly local elements in the inscriptions of the Pāla dynasty and particularly of the Ambari rock inscription of Samudrapāla discovered in Guwahati.[89] This theory adds another significant dimension to the study of the special features of the literary language at the time of Mādhava Kandalī. It explains the ease with which vernacular poets of the region appropriated and gave local colours to models drawn from Sanskrit and, in doing so, created a new popular literary culture of their own.

Mādhava Kandalī's *Saptakāṇḍa Rāmāyaṇa,* which appeared around 1350 CE, has been accepted as the earliest known

87 Dimbeswar Sarma, Introduction, p.173.

88 Ibid, p.173.

89 Ibid, p.175

vernacular rendering of the epic in the whole of northern India. However, there were other fourteenth-century vernacular writers, amongst whom were Baḍu Candīdās, Hema Sarasvatī, and Harihara Vipra, some of whose writings have been claimed by literary historians of both Assam and Bengal.[90] Who was Mādhava Kandalī and why did he decide to take up this mighty task of making the epic known in north-eastern India even before the spread of the Vaiṣṇava movement in the region and elsewhere in the country? In seeking an answer to this, a brief overview is necessary of the geographical location and the scanty information that is available about the history of the region where this text was produced and the ruler who patronized this task undertaken by the poet.

As discussed earlier, the study of Sanskrit texts was prevalent in Assam from the time of Bhāskaravarman (around the seventh century CE), who belonged to the family of Puṣyavarman, followed by the Śālastambha and the Pāla dynasties that ruled over western Assam until the twelfth century CE. That the two epics and the *purāṇas* were familiar to the people of this region either in their written form or as *kathās* that enriched the oral tradition is proved

90 Baḍu Candīdās's *Śrīkṛṣṇakīrttan*(according to linguists from Assam and Bengal this text was composed probably in the 13th or 14th century C.E, after the *Caryāpadas* and before Mādhava Kandalī (see Lilavati Saikia's Introduction to Badu Chandidas's *Srikrishnakirtan*, Assam Publication Board, Guwahati, 2007) and Hema Sarasvatī's *Prahlād Carita* and *Hara-Gaurī Saṃbād* ascribed to the 14th-15th century C.E. (See Ajaykumar Chakravarty's Introduction to Hem Saraswati's *Pracīn Punthi*, ed. by Ajaykumar Chakravarty, Sahitya Akademi, New Delhi, 1996) These texts are some examples of such early vernacular texts.

by the mention of the Rāma-kathās in the *Kālikā Purāṇa*.[91] But it was only in the fourteenth and fifteenth centuries that the *Rāmāyaṇa* was rendered into the local language of Assam by several poets, including Mādhava Kandalī, Ananta Kandalī, Ananta Dāsa, Raghunātha Mahanta, Śaṅkaradeva, Mādhavadeva, and Durgābara Kāyastha. Of these, Durgābara's *Gīti-Rāmāyaṇa,* written in the sixteenth century, has proved to be the most popular version and is still being sung in Assam by the folk minstrels who perform the *Biyāha ojā-pāli.*[92]

The Literary Language of the Vernacular Texts

Linguists have agreed that, though none of the established vernacular authors of ancient Assam have named their literary language as Asamiya or Kāmarūpi, it is certain

---

91 *Kālikā Purāṇa* is considered to be one of the eighteen upa-purāṇas composed in Kāmarūpa in the late ninth century or the tenth century CE. It tells the story of the goddess Kālī, the rituals prescribed for her worship and also contains descriptions of the rivers and mountains of Kāmarūpa. Though this purāṇa is devoted to the '*śakti-mārga*', yet it contains some references to Rāma-kathā which are not based on the Vālmīki *Rāmāyaṇa*. Adhyāyas 36 to 40 of this *purāṇa* relates the story of conception, birth and upbringing of Narakāsura who was the legendary ruler of the ancient kingdom of Kāmarūpa-Prāgjyotiṣpura, but the historicity of whose story is still under academic surveillance. According to the *Kālikā-Purāṇa*, Naraka's birth is linked to Sītā's return to her father's home at Videha after the killing of Rāvaṇa by Rāma and as desired by her mother Vasumatī /Bhūmi (Earth-goddess), she gives birth to Naraka who is the son of Vasumatī and Viṣṇu as Varāha. He was brought up by Janaka, the king of Videha and later conveyed by Vasumatī to Kāmarūpa to rule over the land as a devotee of Viṣṇu. Thus this story seems to de-asurize Naraka by linking him with Sītā, Janaka, Vasumatī and Viṣṇu. Being born in the same sacrificial space in Janaka's kingdom where Sītā was also born, Naraka has been considered a sibling of Sītā. (For a more detailed scholarly study, see B.D. Chattopadhyaya's chapter on "Local and Beyond: The Story of *Asura* Naraka and Society, State and Religion in Early Assam", in his book *The Concept of Bharatavarsha and other Essays,* Permanent Black, Ranikhet, 2017, pp.104–137).

92 For details, see Satyendranath Sarma, *Ramayanar Itibritta*, 1984, p.250 and his *Epics and Puranas in Early Assamese Literature*, 1972, pp.17–18.

that a distinct regional language was in existence in this region as early as the seventh century CE during the time of Yuan Chwang's (Hiuen Tsang's) visit to Kāmarūpa (643 CE).[93] But, as in the case of other regional languages of eastern India that were in the process of formation in the latter part of the first millennium CE, the writers who used the spoken language of the then kingdom of Kāmarūpa for their compositions did not give a specific name to their language. The language spoken in the whole stretch of the territory across the Brahmaputra valley and reaching up to Cooch Behar and Rangpur had no name but was accepted as the language spoken and understood by a mixed population of different ethnic denominations. The *Caryāgīta*[94] compositions that are ascribed to Buddhist writers of eastern India have linguistic elements which have been identified with ancient Asamiya, Bangla, Oriya, Maithili, and Bhojpuri among others. Similarly, the language of *Śrīkṛṣṇakīrttana*, a text written sometime around the beginning of the thirteenth century, before Mādhava Kandalī composed his *Saptakāṇḍa Rāmāyaṇa*, by Baḍu Candīdās, who probably lived in Cooch Behar (Kāmatāpura) during the reign of Durlabhanārāyaṇa, has elements identifiable with the spoken language of ancient Assam and the *deśī-bhāṣā* spoken in western Assam and

---

93 Significantly, the Chinese traveler Yuan Chwang (Hiuen Tsang) in his travel notes does not mention the language spoken in Gauḍa but makes specific mention of the language of Kāmarūpa as "slightly different" from that prevalent in central India (see Banikanta Kakati, *Assamese, its Formation and Development*, DHAS, Guwahati, 1941, p.x of preface).

94 It has been generally agreed upon by scholars that the *caryāpadas/caryāgītas* were composed between eighth and twelfth centuries CE (Satyendranath Sarma, *Asamiya Sahityar Samikshatmak Itibritta*, Guwahati, 1986 [F.P.1981] p.49)

Cooch Behar.[95] Literary historiographers are still battling with the controversy about the linguistic status of texts written in trans-regional literary languages that defy all attempts to place them within the "nation-language literature" category. Banikanta Kakati mentions that the "parallel forms and characteristics of different dialects" that had been freely used by the pre-modern writers of western Assam were discontinued after writers became linguistically self-conscious at a later period.[96]

Political considerations played a major role in this process of separation of the mixed languages into separate entities. It would be interesting to see how a region that for several centuries (probably from the fourth century AD to the eighteenth century CE) experienced concurrent sovereignties exercised by the rulers of Kāmarūpa, Asam, Kāmatāpura, Gauḍa, and Bhutan, developed a vernacular tongue that was spoken, written, or understood by numerous communities spread across the region, from the borders of Mithilā to the eastern limits of the Brahmaputra valley and down south to Śrīhaṭṭa and Chittagong on the Bay of Bengal. The compositions known as the *Caryāpadas* have been claimed by historiographers of Asamiya, Bangla, and Oriya literatures because the language of these verses resembles Old Asamiya as much as Old Bangla and Old

95 Lilavati Saikia, ed., *Baḍu Caṇḍīdāsar Śrīkṛṣṇakīrtan*,'Bhumika', p.14–15. The contents of this text which are primarily based on *śṛngāra-rasa*, do not resemble the Kṛṣṇa-bhakti compositions of Śaṅkaradeva or the Assamese *bhakti* poets of the post-Śaṅkaradeva period (ibid. p.18).

96 Banikanta Kakati, *Assamese, its Formation and Development*, DHAS, Guwahati, 1941, p.11 (see also the discussion in Tilottoma Misra, "Literary Cultures in North-East India: Shrinking Frontiers", *Economic and Political Weekly*, 51:38, 2016).

Oriya.[97] There are other similar texts available that reveal a trans-regional character in language and content. The language of Baḍu Candīdās' *Śrīkṛṣṇakīrttana*[98] resembles the literary language used by Mādhava Kandalī and the fifteenth-century Vaiṣṇava poets of Assam. It also has a strong affinity to the Deśī-Rājbaṃshī *bhāṣā* of western Assam and also to old forms of Oriya, Maithili, and eastern Hindi.[99] The available manuscript copies of the text show that even its script resembles the old Asamiya script (the two letters "wa" and "ra" are written as in Asamiya).[100] The poets who composed these texts were writing for a polyglot literary community whose works

---

97 Suniti Kumar Chatterji, Artavallabha Mahanti Memorial Lectures, First Series, Orissa Sahitya Akademi, Bhubaneswar, 1966, p.30.

98 Banikanta Kakati, while referring to the comments of Suniti Kumar Chatterji on the language of *Śrīkṛṣṇakīrttan* says, "The *Kṛṣṇa Kīrtan* [Śrīkṛṣṇakīrtan] presents a mixture of dialects which have not yet started on courses of independent development but the beginning of which seems to have been well laid down. If it be allowed to represent the pre-Bengali and pre-Assamese dialect groups by the unknown quantity x, then it may be said that *Kṛṣṇa Kīrtan* preserves the specimens of latter day x—dialects which in time developed into distinctive Bengali and Assamese languages." (Banikanta Kakati, *Assamese its Formation and Development*, p.10).

99 Khan Choudhury Amanatulla Ahmed points out the similarities between the language of the Buddhist dohas and songs, the oral tradition of Jugīr-gīt/Maynāmatīr gīt/ Gopīcāndar gīt, Gorakhnāther gīt, the tiger-god Sonārāyar gīt, which may be cited as examples of the ancient Koch language, and the literary language of *Srikrishnakirtan*, Mādhava Kandalī, Śaṅkardeva and other early Vaiṣṇava poets of Kāmarūpa (p.174). He also dwells upon the influence of the languages and dialects of the neighbouring communities with which the Koch kingdom had active commercial and cultural contact (the Tibetans, Bhutias, Garos, Meches, Nepalis) together with the literary languages of the Muslims (Persian and Arabic—"musalmanī bānglā"). See Khan Choudhury Amanatulla Ahmed, "Kochh Biharar Prachin Bhasha", *Paricharika*, Sravan-Bhadra, 1326 (1910), translated from the original Bangla into Asamiya by Anjan Sarma, in B. Mahanta ed., *Shukladhwaja*, Bhabani Books, 2015, p.187.

100 Lilavati Saikia ed., *Baḍu Caṇḍīdāser Śrīkṛṣṇakīrtan*, Asam Prakashan Parishad, Guwahati, 2007, Introduction, p.xv. This text has been claimed by literary historiographers of Bengal as one of the earliest available texts in Bangla.

belonged to a canvas wider than the narrow limits set by modern nationalism. Asamiya, the language of the region was, according to Grierson's *Linguistic Survey of India*, developed from the Magadhi dialect, which is similar to the old Eastern Prakrit. Magadhi Apabhramsa spread in different directions, taking different distinct forms in Orissa, Bengal, and Kāmarūpa-Kāmatāpura. Grierson says that the reason we find some affinity between the languages of northern Bengal (and Assam) and Oriya is that each branch is directly connected to its common parent, Magadhi Apabhramsa.[101] Suniti Kumar Chatterji, basing his thesis on the material collected by Grierson, divides Eastern Magadhi, Prakrit, and Apabhramsa into four dialect groups of which Kamarupiya is the name given to the dialects spoken in northern Bengal and Assam. This linguistic history of eastern India has often been sidelined by powerful votaries of linguistic chauvinism who try to marginalize less powerful varieties of Magadhi Apabhramsa as mere *patois* of their more powerful branch, which received colonial patronage earlier than others.[102]

Early Assamese writers did not refer to their language as Asamiya, but variously called it "*deśī*", "*loukika*", or "own" speech. Thus, in a verse colophon Mādhava Kandalī says that his composition is not in the language of the gods but

---

101 Cited in Banikanta Kakati, *Assamese, its Formation and Development*, DHAS, Guwahati, 1941, p.6.

102 "The comparative obscurity of Assamese and the spread of a powerful Bengali literature almost all over the globe gives an impression to foreigners that Assamese is a patois of Bengali." Banikanta Kakati, *AFD*, p.6. Kakati establishes with meticulous care that the Assamese language does not show any characteristics of being a dialect of Bengali. Rather, both the languages developed on parallel lines , each "with peculiar dialectical predispositions " of its own. He discusses at length the difference between the two languages in the vocabulary system, in the systems of accentuation, in the case affixes, in the completely different negative conjugations in the Assamese language, in the use of plural suffixes and other linguistic features.

in that of the common man.[103] Similarly, Śaṅkaradeva, in his *Uttarakāṇḍa,* seeks forgiveness from the wise for his attempt to render the verses of the epic in his own language, following in the footsteps of Mādhava Kandalī, whom he acknowledges generously as 'the unerring predecessor" ("*pūrba kavi apramādī*").[104] Ananta Kandalī, in a verse colophon added to his translation of *Dasama,* says that he prefers to write in the local speech so that women and *śūdras* may delight in listening.[105] Choudhury Amanatulla Ahmed points out that Pītāmbara Siddhāntabāgīśa, who was a court poet in Naranārāyaṇa's court, translated the *Mārkaṇḍeya-purāṇa* and the *Daśama-skandha* of the *Bhāgavad* as instructed by the king. In the colophon of the *Mārkaṇḍeya purāṇa*, Pītāmbara says that he was requested by the king to translate the difficult verses of the *purāṇas,* which can be understood only by pundits, into the language of the masses so that everyone can partake of the wisdom of the *śāstras* ("*nija deshbhāṣā bande raciyo payār*").[106] It is obvious from this royal command that, whatever may have been the original dwelling place of the poet, the language in

103 Mādhava Kandalī, 'Kiṣkindhākāṇḍa', 26, 72-78 , in *Rāmāyaṇa*, ed., by Kiranchandra Sarma, (1941) Lawyer's Book Stall, Guwahati, 2008.

104 *Uttarakāṇḍa*, 19:4-6.

105 See N.C. Sarma, *The Vaisnava Poets of North-Eastern India*, Punthi-Pustak, Kolkata, 1991, p.4.

106 Khan Choudhury Amanatulla Ahmed, "Koch Biharar Pracin Bhasha", *Paricharika*, Sravan-Bhadra, 1326 (1910), translated from the original Bangla into Asamiya by Anjan Sarma, in B. Mahanta ed., *Shukladhwaja,* Bhabani Books, 2015, p.168.

which he composed the vernacular texts was the language of the common people of the Koch kingdom. [107]

This spoken language had by that time acquired a variety of forms between the eastern and the western boundaries of the kingdom. But the literary form of the vernacular that appears in the writings of Hema Sarasvatī, Mādhava Kandalī, Rāma Sarasvatī, Harihara Vipra, Śaṅkaradeva, Mādhavdeva, Ananta Kandalī, and other Vaiṣṇava poets of the fifteenth and sixteenth centuries drew heavily on Sanskrit. The Sanskrit texts that they translated, adapted, recreated, or re-interpreted necessitated a liberal mixing of *tadbhava* (derived from Sanskrit) and *tatsama* (Sanskrit) words. Many of the writers followed the tradition of dispensing with verbs that impart the local identity to a vernacular language and often merely stringing together nouns and adjectives drawn directly from Sanskrit. Such a blend of Sanskrit and vernacular was used by many Vaiṣṇava poets of pre-modern times elsewhere in India, which gave their language a cosmopolitan character. The literary vernacular used by the Assamese Vaiṣṇava poets would have been understood easily by a wider section of the literate public, extending from the eastern-most limits of the Brahmaputra valley across Cooch Behar, Bengal, Odisham and the Mithila region. The nature and scope of the traditional form of education imparted in the *ṭols* and *catuṣpāṭhīs* of the time were largely responsible for the development of a Sanskrit-based vernacular language in the region. The schools introduced students to the Vedas,

107 Interestingly, it is the neo-Vaishnavite movement which has been credited with the advent of a new consciousness amongst poets and patrons to educate the common people, especially women and śūdras , in the epics and *purāṇas* which were written in Sanskrit, a language inaccessible to them so far. The Kachārī and Koch rulers who were outside the fold of the graded caste order, were originally the worshippers of different Śiva- Śakti cults and must have been gradually drawn towards the Vaiṣṇava movement which made the epics and the classics available to them.

kāvyas, *śāstras*, philosophical texts written in Sanskrit, and also to the basic principles of Sanskrit grammar and the Sanskrit lexicon. So, Śaṅkaradeva, a Kāyastha by birth,[108] learnt the Vedas, Upaniṣadas, the two epics, the *purāṇas*, the *saṃhitās*, the *tantras*, and the *kāvyas* in the *ṭol* of his Brahman guru, Mahendra Kandalī.[109]

With such a grounding in the classics, it is significant that Śaṅkaradeva's earliest composition, *Hariścandra-upākhyāna*, which he completed when still a student at the *ṭol*, was not in Sanskrit but in the vernacular. This text is an adaptation of the *Mārkaṇḍeya-purāṇa*, probably one of the popular *purāṇas* of his time in eastern India.[110] However, Śaṅkaradeva in his later life did compose a few Sanskrit verses in his *ṭoṭaya* hymn "*madhu-dānava*",[111] which he recited in the court of King Naranārāyana, probably to establish his credentials as someone who had scholarly training in the classical language. He also compiled an anthology of philosophical verses in Sanskrit called *Bhakti Ratnākara*. Ananta Kandalī, who has proclaimed in one of his colophons that he was "adept in Sanskrit verses", wrote only two digests containing *ślokas* from the *Dharma-śāstras* (*Nīti-ratna* and *Kalpa-druma*) but did not attempt to write

108 "Many of the Vaiṣṇava leaders of the period, including Śaṅkaradeva and Mādhavadeva, were *Kāyasthas*", Maheswar Neog, op.cit, p.75.

109 Daityāri Ṭhakur's *Śaṅkaradeva-Mādhavadeva Jīvana-caritra* abstains from giving details about all the courses of studies imparted to Śaṅkaradeva in the ṭol, but the *Kathā-guru-carita* mentions the Vedas, Purāṇas and other texts. (see Maheswar Neog, *Early History of the Vaisnava Faith and Movement in Assam*, Lawyer's Book Stall, Guwahati, 1998 (third edition) p.102.

110 Maheswar Neog, op.cit, p.162.

111 A celebration of the divine attributes of Viṣṇu in "rolling alliteration" (M. Neog. op.cit, p.207).

his own verses in that language.[112] As mentioned before, he has stated specifically that, though he was capable of composing verses in Sanskrit, he preferred to write in the local language so that women, *śudras,* and illiterate people could also listen to the verses.[113] Mādhava Kandalī, in order to justify his bold innovation of retelling the Rāma story in the Assamese language, adopts a similar device of asserting his independence from the original "language of the gods" in which Vālmīki had composed the epic. In a verse colophon inserted into the *Kiṣkindhākanda* of his *Rāmāyaṇa,* he says:

"You have so far heard the story of Rāma, which is replete with diverse poetic sentiments (*rasas*) most sacred. May your minds be filled with satisfaction, but do not find fault with the abridgements or elaborations that I have introduced into the text. Vālmīki composed his *śāstra* in poetic metre and prose. I have tried to compose these verses according to my own understanding of his work. Who can ever comprehend each and every sentiment of the poet? A bird can fly only as far as his wings will permit. Poets compose according to the usages of their own time, sometimes guided by their own imagination and sometimes by the available material in society. This composition is not in the language of the gods but in that of the common

112 Nabin Chandra Sarma, *The Vaisnavite Poets of North-Eastern India: Ananta Kandali*, Punthi-Pustak, Calcutta, 1991, p.4.

113 Ananta Kandalī, *Daśama*, v.3094, cited in N.C. Sarma, *The Vaisnava Poets of North-Eastern India: Ananta Kandali*, p.4.

man ("*deva vāṇī nuhi iṭo loukika se kathā*"). Therefore, do not look for its defects everywhere." [114]

Here, Mādhava Kandalī asserts his freedom as a poet to choose his language and to translate Vālmīki's verses into the vernacular, "according to his own understanding" of the text. But, elsewhere, he acknowledges that he wrote in the vernacular to please his royal patron Mahāmaṇikya. Mādhava Kandalī belonged to a village located in the kingdom of Mahāmaṇikya and spoke the language spoken by the king and his subjects. In another colophon attached to his *Laṅkākāṇḍa*, he reveals his identity and purpose in the following words:

"I, who am known as Kavirāja Kandalī, at the request of the Barāha Rājā Śrī Mahāmāṇikya, have rendered the beautiful verses of the *Rāmāyaṇa* into this form for the benefit of the common people. Dispensing with unnecessary details, I have added certain poetic embellishments to the language spoken by Rājā Mahāmāṇikya, like the cream that emerges from churning of milk. If scholars are displeased with my effort, I beseech them to reserve their censure until they have found anything in my work which is not there in the original book."[115]

Mādhava Kandalī was presumably well-versed in Sanskrit. The text of his *Rāmāyaṇa* follows closely the original Vālmīki text. By translating/adapting the earlier text, however, he

---

114 "*Bālmīki racilā śāstra gadya padya chande/ tāhāka bicāra āmi kariyā pravandhe/ aponaāra buddhi artha ji mata bujhilon/ saṅkṣepa kariyā tāka pada biracilon/ samasta rasaka kone janibāka pāre/ pakṣhī saba urai jena pakhā anusāre... kato nija kato lambhā kathā anusāre/ deva vāṇī nuhi iṭo loukika se kathā/ eteke ihāra doṣa nalaibā sarbbathā.*" Mādhava Kandalī, *Kiṣkindhākāṇḍa*, 26, 72-78 , in *Saptakāṇḍa Rāmāyaṇa* [Translation mine].

115 Mādhava Kandalī, *Laṅkākāṇḍa*, 56, 23-25 in *Saptakāṇḍa Rāmāyaṇa*, [Translation mine].

gave the regional text a separate identity. Sanskrit texts in other parts of India, too, had served as launching pads from which vernacular writers set off according to their own genius, freely working with the original renderings. Regional writers found Sanskrit to be a vehicle that enabled them to create their own literary languages by borrowing liberally not only from the vocabulary of Sanskrit but also metrical structures and other aesthetic elements of the language. Therefore, it is not surprising that the language of Mādhava Kandalī's *Rāmāyaṇa* was a fine blend of Sanskrit *tatsama, ardha-tatsama,* and *tadbhava* words and a rich corpus of local colloquial expressions, including even a sprinkling of foreign Parsi words (*dukaan, nukkar, bazaar*, etc).[116] Besides his competent translations of the memorable images used in Vālmīki's *Rāmāyaṇa*, Mādhava Kandalī embellished his text with colourful and highly expressive local idioms, images, and metrical variations that gave his verses a dramatic quality. Later Vaiṣṇava poets often made liberal use of some of these elements found in Mādhava Kandalī's language.[117] Commenting on the early variety of Assamese found in the language of Mādhava Kandalī and his contemporaries, the linguist Banikanta Kakati says that, though the "Assamese idiom seems to be fully individualized" in their writings, in comparison with the Assamese language that was used by Śaṅkaradeva, "a certain archaism" is clearly visible in their works. This archaism, however, is "entirely absent" in Śaṅkaradeva's language.[118] Though the *bargītas* and the *aṅkīya-nāṭas* of

116 See Ramcharan Thakuria's Foreword to Lilavati Saikia's *Madhava Kandalir Ramayanar Bhasha*, Asam Sahitya Sabha, Jorhat, 1993). Also, Choudhury Amanatulla, "Koch Biharar Pracin Bhasha", Dwijendra Nath Bhakat, "Bargitat Rajbangshi Bhashar Samal", in *Shukladhwaj*, 2015, pp.213-218.

117 See Satyendranath Sarma, *Ramayanar Itibritta*, 1984, pp.258–262.

118 Banikanta Kakati, *Assamese its Formation and Development*, pp. 12–13.

Śaṅkaradeva are in the hybrid literary language known as Brajabuli, the language which he uses in his translations from the epics and *purāṇas* is close to the spoken language of the people of the region during his time.

While examining the unique features of Mādhava Kandalī's poetic language, one must keep in mind the compulsions of the new elements that were introduced into the contents of the vernacular version of the epic. For an audience that was comprised primarily of people unfamiliar with the manuscript culture but familiar with oral representations of the epics, recasting and dramatizing characters and scenes in accordance with popular cultural norms was essential. Mādhava Kandalī as well as Śaṅkaradeva in his *Uttarakāṇḍa*, for instance, used a powerful language tinged with forceful local expressions to depict the complexities of the Sītā-Rāma relationship. The poets also tried consciously to retain the oral structure of the text by addressing the audience directly at the beginning or end of the *kāṇḍas* and by mentioning the presence of the sympathetic listener at crucial dramatic moments in the text. Thus, Mādhava Kandalī not only refers to the oral tradition but also invokes the presence of his royal patron before his audience when he acknowledges at the end of the *Araṇyakāṇḍa*, "Thus Mādhava recites while Mahāmāṇikya listens" ("*madhave bhaṇanta mahāmānike śunanta*").[119]

The process of vernacularization of literary culture in northeastern India, however, witnessed a phase of linguistic hybridization when Vaiṣṇava poets who were in search of a literary language more dignified and elevated than common speech as a vehicle of expression for a devotional subject chose an artificial language that was given the name Brajavali (or Brajabuli). Created in the style

119 Mādhava Kandalī, *Rāmāyaṇa*, 'Araṇyakāṇḍa', *adhyāya* 22:21.

of Vidyāpati, the Maithili poet whose works inspired a wide range of poets in eastern India, this language was a blend of Maithili and other local languages in different regions. In the case of Assam, Maithili was mixed with old Assamese to produce a literary language in which all the religious hymns (*bargīta*) of Śaṅkaradeva and Mādhavadeva and all their devotional plays (*aṅkīya-nāṭa*) were composed. This variety of Brajabuli is not the same as the Apabhramsa derived from a variety of western Hindi which is also called Brajabhāṣa.[120] Śaṅkaradeva probably came into contact with the songs of Vidyāpati during his first pilgrimage to northern India and composed his earliest known *bargīta* ("*mana meri Rāma caraṇehi lāgu*") in the artificial language of Brajabuli while he was in the Badrikasrama (around 1490 CE). It was possibly because of the availability of this newly created literary language that Śaṅkaradeva, during his pilgrimages to various religious centres in northern India and his long and fruitful sojourn at Jagannath Puri, could participate easily in religious discourses with other Vaiṣṇava contemporaries.

Royal Patronage of Vernacular Literary Culture

The history of medieval Assam is characterized by a shifting, overlapping sovereignty in the region comprising western Assam, northern Bengal, and some parts of eastern Bengal. The kingdoms of Kāmarūpa and Kāmatā expanded over this whole region at the time when the Ahoms, under the leadership of Sukapha, entered Assam from the north-east and established themselves in the Sivasagar region (1253 CE). After the gradual weakening of the ancient Varman, Śālastambha, and Pāla dynasties that had ruled over Kāmarūpa from around the fourth century CE to the twelfth century CE, the Kachārī powers assumed

120 For details, see Maheswar Neog, *Sri Sri Śaṅkaradeva* (in Assamese), Lawyers' Book Stall, Guwahati, 1963, p.163.

supremacy in the region, and the history of Kāmarūpa and Kāmatā became intrinsically linked from around the time of the Koch king Durlabhanārāyaṇa (second quarter of the fourteenth century CE). It was probably around this time that the capital of Kāmarūpa was also shifted to Kāmatāpur in Cooch Behar because of repeated incursions by the Kachārīs.[121] Both Durlabhanārāyaṇa and his successor Indranārāyaṇa have been widely mentioned in Assamese Vaiṣṇava hagiographies and other writings as great patrons of learning, especially of vernacular literature. During their reigns, many vernacular poets from the Kāmarūpa-Kāmatā region flourished under royal patronage. Hema Sarasvatī of Assam was writing in the fourteenth century in the kingdom of Durlabhanārāyana, while Kaviratna Sarasvatī and Harihara Vipra's writings have been ascribed to the reign of Durlabhanārāyaṇa's son Indranārāyaṇa.[122] Durlabhanārāyaṇa, who probably ruled in Kāmatā and Kāmarūpa towards the end of the thirteenth century CE,[123] was one of the earliest kings to patronize this vernacularization of literary culture in Assam. It is interesting to note that, though this period seems to coincide with the time of Mādhava Kandalī, unlike other poets of Kāmarūpa, Kandalī did not seek the patronage of the Koch kings of Kāmatā but chose to live and write under the patronage of the Kachārī king Mahāmāṇikya. However, about a century later, when the Kachārī kings lost out to the superior Ahom military power and were finally pushed to the margins of the Ahom empire through shrewd diplomacy and military prowess of the Ahoms, the

---

121 Kanaklal Barua, *Early History of Kamarupa*, Shillong, 1933, pp.249–250.

122 Banikanta Kakati, *Assamese, its Formation and Development*, Guwahati: DHAS, 1941, p.12.

123 Edward Gait, *History of Assam*, Thacker Spink and Co., Calcutta, 1963, p.44.

Koch kings emerged as the main patrons of vernacular literary culture.

Naranārāyaṇa (1540–1587)[124] ruled over Kāmarūpa and Kāmatā for almost fifty years in the sixteenth century and consolidated Koch power in both Cooch Behar and Assam, extending his kingdom and his suzerainty over large areas in western Assam after achieving momentous victories over the Ahoms, Kachārīs, and other indigenous rulers of eastern India. He was a great patron of learning, especially of vernacular renderings of Sanskrit texts. Some of the best and most influential Assamese literary works were produced under his direct patronage.[125] Paṇḍit Puruṣottama Bidyābāgīśa wrote the Sanskrit grammar *Prayogaratnamālā*, Rāma Sarasvatī,[126] Pītāmbara Siddhāntabāgīśa[127] and Ananta Kandalī[128] rendered into the

---

124 According to Amanat-ullah Ahmed, he died in 1587 (*Kochhabiharar Itihas*, 2014 edition, Guwahati, p.187), but Gait suggests 1584 (*History of Assam*, p.58) while Kanaklal Barua pushes it to "about 1586", (*Early History of Kamarupa*, p.301).

125 According to Hemchandra Goswami, "The laborious works of this glorious band of scholars were widely circulated among the people of the country as a result of which 'women and Sudras all became learned' (*Darrang-raj-vamsavali*, stanzas 604-612)." *Descriptive Catalogue of Assamese Manuscripts*, University of Calcutta, 1930, p.xiv.

126 "Rāma Saraswati, the most voluminous Assamese writer of the 16th century," says Hemchandra Goswami (*Descriptive Catalogue of Assamese Manuscripts*, p.13). Rāma Sarasvatī, who was a contemporary of Śaṅkaradeva, "prepared the translation of the whole of the Sanskrit *Mahabharata* into metrical Assamese under the patronage of Naranarayana" (ibid).

127 "...the famous Sanskrit scholar of Assam, author of 18 Sanskrit books known as Kaumudis on the rites and ceremonies of Hindus" (Hemchandra Goswami, *Descriptive Catalogue of Assamese Manuscripts*, p.133).

128 Ananta Kandalī, a Vaiṣṇava poet of Assam, was a contemporary of Śaṅkaradeva's. Though he was trained in the Sanskrit *tarkashastra* tradition, he later came under the influence of Śaṅkaradeva's writings and undertook the completion of the translation of the sixth and the tenth *skandhas* of the *Bhāgavata-purāṇa*, probably under Śaṅkaradeva's instructions. He also attempted to re-write Mādhava Kandalī's *Rāmāyaṇa* by infusing it with the *bhakti* element that he found to be lacking in the earlier text.

local languages several verses from the epics and *purāṇas*. The greatest Vaiṣṇava poet from Assam, Śaṅkaradeva, composed most of his religious hymns, the *Bhāgavad* tales and renderings of the *Bhāgavata-purāṇa*, the religious dramas, and a doctrinal treatise (*Bhakti-ratnākara)* during the last period of his life, which he spent in Patbausi, at that time situated in Naranārāyaṇa's Koch kingdom. The *Uttarakāṇḍa* of the *Rāmāyaṇa* that he rendered into vernacular verse and appended to the incomplete text of Mādhava Kandalī's *Saptakāṇḍa Rāmāyaṇa* is also said to belong to this period.[129]

The patronage and goodwill offered by the Koch rulers to all the great poets of eastern India who lived in or migrated to their kingdom in search of a congenial atmosphere has been gratefully acknowledged by many of the poets. Rāma Sarasvatī, one of the most prolific writers in Naranārāyaṇa's court, has paid generous tributes to the greatness of his patron Naranārāyaṇa: "Thus, the saintly king Naranārāyaṇa, the greatest of all kings, summoned me to his presence and ordered me to compose the verses of the *Mahābhārata*."[130] In a verse colophon attached to his translation of the *Vanaparva* of the *Mahābhārata*, Rāma Sarasvatī mentions with gratitude

---

129 According to Maheswar Neog, the *Uttarakāṇḍa* was composed by Śaṅkaradeva during his stay in Cooch Behar in the last part of his life. According to this opinion, this text belongs to the same period as the other work on Rāma-kathā by the poet, i.e, the *Rāma-vijaya* drama (see Maheswar Neog, *Early History of the Vaisnava Faith and Movement in Assam, [1965]* Lawyers' Book Stall, Guwahati,, 1998, p.162). Satyendranath Sarma, however, doubts the information supplied in the *Kathā-guru carita* about the composition of the Adi and *Uttarakāṇḍa* of the Assamese *Rāmāyaṇa*. The signature verses attached to the *Uttarakāṇḍa* of Śaṅkaradeva, in which he reveals his ancestry in details, gives the impression that he completed the *Uttarakāṇḍa* during the early period of his life while he was still at Bardowa, long before he met his disciple Mādhavadeva (Satyendranath Sarma, *Ramayanar Itibritta*, pp.320-321, Dibrugarh University).

130 Rāma Sarasvatī, 'Kulācala-badh', as quoted in Satyendranath Sarma's *Asamiya Sahityar Samīkshatmak Itibritta*, p.168, Saumar Printing and Publishing, Guwahati, 1986 (prose translation mine).

that Naranārāyaṇa offered to send him all the manuscripts and critical commentaries on the *Mahābhārata* that were in his possession so that the poet could undertake the great task. Not only books, which were sent to him piled on a bullock cart, but also other generous incentives like gold, silver, and servants were sent by the king for the poet's personal comfort.[131]

Considering the important role played by the Kachārī rulers in the creation and development of a distinct vernacular literary culture in north-eastern India before the Koch kings began to perform that role, it is bewildering that so little documentary evidence is available on the Kachārī and the Cuṭīya rulers had ruled Assam before the advent of the Ahoms. As stated by the poet Mādhava Kandalī in the verse colophon at the end of his *Laṅkākāṇḍa*, his patron, who requested him to undertake the task of documentation was Mahāmānikya, a Barāhi-Kachārī ruler of central Assam. It may be mentioned here that the interest of the Kachārī king Mahāmānikya in the *Rāmāyaṇa* cannot be attributed to matters of faith alone, because, unlike the Koch rulers of Kāmarūpa and Kāmatāpura, the Kachārī rulers were not worshippers of Viṣṇu, Rāma, or Kṛṣṇa. They were subscribers to the ancient *śākta* and *śaiva* faith. The reigning deity of the Kachārī kingdom was the goddess Tāmreśvarī, aka Kesaikhati, whose temple was situated in Sadiya. Animal and human sacrifices were offered to this goddess by the Kachārī royal family even after they migrated westward to central Assam. The Kachārī kings also built temples dedicated to Bāneśvara and Daśabhujā in their new capitals at Sonapur and Banpur.[132]

131 See Satyendranath Sarma, ibid.

132 Surya Kumar Bhuyan ed., *Kachārī Burañjī*, DHAS, Guwahati, 1984, Introduction, p.vi and p.10.

Scholars have expressed diverse opinions about the identity of this ruler named Mahāmāṇikya and the exact territory over which he may have ruled. As there is no epigraphic evidence or mention in Assamese chronicles of this ruler, it has been surmised by historians from the scattered evidence available that he belonged to a larger Boḍo-Kachārī race and ruled over central Assam around the fourteenth century CE, just before the Ahoms conquered the region. Mahāmāṇikya has also been identified by most Assamese scholars[133] with a king bearing a similar name ruling over Jayantiyapur and parts of the Kapili valley. It has also been conjectured from the information available in the *Kachārī Burañjī*[134] that the capital of the Barāhi kingdom could have been situated somewhere in the Sivasagar district. Mādhava Kandalī, who bore the title Kavirāja Kandalī, was probably a resident of the present-day Nagaon district.[135] But, whatever may have been the identities of the poet and his patron, it is certain that between the thirteenth and fourteenth centuries CE, there ruled a king in Assam belonging to an indigenous community, who entrusted a Brahman poet living in his kingdom with rendering Vālmīki's epic into the local language, thus laying the foundation for the

133 See Banikanta Kakati, *Assamese, its Formation and Development*; Kanaklal Barua, *Early History of Kamarupa*; Hemchandra Goswami, *Descriptive Catalogue of Assamese Manuscripts*; Satyendranath Sarma, *Ramayanar Itibritta*; Maheswar Neog, "Assamese Literature before Śaṅkaradeva", in Banikanta Kakati ed., *Aspects of Early Assamese Literature*, 1953.

134 *Kachārī Burañjī*, edited by S.K. Bhuyan. This chronicle was one of the many *Kaṭaki-burañjīs* or chronicles that detailed the political relationship of the Ahoms with other neighbouring states, prepared by the Kaṭakis or Ahom ambassadors (also available are a *Tripurā Burañjī* and a *Jayantīyā Burañjī*). Most of these *Kaṭaki-burañjīs* were from the eighteenth century [see S.K. Bhuyan's Preface to *Kachārī Burañjī*].

135 Satyendranath Sarma, *Ramayanar Itibritta*, p.253.

vernacularization of literary culture in north-east India.[136] It could also be conjectured, that under the patronage of a ruler from an indigenous community, stories from the two Indian epics captured the imagination of the local people belonging to different ethnic communities and minstrels from those communities recreated oral versions of the epics in the local dialects. *Sabin Alun*, which is a very interesting component of the oral literature of the Kārbi people, indicates such a possibility.[137] It is important to emphasize that when, as a response to the onslaught of more powerful political and cultural forces, an aggressive linguistic nationalism developed in Assam during the colonial period, the contribution of these rulers from the indigenous tribes of the region to the growth and development of the literary vernacular was overlooked. In this way, a historic displacement and exclusion of the tribes from their central position in the development of literary culture in the region took place. But, in the light of the new academic interest in the history of literary cultures in the subcontinent, it would be pertinent to focus attention on the fact that, at a time when the Brāhmaṇas and Kāyasthas dominated the literary world of Assam and eastern India, the gap between the literary and the non-literary world was sought to be bridged through a vigorous effort of translation/representation of Sanskrit texts into the local languages under the active initiative of the indigenous Koch-Kachārī rulers.

---

136 Significantly, a Kachārī queen, consort of the Kachārī Rājā Tāmradhvaja, who was a descendant of Mahāmāṇikya, had commissioned the court-poet Bhubaneśvara Bācaspati to render into Assamese the Sanskrit text of *Nāradīya-Kathāmṛta* [see S. K.Bhuyan's introduction to *Kachārī Burañjī*, p.vii.]

137 *Sabin Alun* (the Kārbi *Rāmāyaṇa,*) consisting of 560 verse couplets available for long as a mysterious oral text belonging to the Kārbi tribes of Assam, was collected, translated, and printed by Samsingh Hanse, Assam Sahitya Sabha, 1986.

Emergence of Women Patrons/Readers/Audiences

An interesting feature of the development of vernacular literary culture in Assam and north-eastern India in the fourteenth and fifteenth centuries CE is the emergence of a readership of literary texts from amongst the lower castes and women, who were either readers or intent listeners of oral renderings of the texts and who often composed songs of their own drawn from the contents of the texts. These songs have become a part of the still-existent rich oral folk literature of the region. The justifications offered by most of the scholars who initiated the process of rendering the epics and the *purāṇas* into local languages bear ample testimony to the fact that the writers were concerned more with the entertainment and involvement of their subaltern audiences, especially women, than the censuring attitude of the learned pundits. There are several recorded stories of influential women living in the Koch and Kachārī kingdoms patronizing the translation and rendition of Sanskrit texts into the local language. One of these illustrious women was the Kachārī queen Candraprabhā, the consort of the Kachārī Rājā Tāmradhvaja Nārāyaṇa and mother of Suradarpa Nārāyaṇa, who commissioned the court poet Bhubaneśvara Bācaspati to translate the *Nāradīya Kathāmṛta* into Assamese.[138] Another instance of romantic lore that has captured the imagination of modern Assamese writers is the story of the beautiful and intelligent Koch princess Suśuddhi (also known as Garamā Kunvarī), the consort of the king of Kāmatā. Suśuddhi became infatuated with Candraśekhara, the son of the royal priest Nīlāmbara, who used to read out to her everyday from the *Hara-Gaurī-saṃvāda.* This relationship between the princess and the Brahmin incurred the wrath of the king, who banished Suśuddhi from his kingdom.

138 S.K.Bhuyan, *Kachārī Burañjī*, Introduction, p.vii.

This incident subsequently led to prolonged battles between the armies of Gauḍa, Kāmatā, Ahom, and Kachārī rulers, which ended with the Ahom king taking possession of Garamā Kunvarī and subsequently sending her to reign in Kachar.[139] Thus, the increasing engagement of women and persons from the so-called 'lower castes' in partaking of the pleasure and instruction provided by literary texts could have led to certain momentous changes being incorporated into the vernacular versions of the texts by some of the best-known writers from Assam who emerged between the fourteenth and sixteenth centuries.

The unique portrayal of Sītā in Mādhava Kandalī's *Rāmāyaṇa* and particularly in Śaṅkaradeva's *Uttarakāṇḍa* may have been influenced by this new awareness of the need to accommodate the woman's voice in literature. Both the poets, in their portrayals of Sītā, showed their sympathy for the wronged wife and were openly critical of the misuse of patriarchal power by Rāma. The voice of Sītā in the Assamese *Rāmāyaṇa* of Mādhava Kandalī, Śaṅkaradeva, and Mādhavadeva emerges as a powerful expression of female resistance against the oppressive patriarchal values embedded in the textual structure of the Vālmīki *Rāmāyaṇa*. This bold depiction of Sītā's voice in the Assamese *Rāmāyaṇa* may have been partly enabled by the comparatively egalitarian structures of the societies of the Koch, Kachārī, and other indigenous groups inhabiting north-east India, whose rulers patronized the vernacularization of the epics in the region. It could perhaps be speculated safely that these early vernacular versions of the *Rāmāyaṇa* in eastern India were influenced by the poets' awareness of the social status occupied by women in north-eastern India, which was significantly

139 Recorded in *Ahom Burañjī*, collected by Hemchandra Goswami (see *Descriptive Catalogue of Assamese Manuscripts*, Introduction, p.xiv.)

different from that of women in other regions of northern India. In the absence of other contemporary accounts that may throw some light on the social conditions of the early modern times in this region, one could refer to some of the early colonial accounts that mention the special status of women in the indigenous societies of Assam and other regions of eastern India.[140]

Structure, the Verse Forms and Selections from the Texts

As I have said earlier, although in a colophonic verse Mādhava Kandalī claims to have composed the "*Saptakāṇḍa Rāmāyaṇa*"[141] yet the extant versions of the Mādhava Kandalī's text consists of only five *kāṇḍas*. These are

140 Edward Gait mentions that "women were placed under no disability in their social life and activities" and that they "were refined and enlightened and active and versatile in their accomplishments." (*A History of Assam*, p.258-259). Rev. Sidney Endle, in his account of the Kachārīs in Assam, observes admiringly that "the position of the wife and mother is far from being a degraded one." He further states, "The Kachari husband and householder has neither sympathy with, nor tolerance for, that degrading and demoralizing creed which says that 'woman is but dust, a soul-less toy for tyrant's lust'. On the contrary, he usually treats his wife with distinct respect, and regards her as an equal and a companion to an extent which can hardly be said to be the rule among many of the Indian peoples. Kachari women, both in early life and as matrons enjoy a large measure of freedom, a freedom which is very rarely abused for evil purposes. On being spoken to on the wayside, the Kachari woman will generally reply at once with absolute frankness, looking the questioner straight in the face and yet with the most perfect modesty..." (*The Kacharis*, Macmillan and Co., London, 1911, p.22).

141 "I have composed the seven *kāṇḍas* of the *Rāmāyaṇa* in verse" ("*sāta kāṇḍa Rāmāyaṇa padabandhe nibandhila*") *Laṅkākāṇḍa*: 55:24.

Ayodhyā, Araṇya, Kiṣkindhā, Sundara and Laṅkā. It is uncertain whether the poet had composed all the seven *kāṇḍas* or only the five extant *kāṇḍas*. As mentioned in the *Kathā-guru-carita*, the *Ādi* and the *Uttara kāṇḍas* were later added to it by Śaṅkaradeva and his disciple Mādhavadeva. Most of the printed versions have been named *Saptakāṇḍa Rāmāyaṇa* because they include the *Ādikāṇḍa* by Mādhavadeva and the *Uttarakāṇḍa* by Śaṅkaradeva. The extant five *kāṇḍas* of Mādhava Kandalī contained in the printed versions consist of 5,226 verses.[142] In the printed version that has been consulted for the present translation,[143] the various *kāṇḍas* or sections have been arranged under chapters or *adhyāyas*. Verse numbers in this edition are not continuous as in the Dattabarua edition, but each *adhyāya* bears a separate set of numbering for the *pada, dularī,* or *chabi* verses.

The metres used in the text of Mādhava Kandalī as well as in those of Śaṅkaradeva and Mādhavadeva are the *pada, jumuḍi, dularī,* and *chabi*, all of which were popular verse forms in old vernacular verse narratives of Assam. In the Assamese *Rāmāyaṇa* of Mādhava Kandalī, Śaṅkaradeva, and Mādhavadeva, the main narrative is carried forward mostly in the *pada* (or *pāyara*) sections, which consist of fourten-syllabic rhyming couplets with two identical syllables at the end of each foot in a couplet. The eight-

142 As computed by Harendranath Datta Barua in his printed edition of the Mādhava Kandalī, Mādhavadeva, Śaṅkaradeva text *Sātkāṇḍa Rāmāyaṇa*, Nalbari, 1952.

143 *Kavirāja MādhavaKandalī Biracita Rāmāyaṇa*, ed. by Kanakchandra Sarma Kavyatirtha, (1941), Lawyers' Book Stall, Guwahati, 2008.

syllabic *jumuḍi* rhyming couplets have rarely been used, the exception being the one instance in the *Ādikāṇḍa* of Mādhavadeva (*adhyāya* 13). The *dularī* and the *chabi* have been used extensively in the Assamese *Rāmāyaṇa* to provide liveliness and variation to the narrative and also to serve as interludes in which the poet reflects on the preceding *pada* section. The *dularī* (or *dulaḍi*) is a four-line stanza with an alternating sequence of rhyme: two sets of short lines consisting of six syllables each and two sets of longer lines of eight syllables each. The *chabi* consists of more slow-moving four-line stanzas with an alternating rhyme scheme: two six-syllabic lines and two eight-syllabic lines. Thus, the vernacular version of the text composed by Mādhava Kandalī, Śaṅkaradeva, and Mādhavadeva experiments with a greater variety of verse forms and metres, unlike the relative uniformity of the Vālmīki text.

Selections and Translations

The present selection is aimed at representing the voice of Sītā wherever she speaks in the Mādhava Kandalī text; but, in order to retain the thread of the Rāma-Sītā story, related verses preceding or succeeding a dialogue or monologue have also been translated. Considering the significance of Śaṅkaradeva's version of the *Uttarakāṇḍa* in the unique representation of Sītā's voice in the Assamese version of the *Rāmāyaṇa*, almost the whole of the narrative from *adhyāya* 1 to 24, which contains the Rāma-Sītā story, has been retained. The only section omitted in this selection from the *Uttarakāṇḍa* is the Rāma-Agastya *saṃbāda* in Lava-Kuśa's song, which contains the stories of the birth of Rāvaṇa, Hanumanta's origin and identity, and the last section of the epic containing Rāma's decision to divide the kingdom amongst his own and Bharata's sons, his banishment of Lakṣmaṇa, Lakṣmaṇa's death and Rāma's sorrow, and finally his decision to leave the world and enter heaven with his faithful followers. The list of selected verses which have been translated in the present work is as follows:

Ayodhyākāṇḍa: adhyāyas 11, 12, 15

Araṇyakāṇḍa: adhyāyas 1 (selections), 11 (selections), 12, 13, 15 (selections), 16, 17, 18

Sundarakāṇḍa: adhyāyas 14 (selections), 15 (selections), 16 (selections), 17 (selections)

Laṅkākāṇḍa: adhyāyas 49, 50, 51

Uttara Kāṇḍa: adhyāyas 1–12, 15 (selections), 16–19, 20 (selections), 21–24

Almost every translator of an ancient epic like the *Rāmāyaṇa* would agree about the impossibility of rendering satisfactorily the original verses into English or any other modern European language. The cultural distance between the source language and the target language is so great that every translator gets disheartened at some point. It is somewhat easier to translate a Sanskrit text into a vernacular language of India because of the cultural resemblances between the old world represented in the original text and the new represented in the vernacular text. Despite these advantages, however, both Mādhava Kandalī and Śaṅkaradeva have humbly accepted the fact that a poet who is aspiring to convey the meaning of the Vālmīki text in his own language can only "fly as far as his wings will permit". It is an even more daunting task to render an ancient vernacular verse text into modern English without diminishing the poetic beauty or the cultural nuances of the original. Realizing the futility of attempting a verse rendering of the original text, because there is no tradition in English literature of composing serious verses for oral rendition (except perhaps ballads), a prose translation seems to be the only way in which the text can be presented to a modern reader who is interested in gleaning pleasure from a well-loved story and at the same time gaining some information about an ancient culture that is considered in some ways to be a living one even today. My aim has been to make the translations as readable as possible in English and to retain the aesthetic beauty of the texts. I have tried to retain the original idiomatic phrases by translating them as best as I could instead of replacing them with English ones. I have also retained the repetitions in the original text, sometimes even at the cost of subjecting the reader to a degree of tediousness. However, for the sake of clarity or readability, I have sometimes shifted around the lines in a verse without disturbing the meaning conveyed by the original.

In this prose translation of selections from the Assamese *Rāmāyaṇa*, I have tried to retain as far as possible the sonorous quality of the original by using a language which is slightly elevated without being archaic. Though it is not possible to bring in the difference in the rhythmic pattern between the *pada, chabi,* or the *dularī* metres, an attempt has been made to indicate the transition from one verse form to another by lengthening or shortening the lines. The line numberings in the print version have been used for this work and have been maintained as far as possible in the translation. This translation had no earlier model to consult or fall back upon, because this fourteenth-century vernacular text has had no reliable English translation until now.[144] Therefore, faults and imperfections in the translation may disappoint the expectations of discerning readers. However, it is hoped that all the shortcomings notwithstanding, the present translation will be able to convey some of the magic that is inherent in the original version of this vernacular epic.

Transliteration

The diacritics in the text have been used in accordance with the IAST (International Alphabet of Sanskrit Transliteration) convention. In the Introduction, diacritics have been used for all non-English words, apart from names of places and words of colloquial Assamese origin or of Persianate origin. In the body of the translation, diacritics have been used for all non-English words borrowed from primary sources. For footnotes, the text follows the policy of using diacritics only for the primary sources, and not for secondary sources.

---

144 The only available translations of the Assamese *Rāmāyaṇa* of Mādhava Kandalī (which includes the later addition of the Ādikāṇḍa and the Uttarakāṇḍa) are a Hindi translation by Navarun Varma (*Mādhava Kandalī Rāmāyaṇa*, Bhuvan Vani Trust, Lucknow, 1979) and an English translation by Shanti Lal Nagar (*Mādhava Kandalī Rāmāyaṇa*, in two volumes, Munshiram Manoharlal, New Delhi, 2000), which is not based on the original Assamese version, but, as is stated in the introductory notes, on the Hindi version published by Bhuvan Vani Press. It is probably because of the translator's unfamiliarity with the original Assamese text that nuances of the poetic language of the original are missing in this translation. The translator also does not mention anywhere that the available version of *Saptakāṇḍa Rāmāyaṇa* in Assamese is a composite work by Mādhava Kandalī, Śaṅkaradeva, and Mādhavadeva.

Selections from Mādhava Kandalī's *Rāmāyaṇa*

Ayodhyākāṇḍa

Adhyāya 11

(Rāma gives Sītā the news about his exile)

Dularī[1]

1. Jānakī, the beautiful wife of Rāghava, was inside her white palace. Like a bright cloud, her beauty was known to the world as comparable to that of the resplendent star Rohiṇī.

2. Decked in precious ornaments, she was joyfully anticipating the moment when her husband would be crowned king that day and she would be his queen.

3. Smiling to herself, the mother of the universe observed all the sacred rituals appropriate to the occasion with great pleasure in her heart.

---

1 *Dularī* is a verse form with a pleasant lilting rhythm, common in old Assamese poetry. It consists of two short pairs of lines that rhyme alternately and also internally.

4. She looked towards the palace gate with happiness spread over her face and eyes and beheld her beloved Rāma, unparalleled in virtues, entering through the door.

5. Rāma's face looked pale, unlike the brightness of the day. It was lustreless, like the setting sun in the evening sky.

6. Sītā, the daughter of Janaka, bowed and circumambulated Rāma with great reverence. Then, with palms pressed together, she stood behind him in anxiety.

7. After a while, Rāghava's most gifted wife, the daughter of king Janaka, considering it to be her duty, began to speak slowly:

8. "Why do you appear so sad at heart, my lord, what misfortune has befallen you? Tell me, my lord, what is the reason for this sorrowful demeanour at a time of great joy?

9. "Why have not all the ministers, Brahmanas, and other blameless ones blessed you by showering on your head flowers and herbs consecrated with holy words?

10. "Why are there no royal jewels on your body, why no white yak-tail whisks for you? Why do you appear so dejected and distraught, my lord, on a day like this?

11. "The powerful elephant, which carries the royal possessions on its back and which has the speed and strength to lift the Meru Mountain[2] with its tusks, why has it not accompanied you today?

---

2 Meru is the mythical mountain occupying the centre of the earth and giving it support.

12. "That supremely beautiful flowery chariot decorated with gold and drawn by eight horses, why is it not with you today?

13. "All the ministers and courtiers who are devoted to you, and all the soldiers experienced in battle, why are they not marching alongside their lord today?

14. "It seems strange that the golden chariot drawn by white horses and decorated adequately for the auspicious occasion, which leaves everyone awestruck with wonder and delight, is not accompanying you today.

15. "Nor can I see all the other individuals and representatives of allied kingdoms who are supposed to accompany you today. Tell me, O lord, why has the royal anointment ceremony been abandoned?"

16. Then the lord Rāmacandra replied to her thus: "Listen carefully, O goddess of my heart, for a mishap that has occurred today.

17. "You who were born into the clan of the holy royal sage, you who are a chaste woman possessing a sinless heart, a beautiful mind and a character imbued with righteousness, listen.

18. "The king, after having given orders for the preparation of the anointment ceremony, went to visit his queen Kaikeyī. Entrapping him with the promise he had made to her once, Kaikeyī asked the king to grant her two wishes.

19. "The first would ensure that I give up my claim to kingship and go to the forest for fourteen years. The second wish that she begged the king for was to hand over the kingdom to Bharata.

20. "Like a venomous serpent, hoarding its poison for long, Kaikeyī thus stung the king and mortally wounded him. She bound him in his own words and robbed him of all his strength and pride.

21. " After hearing those words of my queen-mother, my mind has now achieved a state of calm. Life comes to an end when Time, like the god of Death, arrives to take it away.

22. "I have no other desire left except to submit to my father's wishes. All beauty has fled from my life and I will now leave Ayodhyā instantly and depart for the forest.

23. "Listen carefully with a calm mind, O goddess of my heart, and do not grieve. Come to me, dear friend, and let me look at you one last time dressed in all your finery."

24. When the goddess Sītā heard these unbearably cruel words from her husband, she struck her chest in distress, and crying "O my lord", collapsed to the floor.

25. As when Pārvatī stood before Śiva in grief, or Rati lamented when Mahādeva destroyed Kāma by fire, so Sītā poured forth her sorrow before Rāma.

26. But, though her whole body trembled in fear and the bangles fell from her wrists, yet like a deer when seized with dread stands still before a lion, so Sītā remained motionless and still.

27. Then, regaining her composure, she spoke thus to Rāma: "I have committed many sins. I did not die even when I was buried under the ground.

28. But now for what transgression do you wish to punish me by throwing me into this fire of agony? Why do you wish to abandon a devoted wife like me?"

29. "O leave me not!" she cried and clung to his clothes, as the goddess Lakṣmī falls at the feet of lord Viṣnu.

30. Then Rāma said to her, "Arise my beloved, and listen to my words, which are meant for your welfare. It is impossible for me not to go into exile and disobey my father's words."

31. "I have renounced all my friends and my dear mother Kauśalyā. I am now resolved to go off to the forest this very day, giving up all these illusory domestic pleasures."

32. Salute the greatness of Rāma who has no equal in the three worlds! Chant his name again and again, all ye members of the assembly, and you shall then find respite from all your sorrows.

From Adhyāya 12

(Sītā pleads with Rāma to allow her to accompany him to the forest)

Pada[3]

1. [*Rāma continued thus:*] "I have given up all my friends in the city of Ayodhyā and sacrificed my infatuation for Sītā, who is beautiful in every limb.
2. "Rāhu[4], the demon of eclipses, approaches her with the desire to swallow the nectar of her moon-like face.
3. "But, when she darts her sideways glances, the arrows shot from her lovely bow-shaped brows send him racing up to the height of the heavens.
4. "Even sages are fascinated by her eyes, which are like a pair of blue lotus flowers.
5. "Shapely like the sesame flower is her nose, her face like the *bānduli*[5] flower. Her beautiful teeth are arranged evenly like rows of pearl.
6. "Lovelier than the *bimba*[6] fruit are her lips, her beautiful neck carved with three resplendent lines.

---

3 A *pada* is a rhyming couplet with fourteen syllables in each line.

4 In Hindu mythology, Rāhu is an *asura* with only a head and no body who chases the sun and the moon eternally in order to swallow them, but fails to do so. His futile attempts cause eclipses.

5 *Bānduli* = Sanskrit *bāndhulī*. A bright-coloured flower (copper cups or noon flower).

6 *Bimba* fruit = the bright red fruit of the plant *momordica monadelpha*.

7. "Like lotus-stems are her slender arms, the three lovely wrinkles on her stomach can ignite desire like pyre-wood.

8. "One can imagine that Kāmadeva,[7] burning in the fire of Śiva's wrath, flees for shelter and jumps into the cool pool of your navel.

9. "And arriving at his own destination there, he shuts the doors. The hair on your stomach must be the smoke coming out of Kāmadeva's burning body.

10. "Your waist like the narrow middle of a *ḍambaru,*[8] your wide hips decorated with an ornamented girdle.

11. "This abode of the lord of desire is like a well full of nectar. Your tempting hips shine forth in their exceeding beauty.

12. "Your shapely thighs are like the plantain buds, the beauty of which captures the attention of the beholder.

13. "The soles of your feet are red and the joints of your body are concealed skilfully. Your whole nature is like that of new, tender leaves.

14. "Your graceful gait surpasses that of the elephant. The tinkling of your ankle-bells resembles the notes of the heron's voice.

15. "Your earrings shine like the sun, the precious stones on your body sparkle like stars.

---

7 Kāmadeva: the Hindu god of love.

8 *Ḍambaru* or *ḍamru* is a small drum shaped like an hour-glass, associated with Shiva. It is played by holding it in one hand.

16. "Your beauty can eclipse the lustre of all divine beings, *gandharvas* and *Nāgas*. How can a young man resist such temptation?

17. "Since I am abandoning such a one as you, my condition is like that of someone facing living death. O let me tie a stone round my neck and drown myself in the ocean!

18. "Forsake all your sorrow and concern, O Sītā! A dying man like me can never be released from such a conjunction of fate.

19. "Yet, how can I defy my father's word, Sītā? So, most earnestly do I beg your forgiveness."

20. Then Sītā replied thus: "My lord, tell me where lies my fault that you have decided to leave me behind?

21. "Is it because I did not worship Pārvatī and Śaṅkara in my previous life that my beloved is now forsaking me?

22. "O master who is born into the sun's clan, and who is the lord of Ayodhyā, I am an unhappy woman who worships you;

23. "If you go away to the forest for fourteen long years, leaving me behind, you will deprive me of all the merit I have earned in this life.

24. "You like a black beetle have been enjoying the pleasures of this body of mine, which is beautiful like a *campaka* bud.

25. "Now when it is ripe to bear fruit, why do you wish to abandon this pleasure and make my body barren and fruitless?

26. "Just as the day is lustreless without the sun, and the night loses its splendour without the moon.

27. "Just as the spring is bereft of beauty without the cuckoo, so my life would be in vain without you, my lord.

28. "The very thought of it brings intolerable pain to my heart. O do not bring about this separation between friends, my lord.

29. "Why do you want to reject me and go? Which limb of my body is imperfect for you?

30. "You are a royal prince. How will you face the dangers of the forest alone?

31. "The forest is as hazardous and impenetrable as the kingdom of death. My heart trembles at the very thought of its dark caves."

32. Then Rāghava replied: "Sītā, calm yourself and listen to my words carefully.

33. "When I am gone away to the forest, you must do everything for my welfare by offering prayers to the gods and Brahmins and by observing the fasts.

34. "My two brothers Bharata and Śatrughna are good and intelligent. Worship them like gods with kindness in your heart.

35. "Abandon all pride and try to satisfy their minds. Only then will Bharata provide you adequate protection.

36. "You must wake up and get ready early in the morning and offer your obeisance to my parents.

37. "Harbour no other feelings about them except that they are your well-wishers and friends. Consider all your mothers-in-law as equals to Kauśalyā."

38. Sītā then replied to him thus: "Listen, my lord. Do not disregard my words, but listen to them carefully.

39. "A father's good deeds do not bring happiness to the son. Nor do the son's actions relieve the misery of a father.

40. "But a husband's good deeds are shared and enjoyed by a devoted wife. So, with my master I shall go to the forest to share all his sorrow.

41. "While in the forest, I shall walk in front of him and clear all the thorns in his way.

42. "You know about my intentions now. If you violate the wishes of your devotee, you will face only disgrace for ever.

43. "When you are by my side, how can lions, elephants, bears, tigers, or wild buffaloes bring me any harm?

44. "In the forest I shall see wonderful rivers and lakes and places full of lilies and lotuses of all hues.

45. "O I am full of these happy expectations of going into the forest in your company! Do not deny me this pleasure and break my heart.

46. "I shall travel in the forest with you, just like the king of the gods moves around with his wife Śacī.

47. "In the forest, the wonderful mountains are full of precious gems. There are flowers of different hues which spread their fragrance all around.

48. "They will provide us the arbours where, like Rati playing with Kāma, we can indulge in the game of love.

49. "Before my marriage, my mother taught me that I should not take my meals without my husband.

50. "Now I desire to follow her teaching and roam over rivers and forests in your footsteps."

51. Then Rāma spoke while Sītā stood before him with her head bent low:

52. "Listen, Sītā, daughter of Janaka! It is not possible for me to suffer life in the forest with a woman by my side.

53. "When you will hear the roar of the lion from the forest caves, you will start and tremble with fear.

54. "The elephants there are as huge as mountains, trumpeting incessantly. Every twelve months they will be in a rut.

55. "The loud roars of tigers, lions, and panthers, the call of the wild buffaloes, boars, and *śarabha*[9] strike terror in human hearts.

56. "The king cobra and the mountain snakes, the incomparable python curled up into a sphere;

57. "The very sight of these and other species of dreadful snakes would drain away all your courage and strength.

58. "The forest also abounds in insects, flies, leeches, rodents, and mongooses of all varieties.

59. "There are colonies of tiny ants in the forest whose bite is unbearable even for lions.

60. "The forest contains some species of birds which can even swallow human beings and elephants whole.

---

9 *Śarabha* or *sarabha* in Sanskrit literature refers to a powerful eight-legged mythical creature, part lion and part bird.

61. “You—whose hands and feet are soft like the red lotus, who is always clad in the finest silk garments,

62. “The soles of whose soft feet bleed even while walking in the palace of gold—how can you bear the pain of walking on the thorny forest floor?

63. “For several days you may have to traverse desert countries and for many days live on unclean water.

64. “How will you enter that deep wilderness which is covered with wild grass, creepers, and thorns?

65. “And I would be clad in tree-barks, with unkempt matted hair and overgrown nails.

66. “My body would be reduced to mere skin and bones by the hardship of the forest. What pleasure will there be in making love to you, Sītā?

67. “During the days of sweltering heat, I would have to cool myself in the mud and in the season of autumn remain drenched in dew.

68. “I will be compelled to fast frequently, give up all cereals, and live on fruits and wild roots.

69. “If you go with me to the forest, you will suffer unending pain with these fasts and hardships.

70. “Hence, O beloved daughter of King Janaka, listen to my advice: stay at home and follow the righteous ways of a devoted wife.”

71. Hearing these words of Rāma, Sītā wept aloud and said, “If you leave me behind my life will be in vain;

72. “I will end my life with a knife or drink poison.”

73. Rāma's heart melted before Sītā's grief and he forthwith gave her permission to accompany him:

74. "I have observed all your good deeds, O Jānakī!" he said, "Now get ready at once to go with me to the forest."

From Adhyāya 15

(*Sītā says farewell to Kauśalyā*)

1. Then Kaikeyī gleefully brought the coarse garments made of tree barks for Rāma, Lakṣmaṇa, and Sītā.
2. She steeled her heart shamelessly and said to them, "Put on these barks and leave for the forest at once!"
3. "While you spend fourteen years in the forest, let Bharata come and take charge of the royal sceptre and throne."
4. Then Rāma and Lakṣmaṇa put aside their garments, fit for gods, and attired themselves in the coarse tree barks.
5. Sītā placed the tree-bark garment around her shoulders, as if she were a deer with a rope around her neck.
6. Then, hanging down her head in mortification, Sītā slowly went and stood by her husband's side.
7. "Tell me, O my husband lord Rāma," she said, "how do I wear this garment of bark?"
8. Then she held up the coarse garment in front of her eyes, and all the people cried out in distress.
9. They wept in disbelief that destiny should have ordained that she wear such a garment instead of fine silk.
10. Then the king made reply: "O you sinful woman, your infamy will live forever on this earth."

11. "You had asked only for Rāma's banishment. How heartless and sinful of you to compel Sītā and Lakṣmaṇa to wear those coarse barks!"

12. Then Rāma spoke thus to his father: "My father, I am the only son of my mother and I am leaving her behind now.

13. "Without me, her life will be in danger. So I fall at your feet and beg you to act in such a manner that her life is not imperilled."

14. "See how my mother Kauśalyā is drowned in a sea of sorrow! O give her constant protection during my absence."

15. The king became distraught with grief when he heard these words and he fell unconscious on the floor.

16. When he regained his senses after a while, he gave orders to Sumantrak:

17. "Harness fresh horses to my chariot and bring it hither! Take Rāma to the forest today and be his charioteer."

18. In obedience to the king's orders, the minister forthwith departed and returned with the chariot equipped in every way.

19. Then the king ordered the royal treasurer to bring suitable royal clothes and ornaments for Sītā.

20. The minister departed in haste to act upon the royal orders and soon he brought for Sītā ornaments which were fit for the gods.

21. Then, turning to Sītā, the king said, "O principal daughter-in-law of my family! I wish to see you decked in royal jewellery. So put them all on at once."

22. Sītā at once discarded the bark clothes and dressed herself in clean garments.

23. Five hundred mothers-in-law decked her with precious ornaments—a crown, earrings, and seven-stringed necklaces;

24. Bangles, bejewelled rings, ankle bells, ornaments for the head, and girdles for the waist;

25. Each limb of hers was adorned with a variety of appropriate ornaments.

26. Thus the daughter of Janaka was blessed with auspicious ornaments and Kauśalyā arose and embraced her with affection.

27. It seemed like a mother and daughter were embracing each other fondly as Sītā wiped the tears from her eyes with the fringe of her garment.

28. Kauśalyā, the mother of Rāma, kissed her on the forehead and said, "Listen, O you daughter of Janaka,

29. "Misfortune has come to your virtuous and good husband. So do not stand on any pride or resentment, but always seek to look after his welfare."

30. Sītā replied to her thus: "Abandon your anxiety and grief, my mother. Do not consider me to be like any ordinary woman."

31. "Ornaments look beautiful on a woman who has a good husband. If the husband is absent, then everything is worthless to her."

32. "A woman is given only a limited amount of wealth by her father and brother. The wealth in the possession of a son does not come into the hand of the mother."

33. "It is only the husband's wealth that a wife can enjoy. So which woman can insult her husband?"

34. "The cuckoo's beauty lies in its lovely voice. Women shine in beauty when they follow the righteous path of a devoted wife."

35. "The glory of men shines forth in their learning and the virtue of forgiveness gives beauty to the sage who meditates."

36. "So listen to these words of Sītā, O holy lady—may Rāma be my husband in every life to come and you my mother-in-law."

37. Kauśalyā then shed tears of happiness and sorrow at these good words of Sītā.

38. Then, embracing her son Rāma, she advised him to take great care of Sītā in the forest.

Araṇyakāṇḍa

Adhyāya 1

Rāma, Lakṣmaṇa, and Sītā in sage Atri's āśrama

Pada 38-114

(The sage Atri welcomes Rāma, Lakṣmaṇa, and Sītā)

1. Then the sage sent Sītā inside the hut and there she met the sage's wife.
2. This lady, who surpassed everyone in her beauty and virtues, was known by the name Anasūyā.
3. A devoted wife and pure in mind, she was the mother of Candra. Sītā went forward and touched her feet with a smiling face.
4. The daughter of Janaka stood modestly before the lady, and Candra's mother offered her a seat.
5. Then Anasūyā spoke to her with a pleasing smile: "Why have you come to this forest with Rāma?

6. "He has come at the behest of his father. Why did you not stay behind with your mother-in-law?

7. "You will suffer greatly in the severe conditions of the forest. Your bed will be of grass. Humble roots and fruits will be your food."

8. Sītā replied to her thus: "Why do you belittle my intentions thus? Know that I am a chaste and devoted wife.

9. "What rewards would I have achieved by staying back in my country? Rather, I can achieve my salvation in heaven by being devoted to my husband.

10. "I am a truthful woman, chaste like Sāvitrī. Just as Rohiṇī is for Candra, Arundhatī for Vasiṣṭha,

11. "You for Atri, Māyā for Śaṅkara, I too am firmly devoted to Rāma.

12. "Just as your husband is the most important god for you, so is Rāma for me and I have no one else.

13. "Parents and well-wishers can only lead us to earthly pleasures; but devotion to one's husband ensures salvation and a place in heaven."

14. Hearing these words of Sītā, Anasūyā embraced her with great happiness.

15. She offered Sītā sandalwood unguents to smear on her body, a precious necklace, and thirty two varieties of ornaments.

16. "You have made me happy, lady, with your words. I too am fond of women who are devoted to their husbands. Now ask me for any favour," said she.

17. Sītā replied, "You have looked upon me with kindness. That is the greatest wish that you can grant me."

18. Then Anasūyā said, "All the ornaments that I have given to you, all the vermillion powder and sandalwood, may these always remain with you.

19. "I bless you with eternal youth. May you lead a long and happy life with Rāma."

20. Then Anasūyā blessed Sītā again and said, "May you always remain a devoted wife.

21. "I have received some news about your great *svayaṃvara.*[10] Now tell me more about the customs of Mithilā."

22. Then spoke the chaste Sītā thus: "If you wish I shall tell you my story from the beginning.

23. "My father is the king of the kingdom of Mithilā and his fame has spread amongst gods, *asuras*, and men.

24. "Janaka, my father, was childless and so he went with his wife to inspect a venue for a ceremonial sacrifice.

25. "As he looked up after examining the ground, he beheld a girl of exceeding beauty who had the power to bewitch the three worlds.

26. "This girl, whose beauty and merit has no equal in the three worlds, was the *apsarā*[11] named Menakā.

27. "Seeing her, my father was filled with amazement, and he stood for some time, lost in thought.

---

10 *Svayaṃvara*: a ceremony in which a princess selects her own husband from amongst an assembly of suitors.

11 *Apsarā*: a dancing girl in the court of Indra, the king of the gods.

28. "Then, suddenly, a voice spoke to him from the sky: "this lady has been sent to you for your own good.

29. "If you plough the ground at this spot, you will find a girl child here as beautiful as the *apsarā*."

30. "Hearing this, my father happily began to till the sacrificial ground with a plough in his hand.

31. "Listen, O Anasūyā, about my condition then. I emerged from the earth and lay on the furrow made by the plough.

32. "The king looked upon me with amazement as, covered with dust, I was pushing against the mud.

33. "He picked me up and carried me to his wife. I was named Sītā[12] because I was born in the furrow.

34. "King Janaka called me his daughter and entrusted me to the care of all his principal wives.

35. "I was brought up by them in great happiness and, since none of them had a son, they looked upon me as equal to a hundred sons.

36. "Just as the moon waxes in size, so did I begin to grow until I attained the beauty which can enrapture all the three worlds.

37. "As I blossomed into youth, my father became most anxious about finding a suitable husband for me.

38. "His mind was preoccupied for long with deep anxiety. Then, one day, he decided to hold my *svayaṃvara*.

39. "Long ago, when my father was ploughing the sacrificial ground, Mahādeva had gifted him his own bow.

---

12 Sītā means a furrow made by a plough.

40. "Now the king, my father, invited all the eligible princes and kings, and they assembled at the venue of the *svayaṃvara*.

41. "A thousand men carried Mahādeva's bow to the ceremonial venue and placed it in front of the assembly of kings.

42. "Then King Janaka addressed all the suitors and said, "you have come to seek the hand of my beloved daughter in marriage.

43. "Whoever can string this great bow will become Sītā's husband and my son-in-law."

44. "On hearing this, all the assembled kings bowed respectfully to the bow and then went back to where they had come from.

45. "A few approached the bow to measure their strength; but when they saw its size, they did not dare to try again.

46. "When all the kings had departed in disappointment, my father was sad at heart that the *svayaṃvara* had been in vain.

47. "Then Viśvāmitra arrived with Rāma and Lakṣmaṇa, and Janaka welcomed them with great warmth.

48. "With great happiness I went and sat on my father's lap. I was totally enchanted by the beauty of Rāma.

49. "His magnificent looks were so pleasing to me that I began to hope that this time destiny would not cheat me.

50. "Then all of us proceeded to the venue of the *svayaṃvara* and my father Janaka gave them instructions regarding the bow.

51. "Rāma looked at the bow with a faint smile on his lips and lifted it with his left hand as if it were a mere plaything.

52. "In the twinkling of an eye, Rāma strung the bow and then lightly twanged the bowstring. The sound reverberated through the three worlds.

53. "Then, with a smile on his face, he pulled the bowstring and at once the bow broke into two with a deafening sound.

54. "It was like a rock being hit with tremendous force. The whole earth with its oceans and seven islands trembled at the impact.

55. "While Viśvāmitra and Janaka stared in disbelief, Rāma and Lakṣmaṇa did not bat an eyelid.

56. "All the other kings who were present there accepted defeat and left for their homes.

57. "In deference to my father's wishes, I accepted Rāma with a garland of lotuses.

58. "Then King Daśaratha was invited by Janaka, and, in his presence, my father gave me away in marriage.

59. "King Janaka has another daughter younger to me by the name of Ūrmilā.

60. "Her beauty can enchant all the three worlds. She has a beautiful nose and teeth of pearls.

61. "Her waist is slim and her arms are tender like lotus stems. Her hair is wavy and her eyes are like lotuses.

62. "Her lips are more red than the *bāndulika*[13] flower and her lotus-like face is brighter than the full moon.

63. "Dangling ornaments shine in her ears. Her beautiful neck is carved like a sea-shell, her breasts are firm and raised, her stomach is shapely.

64. "Her neck is bedecked with a seven-layered necklace, its pendant of precious elephant pearl, her arms and wrists are covered with bracelets and bangles of gold.

65. "Jewelled rings shine on her fingers that resemble a row of brilliant slender spindles. Her shining nails are shaped like crescents.

66. "Her thighs are like tender plantain stems, her legs shapely and beautiful, her ankles sport golden bells.

67. "The red soles of her feet shine like lotuses and the beauty of her form surpasses that of the moon.

68. "This girl who has the graceful gait of an elephant was growing in beauty like the moon in Janaka's house. She was lovely like the goddess Lakṣmī and her good qualities pleased even the sages.

69. "This extraordinary beauty in Janaka's house could enchant the whole world with her sideways glances.

70. "This sister of mine named Ūrmilā was called by my father and she was given away in marriage to Lakṣmaṇa.

---

13 *Bāndulika* = a red flower.

71. "I had practised many rigorous austerities in my previous lives as a result of which I was blessed with a husband like Rāghava.

72. "For me Rāghava is my only god and I know of no other like him."

73. Anasūyā was greatly pleased when she heard these words of Sītā, and then she sent her back to her husband Rāma.

74. Rāma and Lakṣmaṇa were very happy when Sītā recounted the details of the visit and showed them the ornaments.

75. They then decided to spend the night happily in that hermitage. The next morning, they bowed reverently to the sage and the three entered the forest of Daṇḍaka.

From *Adhyāya* 11

Pada 27-48

(Mārīca and Rāvaṇa exchange bitter words. Mārīca assumes the form of a golden deer. Rāvaṇa assumes the guise of a mendicant and approaches Sītā)

1. Then Mārīca assumed the form of a magic deer, beautiful to behold, with unblemished golden skin.
2. On both his feet were bands of silver crescent moons and spots like bright stars made of gems glowed from every limb.
3. His jewelled breast glistened like a flash of lightning and his golden skin shone from between the spots.
4. He jumped around gleefully in front of Sītā's eyes and, twisting and turning his body in every way, grazed on the tender grass.
5. Sītā was delighted to see this golden deer and spoke to Rāma in a joyous tone:
6. "Look at this wonderful deer, my lord Rāma! How his unblemished golden skin is decked with shining gems!
7. "This forest of Daṇḍaka must be the best in the three worlds if it can produce a deer like this!
8. "My lord, please do something for my sake so that I can sit on the skin of this animal.
9. "Kill this deer and bring its skin for me. Then I will have something to talk about when we go back to Ayodhyā.

10. "Let me carry the skin back to the city and talk about it in the inner quarters of the palace.

11. "O my master and my wedded husband, I beg of you to bring me this deer which will please my heart.

12. "Do not disappoint me, O my lord! I would be overjoyed if you fulfilled this wish of mine.

13. "If you can catch it live and bring it to me, I would be most happy. Otherwise, kill it and bring me its golden skin.

14. "Then you and I can sit together on that skin, as though we were the moon and the star Rohiṇī in the sky."

15. Hearing Sītā's words, Rāghava replied: "Sītā, I know for certain now that you are a truly innocent person.

16. "Have you ever heard of a deer with a skin of gold? Certain it is that this is a trick of the evil *rākṣasas*."

17. Then Sītā replied: "I am convinced that you are trying to deceive me, thinking me to be a fool.

18. "How can you call that an illusion which I have seen with my own eyes? Have I ever asked for anything else from you, my lord?

19. "I have given up a life of comfort and have followed you around the dark forest faithfully, doing my duty as a devoted wife.

20. "I have asked for a mere deerskin from you and you are trying to deny me that on a false pretext.

21. "If that creature is not an animal but a *rākṣasa*, even then it is your duty to kill it.

22. “For you have come to this forest to do your duty towards the gods and by killing the *rākṣasa* you can fulfil that obligation.”

23. Hearing these words of Sītā, Rāma gladly agreed to oblige her and, turning to Lakṣmaṇa, he spoke thus:

24. “O brother Lakṣmaṇa, you have heard that Janaka’s daughter wishes to sit on the golden deerskin.

25. “I shall certainly fulfil her wishes. For how can I ever think of disrespecting her by denying her something that she desires?

26. “She shall sit on the golden skin and enjoy the same pleasure as that of sitting on the silken petals of a lotus.

27. “So I am leaving now to seek the deer and kill it, while you must stay by her side and protect her.”

28. Then Lakṣmaṇa spoke to him thus: “My brother, I can see something unnatural here. Consider this, how can a deer have such an appearance?

29. “I have heard the sages say that the *rākṣasa* called Mārīca is loitering in the Daṇḍaka forest these days.

30. “This *rākṣasa* assumes the form of a golden deer and devours all the kings who come to hunt here.

31. “Where have you seen a deer whose fleece is the colour of gold and spotted with precious gems and jewels?

32. “So think wisely for your own good and understand that this is the trick of Mārīca, who has come to deceive us.”

33. Then Rāghava said, "If Mārīca has really come hither, I shall get the chance to mitigate all the distress of the sages.

34. "I shall free the Daṇḍaka forest today from the trap laid by the *rākṣasa* and bring Sītā the golden fleece she desires.

35. "I shall certainly try to kill him because I can see on his body gems which are fit for kings.

36. "I know that in heaven there exist similar deer. This one, which looks like them, is now dancing around in the forest.

37. "All the precious jewels which are in our possession cannot match those which adorn the body of this deer.

38. "So I am going this instant to hunt for that deer. Look after Sītā carefully while I am gone."

39. With these words Rāma prepared himself instantly for the hunt.

40. He picked up his bow and arrows and left at once while Lakṣmaṇa stayed behind to protect Jānakī.

Adhyāya 12

Śloka[14]

Wisdom is often determined by action, not action by wisdom.

Rāmacandra's wisdom, too, followed in the tracks of the false deer.

Pada

1. At the sight of Rāma, Mārīca's heart trembled in fear, and he began to flee deeper into the forest.
2. Using all his magical powers, the *rākṣasa* disguised as a deer sped further away, playing hide-and-seek with Rāma.
3. His body, like a burning ember, shone forth occasionally, appearing and disappearing at intervals.
4. It seemed as if this creature of the night had used his magical power to remain invisible for some space of time.
5. Like a moon hiding behind wisps of clouds, he would come into view and again disappear from sight.
6. Rāma became tired of chasing this *rākṣasa*. He finally hid himself behind a tree-trunk and waited in its shade.

---

14 In the original text, this *śloka* is in Sanskrit.

7. When Rāma was thus taking respite from the chase, the *rākṣasa* was grazing amongst a herd of deer in his magical shape.

8. Recognizing the creature from a distance, Rāma then carefully aimed his arrow at the deer.

9. The moment Rāma's arrow pierced through its heart, the *rākṣasa* Mārīca breathed his last.

10. But ere he died, he faithfully tried to serve his brother Rāvaṇa. Imitating Rāma's voice, he cried out desperately to Lakṣmaṇa:

11. "O my sweet-tongued brother Lakhāi,[15] come to me immediately because I am about to die."

12. His desperate cry moved the hearts of all the sages who had heard him. The *rākṣasa* then assumed the size of a mountain and collapsed on the ground.

13. Sītā heard that cry coming from Rāma's direction. Fearing that his life was in danger, she trembled in every limb.

14. With tearful eyes, she looked frantically around and, addressing Lakṣmaṇa, thus she spoke:

15. "Can you hear, Lakhāi, that voice of Rāma? See how destiny has brought that deer to this place!

16. "Alas, alas, that I have committed this crime of bringing death upon my husband in the forest of Daṇḍaka!

17. "Listen to me, O Lakhāi, go at once to Rāma and save his life.

---

15 Lakhāi: a nickname of Lakṣmaṇa

18. "Only your presence can save him from death. So go, my friend, and protect the vermilion[16] on my head.

19. "You have been ever devoted to your brother. So, go now and save him from being killed by the creature of darkness.

20. "Since you know what is best in time of need, I beg of you to save the life of my husband and bring him back to me."

21. While Janaka's daughter was thus overcome by fear, Lakṣmaṇa stood before her with pressed palms and said,

22. "Fear not for Rāma's safety, lady. For there is none under this sun who can defeat him.

23. "Rāghava has the power to defeat single handedly the combined forces of gods, *asuras*, and men.

24. "Rāma is the greatest hero in all the three worlds. So drive away your fears and steel your body.

25. "You are asking me to go to him in response to that cry which you have heard. But, be assured, that voice can never be Rāma's.

26. "Being a woman, you are naturally afraid. But fear not. He will certainly come back to you after killing the deer."

27. Sītā heard him, and her heart was filled with anger. She began speaking to him in words most cruel and unkind:

---

16 The vermilion mark on a woman's head that signifies her marital status.

28. "O most sinful, immoral, and depraved of men! I know now what concern you have for Rāma!

29. "How elated you are at the death of Rāma! You are nothing but a tiger in the guise of a deer!

30. "You possess a nectar-sweet tongue but a poisonous heart. Seizing your opportunity, you have now plotted your evil design.

31. "You are trying to deceive me by saying that the cry is not that of Rāma, as if only this day have I come to my Rāghava's place!

32. "You are a low-caste *caṇḍāla* who has been bribed by Bharata! You have accompanied Rāma to the forest by winning him over with your guile.

33. "A stepmother's son can never be a well-wisher. Rāma accepted you as his own without realizing this.

34. "I know now, you sinful one, that your ultimate desire has been to possess me after the death of Rāma.

35. "But, if my husband dies, I will kill myself instantly by jumping into the fire or slitting my throat with a knife.

36. "Why do you insult me thus, you depraved creature? I will not touch another man even with my feet.

37. "How can an inferior creature like you desire to possess me? For me, Rāma is a powerful elephant in rut and you are a mere deer!"

38. With these words the goddess Sītā beat her breast with clenched fists. She tore at her hair and cried aloud in great agony.

39. Hearing those terrible words of Sītā, Lakṣmaṇa touched the ground with his hands and covered his ears.[17] Then he spoke to her thus:

40. "You are my goddess and Rāmacandra my god, whom I worship before everyone else. I bow before no other except your two pairs of feet.

41. "Women are so cruel and unkind that they seek to create fissures in the relationship between brothers.

42. "On what grounds do you call me unjust? I condemn you for your sharp tongue, which makes you speak to me in such an unkind manner.

43. "Let the sun, moon, earth, and air be my witness that I am forced to abandon Sītā thus.

44. "Driven by fate, you have spoken to me thus in your anxiety. But how will you, on your own, protect yourself in this dark forest?

45. "It is your good fortune that you have had Rāma by your side here. For I have observed many signs of danger in this place.

46. "You yourself know that this place is full of *rākṣasas*. So tell me at once whether I should stay or go."

47. "Go at once, O brave Lakhāi, for I can no longer bear my anxiety for Rāma after having heard his cry.

48. "If I lose my husband I will drink poison and take my life or drown myself in the river Godāvarī."

49. Then Lakṣmaṇa picked up his bow and, circumambulating Sītā thrice, he bowed at her feet.

---

17 A gesture signifying solemn rejection of something that is very reprehensible by making the earth a witness.

50. With an unwilling heart, he then left in search of Rāma. O who can prevent what destiny has ordained for Sītā?

51. Lakṣmaṇa turned back to look at her again with affectionate concern as he went away to meet Rāghava in the forest.

52. Sītā was then left all to herself in the deep forest when Lakṣmaṇa went away in search of Rāma.

53. Without Śrī Rāma and Lakṣmaṇa by her side, Sītā began to weep in anxiety for her husband.

54. Covered with dust, she looked anxiously in every direction, as though in the absence of the moon darkness had descended all around.

55. As soon as Lakṣmaṇa had turned his back on Sītā, Rāvaṇa, like a fisherman, kept his gaze fixed on the float of his fishing line.

56. He clad himself in the garb of a mendicant and approached Sītā, who was seated in her pure and clean dwelling place.

57. With only a loin cloth covering his body, an umbrella on his shoulder and a pair of wooden clogs on his feet,

58. A rag-quilt under one arm and a water-pot in his hand, a garland of *rudrākṣa*[18] beads on his head, he resembled a true ascetic.

59. Meanwhile, Śrī Rāma and Lakṣmaṇa, like the sun and the moon, wandered far away from Sītā, who seemed to remain in the twilight.

---

18 *Rudrākṣa*: a tree considered to be holy because of its association with Śiva (gamble or *eloeocarpuitas granites*).

60. Then Rāvaṇa, who was darkness incarnate, reached her side and was at once fascinated by her beauty.

61. His body began to burn with uncontrollable desire and it seemed as if the lord of the planet Saturn had taken Sītā in his grip.

62. He thought that she was the most beautiful woman in the world and gazed at her spellbound.

63. Frightened by Rāvaṇa's presence, the birds in the forest fell silent and even the wind started blowing gently in fear.

64. The sun gave up its fearful heat and touched his body with gentle warmth.

65. The fearsome *rākṣasa* stood at a distance in his mendicant's garb and recited words of benediction.

66. Then he began chanting aloud some words from the *Vedas* and addressed Sītā thus with excessive humility:

67. "Tell me, whose woman are you and what are you doing here? Why have you come to this deep forest?

68. "Your body is most beautiful to behold. Where have you come from and what is your name?

69. "Your face is like the rising full moon. The brightness of your hair defeats the luxuriance of the yak's tail.

70. "Your eye brows glow like the bow of Madana,[19] and your beautiful side-glance sends forth the arrows of the god of desire.

---

19 Madana is the god of love.

71. "The sight of your dangling earrings agitates my mind. Mistaking your face to be that of the moon, Rāhu[20] approaches your side.

72. "How enchanting is the beauty of your face in its full youth! Your even teeth are like the rows of seeds of a ripe pomegranate.

73. "Your bright eyes are playful like a pair of wagtail birds.

74. "A necklace made of large elephant pearls shines on your beautiful, shapely breasts.

75. "It seems as if the new moon is shining in the sky on its second day and the stars are shining brighter around it.

76. "The soles of your feet are like red lotuses and like *campaka*[21] buds are your beautifully shaped fingers.

77. "Your stomach has three creases to make it shapely and your slim waist resembles Śiva's *ḍambaru*.[22]

78. "Beautiful and well-shaped are your arms, buttocks, and thighs. Even sages would be fascinated by the sight of your red feet.

79. "Shamed by your graceful gait, even proud elephants in rut would hide themselves in the lake.

20 Rāhu is the ascending lunar node, believed to be a planet by Hindu astrologers. It is also a mythical creature that attempts to swallow the sun and the moon, causing eclipses.

21 *Campaka*: a fragrant yellow flower (*michelia champaca*).

22 *Ḍambaru*: a musical instrument shaped like an hourglass.

80. “Entranced by the tinkling sound of the ornaments around your waist, the bangles and the ankle bells, all the swans would slip into the waters of the ponds.

81. “Just as the lotus blooms with the rising of the sun, so ornaments look best on a supremely beautiful one like you.

82. “Are you Mahāmāyā, the wife of Śaṅkara, or are you Lakṣmī, the wife of Mādhava, or are you the shadow of Āditya?[23]

83. “Are you the wife of Bāsava or are you the heavenly dancer Rambhā? Are you the wife of the guru of all the gods? Or are you Tārā the unblemished one?

84. “The Creator must have skilfully combined all the loveliness of the world in creating you.

85. “Like the powerful five arrows of Madana, the god of love, your beauty has the power to defeat all the three worlds.

86. “You who are fit to be the queen of the greatest emperor, why are you living here in the forest?

87. “This forest of Daṇḍaka is full of *rākṣasas*. Tell me whence have you come here.”

88. When Sītā heard these words she was greatly amazed. But seeing that he was dressed like a sage, she replied to him thus:

89. “I am the daughter of Janaka and my name is Sītā. King Daśaratha is my father-in-law and I am the wedded wife of Rāma.

---

23 The sun god.

90. "In deference to the orders of his father, he has come to the forest accompanied by my brother-in-law, Lakṣmaṇa.

91. "All three of us are now suffering the travails of exile in the forest. My husband is now twenty-five-years old.

92. "In all the three worlds, none can surpass him in beauty or in virtues or in the skill of archery, and I am a full sixteen years of age.

93. "Listen, O you revered sage with curiosity in your heart. This place had been attacked by many *rākṣasas*;

94. "Triśira, Dūṣaṇa, and Khara, powerful in their strength, have been dispatched by Rāma to the abode of Death.

95. "Fourteen thousand *rākṣasas* came to attack him, but Rāma sent them all to the land of Death.

96. "Every single *rākṣasa* encountered by Rāma was chased and killed by his arrows."

97. Then Rāvaṇa said, "Sītā, your beauty surpasses everything. In all the three worlds there is none who can match your loveliness.

98. "Your face is bright like the full moon and every young man pierced by the arrow of desire can die for you."

Adhyāya 13

(*Rāvaṇa reveals his identity to Sītā*)

1. Then Sītā replied: "Listen, O you holy man, both Rāma and Lakṣmaṇa have gone to kill a deer.
2. "They will return soon. So, please rest for a while.
3. "They will be interested in meeting a sage like you and will greet you with due respect and offer you water and fruits."
4. Then Rāvaṇa the ten-headed one spoke to her thus: "Listen to me, O Sītā! I am the king of Laṅkā who has come to your dwelling place.
5. "I had heard many stories about you in my own country. Now that I have seen you in person, I am mightily pleased.
6. "All the denizens of the underworld bow down to me in supplication. I have defeated the three hundred million gods in heaven.
7. "I am afraid of neither Hari nor Śaṅkara and my golden kingdom of Laṅkā is situated in the midst of the ocean.
8. "I have acquired the knowledge of all the sixty four arts and the fourteen *śāstras*. All the twenty-five super-human powers of this world are in my possession.
9. "I am Rāvaṇa, the powerful elephant who defeats the might of all his enemies. So, Sītā, leave this human Rāma and accept me now.
10. "I will win all the queens of all the other kings on earth and bring them to serve as your handmaidens.

11. "What more can I do for you? I can even bring Indra's wife Śacī to be your servant.

12. "I can win over all the ten *digpālas*[24] of this world and put their women at your service.

13. "Mandodarī, who is my principal wife, will also serve you with all the other women in the palace.

14. "All your sufferings will come to an end from this day. I rule over millions of *rākṣasas*.

15. "So, lift your head, Sītā, and look at my face. Give up the wild fruits of the forest and taste the best fruit that the three worlds can offer.

16. "I have abducted the most beautiful women in all the three worlds after killing their husbands.

17. "Let them all live happily as your servants. You can shine in their midst like the full moon amongst the stars.

18. "By the blessing of the Creator, let me become the god of love. Let the two of us together rule over the kingdom of Laṅkā.

19. "Discard the company of humans and accept me, Sītā. Come quickly and let us go to my kingdom.

20. "I am so overcome with desire for you that I cannot bear it any longer. Accept me as your husband at once because I am Rāvaṇa, the master of the three worlds."

21. Hearing these words of Rāvaṇa, Sītā was struck with terror. She trembled with fear when she realized that he was a *rākṣasa*.

---

24 *Digpāla*: The gods who are in charge of the various cardinal directions of the universe.

22. His dreadful speech made her angry beyond measure and thus she spoke to him in a harsh and ruthless manner:

23. "O you savage creature of darkness, Rāvaṇa! Is it your desire to depart to the realm of Death at once?

24. "Rather than court me, the wife of Rāma, you should go and drink some deadly poison!

25. "You who wish to dance atop the trident are like a grave sinner who desires heaven!

26. "Being a mere firefly, you wish to lend light to the moon! How dare you aspire to carry away fire by tying it in a rag, you fool!

27. "You are trying to sharpen your tongue by rubbing it on the blade of a sword! O you are nothing but an insect jumping into a burning fire!

28. "The very idea of a low-bred *rākṣasa* desiring to possess Rāma's wife is like trying to press one's eye against a needle head.

29. "You are trying to swim the ocean with a stone tied around your neck! Your desire is like a small bird daring to lend its strength to the mighty Garūḍa!

30. "You are a mere frog that is trying to confront a snake! You are a tiny snake aspiring to swallow a mountain!

31. "Being a cat, you are trying to mock a tiger! You who are nothing but an animal of this earth have the audacity to approach the sun!

32. "Your desire for me is like that of a jackal for the lion's spouse! How dare you make such a proposal to Sītā, the pure one?

33. "A life of indulgence has turned your mind perverse. Now all your ten heads will be decapitated by Rāghava!

34. "My lord Rāma will see in you all the differences between a crow and Garūḍa, between the jackal and the lion,

35. "Between the mighty ocean and the small mountain rivers!

36. "Why should I leave Rāghava and submit to you? Why should I accept a small pond instead of the mighty Gaṅgā?

37. "Why should I accept a donkey instead of a lion? Why should I reject divine nectar for the sake of the bitter leaves of the jute plant?

38. "Know that I am the devoted wife, Sītā, the pure one. Why do you speak such insulting words to me?

39. "In my dreams, in my senses, in my thoughts I am firmly dedicated to Rāghava. I will not touch even the shadow of another man with my feet.

40. "Why should I forsake clarified butter for the sake of a distasteful muddy concoction? I would rather throw Rāma's unsightly loin-cloth on your head!

41. "Rāma's arrows will tear off your tongue! Can the *rākṣasas* do anything to help you then?"

42. Hearing these words from Sītā, Rāvaṇa's anger rose, as though clarified butter had been poured into a fire.

43. "You know nothing about my power, Sītā. That is why you are singing the praises of Rāma's manly prowess.

44. "Rāma is neither a great archer, nor does he possess physical strength. He knows little about the holy śāstras or about the rules of *dharma*.

45. "That is why he remains bound by his father's words and, knowing him to be inferior in strength and wisdom, king Daśaratha has sent him into exile.

46. "Bharata, who possesses many virtues, has been entrusted with the power of governance while Rāma, the unworthy one, has been sent to the forest.

47. "If your husband Rāma is a proper man, why doesn't he kill his brother and get back his kingdom?

48. "It makes me laugh when I see someone belonging to the Kṣatriya caste bearing the burden of a knot of matted hair on his head!

49. "How long will your husband live? He is after all a mere human being and soon his life will come to an end!

50. "So give up the house of your mortal husband, Sītā, and reign happily forever in my Laṅkā.

51. "By the blessings of Brahmā, I possess an indestructible body. There is none in heaven, earth, and the underworld who can match my valour.

52. "I have defeated the gods and I fear nobody now. I have snatched away Laṅkā from my elder brother Kubera.

53. "From him I also seized the Puṣpaka, the most famous divine chariot on earth, and grabbed plenty of riches and men.

54. "Kubera saved his life by taking shelter at the feet of Śiva on the Kailāśa mountain.

55. "Listen to my other deeds of valour, o Sītā! I have defeated the Bāsava, Yama, and Varuṇa.[25]

56. "I have defeated all the *asuras* and the *rudras*[26] and there is none who can equal me in heroism in the three worlds.

57. "All the divines serve me in Laṅkā and you will enjoy seeing them thus, o Sītā.

58. "Although you are human, come and enjoy all the pleasures of the *rākṣasa* kingdom. The travails of this forest life are not for you.

59. "Willingly am I offering myself to your service. Do not be so cruel to me, beautiful one!

60. "If you do not accept me as your master right now, you will remember me and repent for the rest of your life.

61. "I have compelled all the kings of this earth to submit to my power. I have lifted the Kailāśa mountain with Śiva on it.

62. "The essence of the whole world is added to my being. So, come to Laṅkā and enjoy all its pleasures.

63. "I, the emperor of the three worlds, have willingly become your slave. Why do you wish to reject someone who has submitted himself to you?

64. "If you disappoint me by rejecting my proposal, then, come joy or sorrow, I shall certainly abduct you today."

---

25 Bāsava: Indra, the king of the gods; Yama: the lord of death; Varuṇa: the god of rain.

26 Rudras: the eleven demi-gods sprung from the body of Śiva to destroy all creation.

65. Hearing these words of Rāvaṇa, Sītā was overcome with fear. She began to speak to him thus in anger and trepidation:

66. "Even if you try to enter the underworld after abducting me, Rāghava will certainly seek you out there and destroy you.

67. "Being a *Hāḍī,*[27] how dare you aspire to read the Vedas? You will soon be decapitated by Rāma.

68. "You may hope to live after abducting the consort of Śiva, or bring your own death by abducting Śacī, the wife of Indra.

69. "You may be able to abduct the moon god's Rohiṇī or Sāvitrī, the virtuous wife of Satyavāna.

70. "You may even snatch away Arundhatī, who belongs to Vasiṣṭha. But you will never be able to abduct me, the wife of Rāma.

71. "Fool, you will certainly die at Rāma's hands if you dare to carry me off to Laṅkā. I will be a blazing fire for your Laṅkā.

72. "If you are the son of good parents, you should stop and ponder awhile. Try and face at least one arrow from my master's hand.

73. "But how will you ever face Rāma's arrows? Lakṣmaṇa's arrows are capable enough of inflicting mortal wounds on you.

---

27 Hāḍī: a professional caste of goldsmiths in Assam, considered to be low-caste by Brahmins and Kshatriyas.

74. "You are trying to boast about the superiority of your manly prowess in front of a woman, knowing nothing about my master's qualities.

75. "You have harmed all the gods and *asuras*. Now all your pride will be destroyed by Rāmacandra's arrows!"

76. Sītā's words angered Rāvaṇa beyond all measure. He gave up his mendicant's disguise and assumed his true form.

77. Twenty ears, ten noses, and twenty arms! Ten heads were painted on his huge forehead.

78. Twenty pairs of eyes shone in their orbs from the ten faces, as though twenty furnaces were burning on a mountain.

79. His dark body looking like a mountain of *kohl*, Rāvaṇa stood before her in his fearful form.

80. He gnashed his twenty rows of teeth in anger, as though twenty grinders were working at the same time.

81. In great anger, he began to speak menacingly thus: "I shall abduct you, you sinful woman! The three worlds cannot save you now!

82. "You have insulted me in this manner, you sinful one! I can decide to break all your teeth with a single slap of my hand!

83. "You don't know who I am! I am the mighty Rāvaṇa who embodies the fire that surpasses all fires and the death that annihilates the lord of death!

84. "You are trying to praise the mortal Rāma in front me! Even a thousand Rāmas cannot inflict any harm on me!"

85. Listen, all ye courtiers, to the story of Rāma. In this dark *Kali* age there is no other path to salvation except chanting his name.

86. Since Rāma's name is the only essence of this life, so chant his name aloud. Only thus will you be able to consign to the flames all the sins you have accumulated in this life.

Adhyāya 15

[from verses 1–12, 110–117]

(*Rāvaṇa abducts Sītā*)

Pada

1. Then Rāvaṇa in his anger went towards Sītā and, holding her by her hair, he pulled her to himself.
2. With great care, he lifted her in his arms, as though the moon's beloved Rohiṇī was in Rāhu's grip.
3. Placing his hands on her thighs, he lifted her up gently and carried her swiftly to his chariot.
4. Seized by great dread, Sītā cried out loudly as the chariot sped away across the sky.
5. She sobbed incessantly in uncontrolled grief and all her limbs trembled in fear and agony.
6. Crying out to Rāma for help, she said, "Alas, alas, Rāma that it should be so, that your own wife is being abducted by the evil Rāvaṇa!
7. "You who have been incarnated to punish the evil, now come to my help when Rāvaṇa abducts me.
8. "O Lakṣmaṇa, come to my help at once! A creature of darkness resembling a goat is carrying away the lion's consort.
9. "O Destiny, why have you brought upon me such misfortune that I have lost my own husband?

10. "O my good husband, how will you live when Rāvaṇa has abducted the beloved daughter of Janaka?

11. "Kaikeyī, my mother-in-law, has at last succeeded in her intention and my father-in-law has embraced death in terrible sorrow.

12. "I pray to you, all ye forest gods! Please convey to Rāma the news of my misfortune."

[verses 13–85 concern Jatayu bravely attempting to rescue Sita and being defeated by Rāvaṇa after a fierce fight]

110. Distraught and pale with grief and agony, Sītā began to speak in a dejected voice to Rāvaṇa.

111. O sinful one, you will never be able to attain salvation. You who claim to be a great emperor have proved to be a mere woman-snatcher!

112. "I have pondered long and come to the conclusion that it was you who sent that magic deer in order to remove Rāma from my side.

113. "That *rākṣasa* of yours mimicked the voice of Rāma so that Lakṣmaṇa too would abandon me.

114. "Had Lakṣmaṇa been with me then, his arrow would have dispatched you to Death's abode at once.

115. "Woman-snatcher, sinner, eating the leftovers from the plate of a *hāḍi*! You have chosen to drown with a stone tied round your neck!

116. "How can you carry me off thus without having defeated my husband? You sinful one! Go at once and follow the path of a low-caste man.

117. "Even at this moment of death, you are bereft of wisdom. You are nothing but a mere drop of dew which will soon be evaporated by the might of Rāma, the sun."

Adhyāya 16

Sītā in Laṅkā [verses 33–55]

(Rāvaṇa speaks to Sītā)

1. "Whatever may be your order, o Sītā, I shall carry it out. I am now the provider of your food and sustenance.
2. "So, abandon your sorrow, beloved, and accept Rāvaṇa, the master of the three worlds, as your husband.
3. "Forsake the hope that Rāma will come and kill me. Have you ever heard, Sītā, that I have been imprisoned by anyone?
4. "Who will ever wish to be consumed by the flames of fire? Which hero will ever be able to defeat me?
5. "I am secure in this invincible fortress, which is surrounded by the mighty ocean on all sides.
6. "So give up the hope that Rāma will come and rescue you. I fall at your feet, Sītā, and seek your favour.
7. "Let us consummate our union on this Puṣpaka chariot, which is the best in all the three worlds.
8. "I bow and touch your feet with my ten heads and humbly plead with you, holding a straw between my teeth.
9. "Being a king of kings, I have become your slave. What more honour do you expect from me?
10. "My whole body burns with the fire of unfulfilled desire. Extinguish it with the nectar of your lips."

11. Hearing these words of Rāvaṇa, Jānakī burst out in fury, like dry leaves set suddenly on fire:

12. "I am the daughter-in-law of King Daśaratha and the wife of Rāmacandra. I have arrived here now to be the cause of destruction of your entire clan.

13. "Long-armed, brave, and good is my husband. He is exceedingly handsome, like an incarnation of the god of love.

14. "You cannot compare yourself with him in any way. You are like an iron flower in front of a precious jewel.

15. "Jānakī's mind will not change even if the sun rises in the west and sets in the east.

16. "Rāvaṇa, you are a savage who is not aware of his own deeds. That is why you speak such base and improper words to me, you shameless and sinful one!

17. "You are trying to put an elephant goad through the matted hair of Śiva! Being a worm of the underworld, how can you aspire to live in heaven?

18. "You are aware that your end is now drawing near. That is why you are making such a request to me.

19. "My only master is my beloved Rāma. I shall not allow my feet to so much as touch the head of another man.

20. "Although you have sought protection from Śiva and Brahmā, you will certainly die at the hands of Rāma.

21. "Even if the keepers of the ten corners of the universe seek to guard you, Rāma will still prove to be your death incarnate.

22. "Had you dared to abduct me in the presence of my husband, you would have met the same fate as that of Virādha[28] and gone limping to the kingdom of Death.

23. "Woman-snatcher and sinner, I denounce you from the bottom of my heart! In vain do you come and boast to me about your heroism."

---

28 Virādha: a fearful demon who had tried to abduct Sītā but was killed by Rāma in Daṇḍakāraṇya, thus freeing him from the curse of Kubera, who had transformed him from a *gandharva* to a *rākṣasa.*

Adhyāya 17

(Sītā pronounces her curse on Rāvaṇa)

Jumuḍi[29]

1. "Rāma will kill you and save my honour.
2. "He will burn down Laṅkā and deliver me from my misfortune.
3. "He will wound your heart and fill you with remorse.
4. "He will hold his bow in his hand and destroy all evil beings.
5. "He will cross the ocean with ease and banish my sorrow.
6. "He will destroy his enemies effortlessly as though he were playing a game."

29 Jumuḍi: a couplet verse with eight syllables in each line.

Adhyāya 18

[verses 1-4]

(Sītā reprimands Rāvaṇa further)

Pada

1. "You evil-natured Rāvaṇa, I would rather fast unto death than obey your orders.

2. "You may claim to be a holy man, but I shall desist from destroying you with my curse because I am afraid of deviating from the righteous path.

3. "By trying to possess the chaste Sītā by force, you are preparing your own death-noose.

4. "Move away, creature of darkness, from my side, or else I shall reduce you to ashes with my curse."

Sundarakāṇḍa

Adhyāya 14

(Hanumanta searches for Sītā amidst the beautiful women asleep in Rāvaṇa's harem and fails to find her there)

[verses 91-95]

Hanumanta discovers Sītā in Aśokavana

1. Hanumanta then heard the sound of ornaments tinkling, and, lifting his head, he saw Rāvaṇa approaching the place.
2. He instantly reduced the size of his body and jumped up to the branches of the *śiśu*[30] tree and covered himself with the thick foliage.
3. Meanwhile, Sītā saw the indications of Rāvaṇa's approach and she began to tremble like a plantain tree that shivers when the wind passes through it.

---

30 *Dalbergia sisoo* or Indian rosewood.

4. She sat crouched beneath the *śiśu* tree, covering her thighs and abdomen and shielding her breasts with her arms.

5. In fear and shame, her eyes filled with tears. Rāvaṇa stood apart, enchanted by the sight of Sītā.

Adhyāya 15

Rāvaṇa tries to persuade Sītā to change her decision.

Dularī

[verses 1-26]

1. Looking at her face from a distance, Rāvaṇa called out to Sītā thus: "There is no other man present here. So abandon your shyness, o most beautiful woman in the three worlds!

2. "Totally enthralled am I by your exceeding beauty, and my body trembles in anticipation. Have you not yet overcome the adverse feelings which you have harboured towards me because of the abduction?

3. "Lift your head, o you who possess a nectarous face, and speak to me so that I may view the rising of my moon and be relieved of the terrible darkness within me.

4. "Who can ever describe your beauty, you who possess all virtues and talents? I have not yet seen anyone more beautiful than you in the whole universe.

5. "A beautiful woman like you is now sitting on the ground while Queen Mandodarī is lying on her golden bed! But she cannot match your beauty because you are born of the gods.

6. "Even without any ornaments, your limbs shine forth with loveliness befitting a goddess. Had they been

embellished with ornaments, who could have ever controlled his desire for you?

7. "Leave for the ascetics those matted tresses of a forest dweller and accept me, o Sītā! I shall make King Janaka, your father, the ruler of the whole earth.

8. "Then, when he becomes my father-in-law, let everyone see how great he is. Let all other kings on this earth come and serve at Janaka's feet."

9. Turning her back on Rāvaṇa in fear and modesty, Sītā replied to him thus: "You who are the son of Brahmā, the grandson of the great sage Pulastya, and the king of Laṅkā,

10. "You who are well-versed in all the fourteen śāstras and know the difference between the righteous and the evil path, why are you trying to hurt the feelings of a chaste woman like me by speaking such inappropriate words?

11. "Give up your immoral desires, king of Laṅkā, and follow the path of righteousness. Take me away from here and at once offer me at Rāghava's feet.

12. "I shall use my miraculous power to instil reverence in your heart for my master and get assurance from him to grant you safety. You shall be able to enjoy unimpaired happiness for eternity and by Rāma's blessings the three worlds will be without any danger for you.

13. "Or else, you will soon suffer the consequence of having stolen someone else's wife. The gold-feathered arrows of my master will at once destroy you and all your allies.

14. "All your sons will die too and there will be no one alive to perform your last rites. Even now, blind sinner Rāvaṇa, do not try to deceive me about my husband.

15. "Your eyes should fall out of their sockets when you dare to look upon me to fulfill your base desire! Your tongue should drop off when you speak such foul words to Rāma's wife!

16. "My master is present in every place. It's your good fortune that I am not going to set you ablaze today with my curse because I am following the path of righteousness."

17. Rāvaṇa looked at Sītā and said: "o you unfortunate one! You continue to speak fearlessly even now because you know that I shall not kill a woman.

18. "You can look upon my face and answer me, you evil woman! Are you a pious saint that you pretend to explain to me the essence of all the ancient texts of wisdom?

19. "I have conquered the earth, the underworld, and the heavens. The thirty gods fall at my feet and worship me. Who are you to teach me the virtues of the pious and saintly man?

20. "I could, by myself, kill both your husband and his brother at this very instant; but that they are helplessly roaming in the forest after having lost their kingdom."

21. Then Sītā replied: "You vile Rāvaṇa! Do not boast so much! You have abducted a chaste woman, as a consequence of which evil act you will suffer much.

22. "You who lack courage to confront my lord, do not try to beat your own drum before me! Rather, go and boast about your valour in front of others!

23. "You are a fool compared to my husband and brother-in-law! You have abandoned your manliness and left your shame at the washerman's door when you abducted me secretly!

24. "I am the true wife of my husband Rāghava and you are fuelling the fire of my sorrow with your words. Had I received a signal from my husband, I would have burnt you down to ashes with my curse.

25. "O Rāvaṇa, you are boasting loudly about your prowess in front of a fearless woman like me. Only a shameless creature who has no other means to survive would be happy to stay with you.

26. "Your only quality is to behave in a shameless manner. I trample upon your valour with my left foot! Go drown yourself with a pitcher tied round your neck!"

Adhyāya 16

[Verses 1-20]

(Rāvaṇa is angry and orders the rākṣasa *women to frighten Sītā)*

Pada

1. The ten-headed Rāvaṇa was crestfallen when he heard Sītā's words. His eyes became angry and bloodshot.

2. He shook his thighs and rubbed his palms menacingly. Casting angry sideways glances at Sītā, he scratched all his ten heads.

3. Then he spoke to her in an abusive tone: "Today I shall obliterate your fame as a chaste wife! Let Rāma come and protect you if he can!

4. "Let Earth be witness to how I am going to force myself upon this sinful woman! She must be blind not to accept me as her husband!

5. "Only superior creatures are capable of making the right choices. The base ones must be made to bend so that their thoughts can be refined through coercion."

6. Thus boasting and ranting, the demon king of Laṅkā left the place. Hanumāna, the son of the wind-god, heard him, and his anger began to mount.

7. He fretted and fumed silently in unbearable agony. "Let him but try and touch Sītā the goddess!"

8. "Where will you hide yourself, Rāvaṇa? If I am the son of the wind-god, I shall punish you suitably!" he said to himself.

9. "I shall stamp on your foot and maul you. Or else I shall pull at your other leg and throw you down on the ground. I shall then tear you to pieces.

10. "I shall crush your ten heads with my kicks, or break all your ribs and kill you.

11. "I shall crush the enemy of Rāma this very day! I shall tie him to my tail and roll in the ocean."

12. When Rāvaṇa left the place raving and seething with anger, Mandodarī told him that his action was not proper.

13. "Long ago, Kubera's son Nalakubera cursed my husband to die if he used force on a woman."

14. So Mandodarī came forward and tried to soothe her husband: "My lord, it is not proper of you to display your anger before a woman.

15. "Even the gods are afraid to face your anger. Do you not remember the ancient story?"

16. Thus Mandodarī intervened and at once Rāvaṇa's anger was reined in, as though an elephant were being controlled by the goad.

17. He spoke thus to the *rākṣasa* women: "I order you, women, to try your best to make Sītā change her feelings towards me.

18. "I am granting you two months' time for this task. Let Sītā submit to me within this time.

19. "You may use all the tactics of the hawk or the dove; but compel her to surrender to my wishes at last.

20. "If you are unable to convince her in any way, then I give you permission to kill Sītā and feast upon her flesh."

21. With this order, the king of Laṅkā left that place and, accompanied by all his women, he entered his royal palace.

[Verses 55-68]

(Sītā speaks to the rākṣasa *women after they threaten her)*

1. Sītā trembled in fear and apprehension when she heard these hurtful words of the *rākṣasa* women.

2. Thus she addressed the *rākṣasa* women from her seat under the *śiśu* tree:

3. "You evil, base, and barbarous daughters of the night! You have no knowledge of what is happiness and sorrow in the three worlds.

4. "You who have no compunction in killing living beings, how can you understand what is the righteous way of the devoted wife?

5. "I am an unfortunate sinner who does not know what is the best course of action for me. How can I survive so long without my husband Rāma?

6. "My lord does not know that I have been abducted and brought here. Or else Rāvaṇa would not be alive now.

7. "Neither Rāma nor Lakṣmaṇa knew about my abduction by Rāvaṇa.

8. "That is why the ruler of Laṅkā, that sinful, base, barbarous, abductor of women, is still alive.

9. "My lord may be dressed like a mendicant with matted hair, he may be living in the forest and in great distress.

10. "Even then, he is my lord and my only god. I am a chaste, married woman and forever devoted to my husband.

11. "Oh, when will I see this Laṅkā being burnt down to ashes and all the *rākṣasa* women being consumed by the jackals?

12. "When will I joyfully witness the *rākṣasa* women lamenting over their husbands?

13. "Rāvaṇa may be the ruler of the three worlds, but I shall not step even on his shadow!

14. "What more harm can you do to me except kill me and eat my flesh?"

[Verses 94-108]

(*Hanumanta has been listening to all that the* rākṣasa *women have said to Sītā and Sītā's brave response*)

1. The most powerful Hanumanta heard everything from the beginning to the end.

2. "Blessed am I" he said, "that I have been born on this earth to see the chaste goddess Sītā with my own eyes!

3. "I have now looked upon the divine Sītā. Thinking of her, Rāma is enduring every possible misfortune.

4. "She, for whom thousands of bears and monkeys are searching every corner of the earth, is now in front of my eyes.

5. "How can I perform my mission now in such a way that I remain invisible to the *rākṣasa* women?

6. "If these creatures happen to see me and recognize me, there will be a great uproar. They will report to Rāvaṇa and have me imprisoned.

7. "Yet I cannot leave this place without speaking to Sītā; but I do not know how it will be possible to talk to her.

8. "If I appear before her and speak now, she will suspect me to be an agent of Rāvaṇa who has been sent to deceive her.

9. "If I leave this place without speaking to her, how will I convince Rāma that I have seen her?

10. "He will think that this monkey has come to cheat him by claiming to have seen Sītā without having met her.

11. "So I shall do what I consider to be most appropriate. May the thirty gods give me the strength to carry out my duty to Rāma!

12. "I shall speak such words that will convince Sītā and my voice will be soft and musical.

13. "If this attempt fails then I shall think of other ways." With these words Hanumāna shrunk his body to a minuscule size atop the tree.

14. He folded his hands in supplication to Sītā and began to speak softly thus:

Adhyāya 17

Sītā-Hanumanta dialogue

[Verses 1-45, 80-113,121-156]

1. "There was a great king named Daśaratha and among all his sons Śrī Rāma is the best.

2. "King Daśaratha was preparing to anoint Rāma as the king, but his younger queen Kaikeyī snatched away the kingdom at the auspicious moment.

3. "From her husband, she begged for the kingdom for her son Bharata and got Rāma banished to the forest.

4. "Rāma then took his brother and his wife with him to the forest. In the forest, Rāvaṇa abducted Sītā."

5. Hanumanta fell silent after this and Sītā looked all around when she heard these pleasing words.

6. She looked towards the east, then to the west, north and south; but she could not see anybody.

7. Then she looked upwards at the tree, shading her eyes with her left hand. There she saw a monkey with his palms folded together reverentially.

8. Sītā then began to speak thus: "I pray to you, o Harihara, Sūrya, Kubera, and Purandara!

9. "May the words that I hear from the mouth of a monkey be true and not an illusion."

10. Then, addressing the monkey, she said: "Where have you come from, my dear friend, and how do you know about my husband?"

11. Then Hanumanta replied from his perch on the *śiśu*: "which goddess are you and whom do you belong to?

12. "Why are you sitting under this *śiśu* tree and why are you shedding tears incessantly?

13. "Are you Śacī, the fortunate wife of Bāsava, or Chāyā, the wife of Āditya,[31] or Candra's wife Rohiṇī?

14. "Are you Lakṣmī, the wife of Hari, or are you Pārvatī, the wife of Śiva? Or are you Vasiṣṭha's wife Arundhatī?

15. "In the entire universe, I have never seen such beauty as yours, with your bright face resembling the moon and your wide eyes.

16. "I shall speak a few words to you if you reveal your identity to me. Are you not the beloved daughter of King Janaka?

17. "Is your name Sītā and are you the one who was abducted by Rāvaṇa?"

18. Sītā regained her composure and made reply: "I am the daughter-in-law of Daśaratha and the wife of Rāma.

19. "Kauśalyā is my mother-in-law and Lakṣmaṇa my brother-in-law. My name is Sītā and I am the daughter of Janaka.

20. "King Daśaratha thought it fit to hand over the kingdom to his eldest son but his younger wife Kaikeyī snatched it away from him.

31 Āditya: the sun.

21. "She begged for the kingdom on behalf of her own son and got Rāma banished to the deep forest.

22. "Rāma spent several years in the forest of Daṇḍaka until one day Rāvaṇa forcefully carried me off when I was alone.

23. "I am suffering such pain and agony in the midst of the *rākṣasa* women that I wish Yama had taken me away instead.

24. "Tell me, my good fellow, whence have you come? Are you a messenger from Rāma or from Rāvaṇa?"

25. Hanumanta then folded his palms respectfully and said: "Your husband Rāma is safe and well.

26. "He has searched for you far and wide but could get no news about you. I am Hanumanta, a messenger of Rāma.

27. "Sumitrā's son is Lakṣmaṇa. There is not a more unwavering archer than he in this world.

28. "This handsome man named Lakṣmaṇa has sent you a message. Please accept it, o mother."

29. With these words Hanumanta placed his forehead on the ground before her and repeated the message sent by Lakṣmaṇa:

30. "The golden deer that you had seen was not a real deer but an illusion created by a *rākṣasa*.

31. "There was a creature of darkness called Mārīca who made Rāma chase him quite a distance away.

32. "When Rāma drove an arrow into his body, inflicting a mortal wound, he cried out, imitating Rāma's voice.

33. "At this, you were distraught with grief and used improper words to send Lakṣmaṇa to go in search of Rāma.

34. "In this way, after removing the two brothers from your side in a planned manner, Rāvaṇa abducted you when you were alone."

35. Then Sītā replied, "Rāvaṇa came here once to deceive me. Now he has come again to trick me.

36. "Go away from hence, you sinful creature. Do not disturb me anymore. What connection could there be between Rāma and a monkey?

37. "You came here earlier and I will not forgive you for that. O how much more insult can I bear from such degraded creatures?

38. "What will you gain by cheating me in this way? You will be degraded further for your sinful behaviour.

39. "Try and understand the true essence of a chaste woman like me," she said. Hanumanta trembled in fear and prayed silently to *dharma*.

40. Fearing that the goddess would burn him down to ashes with her curse, he spoke to her in a fearful, plaintive tone:

41. "I am not a *rākṣasa*, o mother, but a messenger of Rāma. I am the son of Pavana who has come in search of you.

42. "If you abandon your doubts and look at me carefully, you will be convinced that I am not a *rākṣasa*."

43. Sītā then spoke to him thus: "Give me some proof of your identity by describing the beauty and virtues of Śrī Rāma.

44. "Tell me about his character and the greatness of his heart. Describe also the beauty and virtues of Lakṣmaṇa."

45. Then the son of the wind-god said, "Listen carefully o ye mother. I shall describe Rāghava's qualities as I have perceived them.

(Hanumanta recounts Rāma's great qualities and narrates all the events that took place after Sītā's abduction, how Rāma procured new allies and how he was preparing to fight Rāvaṇa—verses 46-72)

[Verses 73-156]

1. "I have now told you the whole story from the beginning till the end. Now accept with happiness this ring on which Rāma's name is engraved."
2. With these words Hanumanta placed Rāma's ring in Sītā's palm and, as she stared at it, she seemed to have lost her senses for a while.
3. When she gained control over her feelings, she touched her head with Rāma's ring.
4. Her pure and unblemished face lit up with happiness as though the moon's bright orb had reappeared after an eclipse.
5. Though her body seemed to shrink from the unbearable pain inflicted by grief, her face showed signs of joy and eager curiosity.
6. Tears streamed down from both her eyes as though dew drops were tumbling down lotus leaves.
7. "How happy I am and curious to know the truth. Your words are nectar to my ears, dear brother.
8. "I am totally convinced by what you have said and, abandoning all my sorrow, I am now in full control of my senses.

9. "Tell me in brief, o Hanumanta, whether my husband Rāma is safe and well.

10. "Before you talk of other things, tell me, o Hanumanta, whether my brother-in-law Lakṣmaṇa is well.

11. "Kauśalyā, Sumitrā, and the lady Kaikeyī, are they all healthy and well?

12. "Now tell me also about Bharata. Is he prepared to come and rescue me with all his forces in complete array?

13. "The king of the monkeys whom you call Sugrīva, will he remember to come and liberate me?

14. "On only one count do I still have doubts, my brother. How did you manage to cross the ocean and come hither?

15. "This ocean, which is the home of the god of rains, is hundreds of *yojana*[32] in width and its depth is frightening for humans to comprehend.

16. "Crossing such a fearful, inaccessible ocean, how did you arrive in this kingdom of Laṅkā?

17. "You appear to me quite small and weak!" Hanumanta then made reply, "Listen, o mother, by your blessings my power is like that of the wind.

18. "Dismiss these doubts from your mind, o mother. By Rāma's blessings, I can stride over the ocean as though it were a puddle in a cow's hoofmarks."

---

32 *Yojana*: a measure of distance, approximately nine miles.

19. Sītā said: "Tell me in a few words, o Hanumanta, how is my husband and how is he managing his daily life, what thoughts do trouble his mind?"

20. Hanumanta said: "Why do you ask me such questions which cannot be answered? Śrī Rāma has almost lost his speech in sorrow.

21. "His hair is matted with dirt and mud and on many days he lives only on fruit. He neither speaks in joy nor laughs and each day without you seems to him like a year.

22. "Thinking of you, he has lost all serenity of mind. He roams around the forest restlessly in search of you."

23. The mother of the world then wept uncontrollably in pain when she heard about the sufferings of Rāma.

24. The monkey Hanumanta could not bear the sight of Sītā's sorrow. Placing his head at her feet he said:

25. "Be not so distraught with grief, o mother. For Rāma has sent words that he is in sound health.

26. "Lord Rāghava is sober and deep like the ocean and as unswerving in his courage as the greatest hero on this earth.

27. "He thinks of you day and night without a thought about enjoying other pleasures."

28. Hearing these words, Sītā shed many a tear and the brave Hanumāna joined her in her grief.

29. Then he said hesitantly: "I would like to speak a few words to you mother, though I am afraid to do so.

30. "When I see your grief I am extremely pained. That is why I shall speak these words to you, come what may.

31. "Sit on my back, o goddess of the universe, and hold on to my hair with all your might. This instant will I carry you to my master Rāma.

32. "Thus, by uniting you two, I will be able to put an end to all the sorrow and agony that you and Rāma are bearing."

33. Sītā stared at the monkey in disbelief and said: "This is like my little son talking big indeed!

34. "You are not strong enough to bear the weight of a handful of cotton, how can you lift big stones? It is as absurd as little ants trying to swallow elephants,

35. "Or a small bat trying to lay eggs the size of big drums, or a little sparrow lifting a mountain."

36. Then Hanumanta said: "Fear not, o mother, for I am the brave Hanumanta. My infinite power can defeat all foes.

37. "My father was a great hero named Keśarī. I shall now tell you the famous story about his strength and courage.

38. "Once, he made a great leap to reach Gandhamādana Mountain, but landed on the peak of Gokarṇa instead.

39. "There I was conceived through the mediation of Vāyu, the lord of the winds who is the friend of Agni,[33] the lifeblood of the world.

---

33 Agni: the fire-god.

40. "I am capable of carrying you across the world. I can even carry away the whole of Laṅkā with all its men and soldiers.

41. "I have been watching you silently, chaste goddess, from my perch on the *śiśu* bough.

42. "I saw in my imagination Lakṣmaṇa pleading with you with folded hands and I saw the monster Rāvaṇa talking to you at length.

43. "You withstood all that with a fearless heart. Can anyone shake the mighty Meru Mountain with the gentle breeze of a fan?

44. "What I heard with my own ears and saw with my eyes, I shall report to Śrī Rāma."

45. With these words he tried to raise Sītā's confidence in him. He leapt from the tree and stood before her, expanding his body to the size of a mountain.

46. Then, shrinking back again to his former size, he bowed respectfully before Sītā and leapt back to the tree.

47. Sītā then addressed him thus: "Friend, you are a true messenger of Rāma. Son of Pavana, you have crossed the deep, vast forest.

48. "You have travelled across hundreds of *yojana* and without a doubt you are capable of crossing millions more.

49. "I know that you can easily carry me on your back. But, consider carefully what I have to say.

50. "What purpose would be served if you carried me off from hence? People would make fun of Rāma's courage and strength.

51. "Everybody would say that he could not win the battle and take his woman back victoriously.

52. "They would laugh at him and say that he is a sinful woman-stealer who had to bring back Jānakī by stealth.

53. "The whole world knows that I am a chaste woman who will not consciously touch the body of another man.

54. "You may say that when Rāvaṇa abducted me I did touch him. But that was because women are never free agents but are always subject to others.

55. "I no longer have any doubts about how you crossed the vast seas. Now, go and bring Rāma-Lakṣmaṇa to me when I am still in my senses.

56. "With my orders go at once from hence while I am sitting alone steadfastly under the *śiśu* tree.

57. "Go tell Rāma that I will be eaten up by the *rākṣasa* women if my husband fails to come within another month.

58. "Tell him that I am ready to take my own life if my husband Rāma does not come to me even then.

59. "Go and tell all this to Rāma, how I am spending my days under this tree,

60. "How the *rākṣasa* women are trying to break my resolution and how I am facing the threat of being punished after a month.

61. "O how will I escape from all these dangers and find Rāghava by my side again?"

62. Māruti[34] heard her and said, "Worry no more, for, Rāvaṇa with his whole army may be considered annihilated already.

63. "Rāma's army contains thousands of brave monkey soldiers, whose strength can match the powers of hundreds of mountain-sized elephants.

64. "Why should you be doubtful and full of despondency when there are many more heroes like me in Rāma's army?

65. "The monkey king Sugrīva will set sail in the ocean with his well-armed soldiers.

66. "And Śrī Rāma with Lakṣmaṇa will come at once to destroy Rāvaṇa and take you back from here.

67. "Now, so that I may win the confidence of Rāma, tell me in brief about some secret of yours which is known to none else but Rāma.

68. "I shall leave this place instantly if you tell me of such a secret which is shared by you and Rāma."

69. Then Jānakī said, "Listen, o son of Vāyu, I shall tell you about some of our secrets now,

70. Sītā then narrated before Hanumanta some of those secret stories about Rāma and herself.

71. "Once, in Citrakūṭa, when Rāma was sleeping with his head on my thigh, a crow flew down and pecked at my breast, injuring it.

---

34 Māruti: the son of Mārut or the wind-god, another name for Hanumāna.

72. "Rāma immediately shot at the bird an arrow made of *kuśa*[35] grass and blinded him in the right eye.

73. "Once, I had put a mark on his forehead with the *mānasa stone*[36] and it had aroused his desire for me. He folded me in his embrace.

74. "And I had then hit him hard with both my hands. Consider, who else but me can talk about these things to you?"

75. "Whatever you have said, I shall convey it all to Rāma. Meanwhile, if you have anything to offer me as food, I shall be obliged."

76. "Also give me something of yours which I may carry to Rāma so that he will be convinced that it is you," said Hanumanta.

77. Praise be, Lord Raghupati, the ultimate refuge for the destitute, at your feet may I surrender my will.

78. May I never cease to sing your praises and to listen constantly to your voice.

79. Only then will all my wishes come true. So, all ye people present here, raise your voices and sing the praises of Rāma.

---

35 *Kuśa*: a kind of grass considered sacred by Hindus.

36 *Mānasa* stone: a stone associated with desire or a wish.

Laṅkākāṇḍa

Adhyāya 49

(After the battle has ended and Rāma has destroyed Rāvaṇa and his forces, Sītā arrives and stands before Rāma)

Dularī

1. Śrī Rāma then said to Lakṣmaṇa: "Listen to my orders,, o Lakṣmaṇa. Go at once and make preparations to celebrate the handing over of the kingdom to Vibhīṣaṇa at this auspicious moment."
2. In obedience to Rāma's orders the brave Lakṣmaṇa departed at once. *Nāndī*[37] verses began to be chanted and victory music was played while loud shouts of victory resounded all around.
3. Sounds of conch shells, trumpets, and cymbals, accompanied by the beating of drums, reverberated in

37 *Nāndī*: verses sung at the opening of a play in praise of a deity, king, or patron.

every direction. *Rākṣasas* and demons, forgetting their mourning over Rāvaṇa, began to dance in happiness.

4. Young women waved white whisks as an auspicious act and an umbrella as white as the moon was held above the head of Vibhīṣaṇa.

5. Brāhmaṇas blessed him by offering clarified butter to the fire. The sweet-smelling breeze, blowing gently, created an atmosphere of happiness all around.

6. Dancing girls danced, the singers sang their songs, and the *bhāṭa*[38] recited the *capaya*[39] verses. Thus, Vibhīṣaṇa was anointed king and all the sorrows which had once become his destiny came to an end.

7. He sat on his golden throne surrounded by all his ministers while Lakṣmaṇa joyfully performed the anointing ceremony by pouring out water from a golden pitcher.

8. All the soldiers raised a victorious shout to the accompaniment of the five musical instruments, and their salute to Rāma reached as far as the heavens.

9. Then Vibhīṣaṇa, with all kinds of delicious offerings, rushed to the side of Rāma and, after respectfully placing them before Rāma, partook of the savoury delights.

10. Rāma happily accepted the offerings and shared the sweets with the bears and monkeys.

11. Addressing Hanumanta, Rāma then said: "Go and give Sītā all the news about how I destroyed Rāvaṇa."

---

38 *Bhāṭa*: a minstrel who sings panegyrics in praise of a king.

39 *Capaya*: a verse in four-foot rhyming metre.

12. Obeying Rāma's orders, Hanumāna immediately went to the Aśokavana to meet Sītā.

13. Sītā, clad in her dusty attire, was sitting in the midst of the *rākṣasa* women, like a garland of lotus flowers encircled by dark hair.

14. Māruti bowed before her and said: "Rāma is safe and sound, lady. The creature which had abducted you and brought you here has been dispatched to the lowest level under the earth.

15. "Your brother-in-law Lakṣmaṇa has killed Indrajit and all the bear and monkey soldiers have sent the *rākṣasa* forces to death.

16. "Lord Rāma, after killing Rāvaṇa, has handed over the kingdom of Laṅkā to Vibhīṣaṇa. Now all is well with Lakṣmaṇa, Sugrīva, and the monkey soldiers.

17. "All the promises which I had made to you, o goddess, have been fulfilled. I crossed the ocean, brought Rāma here, and got the evil Rāvaṇa killed.

18. "Rāma has now sent you this message: let the daughter of Janaka hear this news of my victory. He who had abducted you has been sent to the abode of death."

19. When the chaste Sītā heard this news she fell silent for a while, though her tearful eyes were filled with happiness.

20. Then Māruti said: "Why don't you speak, o goddess of the universe? Rāma has truly destroyed the king of Laṅkā."

21. Sītā replied: "O my dear brother Hanumanta, I cannot speak to you out of shame because I have nothing with

me which I can offer to you as an appropriate reward for bringing this happy news."

22. "Give me that reward," said Māruti , "which providence has reserved for me. If you smile now with happiness, it would be for me the most precious gift on earth.

23. "These *rākṣasa* women, obedient to Rāvaṇa's orders, have abused and insulted you. They have threatened you in different ways in order to frighten you into submission.

24. "I am deeply anguished even today when I remember those insults heaped upon you. I want to thrash them all to death, let Rāvaṇa come and save them if he can!

25. "I shall kill some of them with punches and some with blows, some I shall I strike with my elbows, some I will beat to death with slaps or sticks, and some will I destroy with stones.

26. "If you give me permission to gouge out the eyes of some of them or cut off their noses and drag them away, I shall consider that to be an appropriate reward for me."

27. Then the goddess Sītā said: "My brother Hanumanta, why are you so angry with these women? The *rākṣasa* women are all slaves of Rāvaṇa, they have no independent agency.

28. "Had they dared to defy Rāvaṇa's orders and desisted from threatening me, Rāvaṇa could have even then put me to sword instantly and no one in this universe could have saved me.

29. "These women now can do me no harm but are themselves frightened to death. They have fallen at my feet and have begged for mercy.

30. "Who has the power to kill or save anyone? The sins we have committed in our previous lives will determine whether we will live or die."

31. Then Māruti said, "Praise be to your wisdom, o mother goddess Sītā! You are truly the progeny of the clan of the moon and a daughter-in-law of the sun's clan.

32. "You have said what is right and I am mightily pleased with your nectar-like words. Now tell me quickly what message I may convey from you to Lord Śrī Rāma and I shall leave at once,

33. Then Sītā said: "Hanumanta, your words remind me of my father Janaka. My heart is now impatient to see him by whose blessings all my sorrows have been wiped away.

34. "Go and tell my true and wedded husband to come at once and take me away from here without any delay."

35. Receiving this order from Sītā, the son of Vāyu touched her feet and sped away at once. Soon he landed in front of Rāma like the great Meru Mountain.

36. He circumambulated Rāma reverentially with pressed palms and paid homage at his feet. Then he narrated thus from the beginning to the end all that Sītā had said:

37. "Listen, o Lord of the Raghu clan at whose feet I offer my prayers, the goddess Sītā is the reason for which you had crossed the ocean and destroyed Rāvaṇa,

38. "Now bring her here at once, there is no reason to delay further. The goddess has always been eagerly waiting to behold your two feet.

39. "Her heart was overjoyed to hear the tale of your victory and she has sent me to you eagerly so that you may give her permission to come to you at once."

40. Hearing this, Rāma was overcome by waves of sorrow. He slapped his forehead and rested his cheeks on his hands while tears streamed down his cheeks.

41. Māruti's words suddenly brought a pall of gloom to his happiness and he sat dejected and downcast, in deep thought.

42. His mind overcast with sorrow, he looked down at the ground and then, looking up at Vibhīṣaṇa, he said, "Listen to me, o brave Vibhīṣaṇa,

43. "Go with my orders to the daughter of Janaka. Let her go bathe herself and wash her hair in the ocean and then come here in a palanquin."

44. At once Vibhīṣaṇa went to the Aśokavana and, with folded hands, said reverentially to Sītā: "Listen to your husband's orders, O goddess—

45. "Bathe in the ocean and wear all your ornaments and then go to Rāma immediately in a palanquin."

46. "What kind of an order is this?" she said. "I shall meet my husband in my present dusty attire and I see no reason to put on my ornaments. Bring the palanquin at once and I shall go."

47. Then Vibhīṣaṇa replied, "You should obey Rāma's orders, o mother. Bathe and wash your hair and

go to Rāma after decorating yourself with all the ornaments."

48. Then Sītā was given a ceremonial bath with fragrant water brought in golden pitchers by the attending girls.

49. Vibhīṣaṇa brought a variety of ornaments made of gold and placed them before her. Sītā, the daughter of Janaka, put them on joyfully in obedience to Rāma's orders.

50. Resplendent with new clothes and ornaments, Sītā climbed into a covered palanquin, while Vibhīṣaṇa led the way.

51. Thus she left Aśokavana and proceeded quickly towards Rāma, while the road was cleared of crowds by baton-wielding escorts.

52. Vibhīṣaṇa went forward and informed Rama: "I have brought Sītā here according to your orders. Now, if you permit me, I shall produce her before you."

53. Hearing this, Rāma looked to his left and right with mixed feelings. Joy and sorrow in equal measures wrestled within him.

54. After a while, sighing deeply he said: "Vibhīṣaṇa my friend, bring Sītā before me at once."

55. So the new king of Laṅkā went forward and ordered his servants to remove the soldiers from the path.

56. Thousands of his men, clad in bright clothes with long-tailed turbans on their heads, waved their canes and gestured to the soldiers of Rāma to clear the way.

57. And some began to hit the monkey soldiers with their canes and tried to drive them away from Rāma's side.

58. All the bear and monkey soldiers were eager to catch a glimpse of Sītā. They tried to approach her but the fear of being beaten forced them to flee.

59. I bow a hundred times at the feet of Rāma and sing his praises. It was he who killed Rāvaṇa, the enemy of the gods, and rescued Sītā.

60. May he, who is the lord Dāmodara[40] to all who worship him, grant me all my wishes. You who realize the divinity of Rāma, abandon all your futile labour and chant aloud his praises.

40 Dāmodara: another name for Śrī Kṛṣṇa.

Adhyāya 50

(Sītā's test by fire)

Pada

1. When Rāma saw that Vibhīṣaṇa's servants, wielding canes and sticks, were mercilessly driving away the monkeys and the bears.
2. He was anguished at the pain suffered by his monkey soldiers. Addressing Vibhīṣaṇa angrily, he said: "Friend, you are a lesser creature than they.
3. "The monkeys are my true friends, my fathers and grandfathers. It is because of them that I could tide over the great crisis.
4. "You have wounded my soul beyond measure by ordering your servants to beat up my monkeys.
5. "I am greatly displeased with your action. I see no harm if sons wish to look at their mother's countenance.
6. "Go and reassure them and bring them back at once. Let them look upon Sītā to their hearts' content.
7. "The bears and the monkeys wish to see her for whom they have suffered so much pain.
8. "During wedding ceremonies or sacrificial rites, or when women make their choice at *svayaṃvara* sites,
9. "There is no bar on women being seen by everyone in public and it does not go against the sacred laws."

10. Vibhīṣaṇa was crestfallen on hearing this and he ordered all the monkeys to be brought back at once.

11. Then Rāma gave his orders, in a voice full of anger and displeasure: "Let Sītā alight from the covered palanquin and walk barefoot hither."

12. Knowing this to be an ominous signal, the crowds exchanged glances in fear and apprehension.

13. Their eyes full of tears, they looked down upon the ground and, uneasily shuffling their feet, whispered thus to each other: "Does Rāma intend to reject the angelic Sītā after all?"

14. Then Vibhīṣaṇa removed the cover of the palanquin and the crowds beheld Sītā weeping in distress.

15. The monkey soldiers could hardly bear the heartrending sight when they beheld Janaka's beloved daughter in tears.

16. Lakṣmaṇa covered his face and wept. Vibhīṣaṇa and Aṅgada too looked down and cried.

17. Nala, Nīla, Keśarī, Panasa, Hanumanta, Gabākṣa, and Jambawanta could not hold back their tears when they saw the grief-stricken Sītā.

18. Seeing Sītā's plight, all the people cried out in distress and in vain did the bears and monkeys try to hide their tears.

19. Pricked by thorns, her tender soles bled as Sītā walked barefoot behind Vibhīṣaṇa.

20. The jewels that adorned her body tinkled merrily as she advanced like Lakṣmī to meet her Nārāyaṇa.

21. Just as the goddess Durgā appeared splendid when she went to meet Śaṅkara, so Sītā's beauty was luminous like burning gold as she approached Rāma.

22. Sītā, the chaste and sinless one, shrinking from public gaze, seemed to hide within herself in doubt and shame.

23. Thus the mother of the universe, her form tender like butter, walked along silently without looking at anyone.

24. The bears and monkeys were overwhelmed with joy when they saw the beauty of Sītā, their goddess.

25. "We are blessed by the sight of Jānakī," they said, "and happy that we have come here with Rāma."

26. Amazed by her exceeding beauty which could enchant the universe, the monkeys, bears, and *rākṣasas* gazed at her in wonder.

27. The sight of Sītā filled Rāma's heart with love, but he steeled his body against her and contrary emotions assailed his heart.

28. Seeing Sītā's sorrow, tears welled up in his eyes which he tried to suppress with a show of rage.

29. Sorrow and anger mingled in his heart as he tried desperately to control his tears.

30. As Sītā drew near, he was silent and grim, displaying his lack of affection for her.

31. Gently lowering her head, the modest Sītā quivered like a plantain leaf in anxiety and fear.

32. Then, emboldened by her love and faith in her own purity, she cast off all fear and stood upright.

33. She, who had been pining so long to look at his dear face, now stood apart uncertainly and gazed at him sideways.

34. At last Rāma raised his eyes to Sītā's face. His heart was in turmoil behind his stern gaze.

35. He spoke to her in a voice full of anger: "Listen to me, you, Janaka's daughter,

36. "I killed Rāvaṇa in battle and cleared my name. By bringing you back, I have recovered my family's fame.

37. "Had I not killed my wife's abductor, people would have thought I had silently accepted defeat.

38. "By silencing all the scurrilous gossip of common men, now I have freed my illustrious family from all blame.

39. "Your abduction by King Rāvaṇa was ordained by fate, and by annihilating your abductor I have asserted my might."

40. Guessing the intention behind Rama's words instinctively, the divine Sītā trembled and perspired in anxiety.

41. As the full moon darkens when it is suddenly covered by clouds, her fair countenance lost its lustre and brilliance.

42. "Listen to me, Jānakī," Rāma said, "I will have nothing more to do with you. I have kept my promise to Vibhīṣaṇa by installing him on the throne of Laṅkā.

43. "I have helped great Māruti keep his pledge and I have fulfilled the aspirations of my friend Sugrīva.

44. "Not for your sake did I perform my heroic deeds, but to clear my fair name have I asserted my masculine prowess.

45. "Now open your eyes and behold! The whole world is rejoicing at my victory. So I discard you now, Sītā. You may go where you please.

46. "Rāvaṇa abducted you and kept you with him for a long time. Who would ever believe in your chastity after all that?

47. "Taking you back now would seem as foolish as to try and swim with a stone tied to my chest.

48. "It is impossible for me to accept you again after your long sojourn in the palace of Rāvaṇa.

49. "If I do take you back, my reputation would suffer. I cannot accept you because I fear scandalous gossip.

50. "So, you may go and offer yourself to Bharata or Lakṣmaṇa, or even to Vibhīṣaṇa or Sugrīva.

51. "It is unbelievable that a woman of surpassing beauty like you would have been left untouched by Rāvaṇa."

52. Hearing such cruel words from her husband, Sītā's heart became heavy with grief and shame.

53. Rāma's cruel words like arrows pierced her heart and Janaka's daughter at last slowly began to speak:

54. "I was born into an excellent family and my father gave me in marriage to a *mahanta*[41]clan.

---

41 *Mahanta*: a reputed and respected person.

55. "But you have seen in me only a common woman, offering me to others as though I were a mere courtesan.

56. "The sinful Rāvaṇa abducted me and, being a woman, I had no freedom to assert my self.

57. "But my inner self I have always kept inviolate. My heart has remained faithful to you night and day.

58. "Sacred *dharma* and the earth herself shall bear witness that I am not what you suspect me to be.

59. "Let ordinary men hold what opinion they will. I know in my heart of hearts that I am chaste and pure.

60. "If you had let me know about your intentions, then when Hanumanta had come in search of me,

61. "I would have given up my life in his very presence and spared your soldiers all the trouble they have taken for my sake.

62. "How heartless and cruel are all men! You do not have the sensitivity to remember any of my good qualities.

63. "I know that iron once broken can never be moulded back into shape again. So let me decide upon a medicine to put an end to my suffering."

64. Then, calling out to Lakṣmaṇa, the hapless Sītā said, "I, the unlucky Sītā, appeal to you, my brother! Build me a pyre as soon as you can.

65. "I shall find my own salvation by jumping into the fire. What use is there for a life like mine?"

66. When Lakṣmaṇa heard these words, he looked at Rāma for his orders. Rāma with his eyes signalled his consent at once.

67. Then Sumitrā's beloved son quickly built a pyre with fragrant sandal and agarwood.[42]

68. Let all men listen carefully to Rāma's story and chant again and again the name of Hari.

42 Agarwood or aloeswood is a fragrant wood used in incense and perfume.

Adhyāya 51

Chabi

1. Lakṣmaṇa brought pitchers full of clarified butter and poured them on the pyre. Then he lit the fire and, as the blazing flames leapt up, Sītā prepared herself for the sacrifice.

2. Rāghava's heart seemed to have been pierced by an arrow as tears streamed out of his eyes. All the soldiers wailed out in dismay when they beheld the heart rending sight.

3. Sītā joined her palms and, with her head bowed in respect, circumambulated Rāma, saying, "May you remain my good husband in all my lives to come and may I always have Lakṣmaṇa as my brother-in-law.

4. "May King Daśaratha again be my father-in-law and may my mother-in-law be Kauśalyā again. But, now without a glimpse of her divine self, I must enter the fire and die far away from home."

5. Then, bowing to the thirty gods with folded hands, thus she offered her prayers to Agni, the god of fire: "In my dreams or in my senses, I have known no other but Rāma. Night and day, I have thought only of him.

6. "I have never committed any sins with my body, mind, or speech and I have retained my purity always. So, o Agni, who art the witness of the world, grant me such reward as you may consider my due."

7. Knowing in her heart of hearts that she was pure and chaste, Sītā jumped into the fire with a happy and fearless face, while all the gods in heaven watched.

8. The people of Laṅkā all came out, the young and the old, the children and all the legions of soldiers. They cried out in shame and sorrow. Their loud lamentation seemed to fill the sky's vast expanse.

9. And all the bears and monkeys in the three worlds who had been watching from the earth and skies shouted out the name of Hari in distress, and their cries reached up to the heavens.

10. All the young women surrounded the pyre and raised a sorrowful cry in praise of Sītā. The gods in heaven became distraught with grief as they recalled the righteous path of *dharma.*

11. Seeing Sītā entering the burning pyre, the divines in heaven, led by Brahmā, Viṣṇu, Maheśvara, and Indra, the king of the gods came down hastily, riding their chariots.

12. Rāghava bowed to them with reverence and stood lost in his own thoughts. From their position in the sky the divines raised their right hands and addressed Rāma thus:

13. "You who are the best of human beings, possessing wisdom which is the greatest remedy for all ills, have come to this earth in the service of the divines. Why are you ignoring Sītā thus after you have seen her entering the burning pyre?

14. "All of us know too well that she is a chaste and devoted wife and no other woman can equal her. Even the wise

commit errors sometimes. You have done this misdeed without being aware of your own true identity."

15. Then, addressing the divines, Rāma said: "You are recounting my good qualities. But please tell me, each by turn, which divine being am I?

16. "I know that I am the son of King Daśaratha and his queen Kauśalyā Devī. I have destroyed all my enemies in this human form which I have assumed."

17. Then lord Brahmā offered him his unfailing prayers and said: "You are the supreme god Nārāyaṇa Hari. You have been born as a mortal being so that, holding the conch-shell, the discus, the mace, and the lotus in your hands, you may destroy the *asuras*.

18. "Sages worship your mighty form because they are unable to comprehend your vision as the supreme liberator. Sītā, who dwells in the folds of your heart, is the goddess Lakṣmī who wipes away the sufferings of the poor.

19. "You were born on this earth, o lord and master, according to the wishes of the thirty gods, so that you may kill Rāvaṇa. You, who are the bridge of life, were born to bring about the apocalypse and destruction of all the evil ones."

20. At this moment, Agni appeared in human shape and, lifting Sītā in his arms, he placed her before Rāma. Clad in the same garments and ornaments, she looked ten times more radiant than before.

21. Listen, o ye people, to the holy story of the *Rāmāyaṇa* and observe the beautiful character of Rāma. Drink in the flavour of the story through this offering made to

your ears only and let your minds be alert and ready to be placed at Rāma's feet.

22. The merciful God will absolve you from all your grave sins and find you a blissful place in heaven. Knowing this, all ye who are present in this court, raise your voices and chant Rāma's praise and thus from all your sins may you attain the final liberation.

Selections from Śrī Śaṅkaradeva's *Uttarakāṇḍa*

Adhyāya 1

(Sītā's exile)

"Om Namaḥ Śrīkṛṣṇāya"[43]

1. Glory be to Śrī Rāma, the ruler of the world, whose attributes were celebrated by his servant Uddhava.[44]
2. I bow my head at the feet of Rāma, the chanting of whose name enables all to escape from the miseries of life.

43 Kṛṣṇa is the Supreme Being and the only object of all devotion in Śaṅkaradeva's *ekaśaraṇa-nāmadharma*. But the names Rāma and Kṛṣṇa are often used simultaneously as manifestations of the same Being. According to some of the *caritas*, Śaṅkaradeva admitted that, since his mind was totally occupied with Kṛṣṇa, whenever he tried to narrate the story of Rāma, he would unconsciously slip into the story of Kṛṣṇa. (see Maheswar Neog, *Early History of the Vaisnava Faith and Movement in Assam*, Lawyer's Book Stall, Guwahati, 1965, p.194).

44 Brother of Vāsudeva and a friend of Kṛṣṇa. Kṛṣṇa is said to have expounded the essence of the *antaraṅga* devotion to him and this is said to be the essence of all the *upaniṣadas* (Maheswar Neog, *Early History of the Vaisnava Faith and Movement in Assam*, p.219).

3. I worship Keśava, the supreme pride of the clan of Raghu,[45] and sing the praise of Kuśa and Lava, the two sons of Sītā.

4. After Rāma left for his heavenly abode and Sītā entered the netherworld, Śaṅkara composed these verses, dedicated to the feet of Śrī Rāma.

5. Holding on to the lotus-feet of Śrī Rāma in my heart, and offering my silent prayers to my Guru,

6. I am composing this essence of the *Uttarakāṇḍa* story so that the verses may be disseminated with the blessings of Rāma's holy feet.

7. All ye who cherish the desire to rest in the contemplation of Vaikuṇṭha,[46] listen intently to this *Rāmāyaṇa* story.

8. Try to comprehend the true essence of this narrative of Rāma's deeds, knowing that in this *kaliyuga,*[47] chanting the name of Rāma is the only way to seek deliverance from all sins.

9. All the legions of sin flee like a herd of elephants in distress when you chant hymns in praise of Rāma which produce the mighty roar of a lion.

10. All religions reside in the songs chanted in praise of Rāma, and truly great are those who rest in this faith.

---

45 Rāma has been referred to variously as Raghukula-tilaka, Raghu, Rāghava, Raghunātha, Raghupati. In this text, for the sake of convenience the translator has mostly used "Rāma" instead of the other variations.

46 The paradise of Viṣṇu.

47 The fourth era of the world according to Hindu religious texts, when Viṣṇu will appear in his Kalki incarnation and destroy all sinners on this earth. Amongst the four *yugas*, Kali is believed to be the worst, a time when the world will be filled with evildoers.

11. Listen to the end of the Rāma story in the *Uttarakāṇḍa*. How Rāma went dutifully into exile in obedience to his father's wishes;

12. How Sītā was abducted thence by the king of Laṇkā and how Rāma made alliance with Sugrīva;

13. How he killed Rāvaṇa after building a bridge across the sea, and how he tested Sītā's purity by subjecting her to the fire ordeal;

14. Then he ruled over his kingdom for ten thousand years, his palace enlivened with the presence of monkeys and wild bears.

15. In Jānakī's company he enjoyed the fulfilment of all his desires and she became pregnant with his future progeny.

16. Rāghava's heart was filled with joy when he saw Kauśalyā and the other queen-mothers celebrating the news of the happy event.

17. But then fate conspired to spoil this happiness when Sītā confided to Rāma her latest dream:

18. "Listen, my master, please grant me this wish", she said. "In my dream last night, I saw myself in the *tapovana*.[48]

19. "I saw all the wives of the sages welcoming me to their midst and I spent my time happily in their company.

20. "Only if I can find that happiness in your palace which I found in the forest of meditation, then will my dream truly become a reality."

---

48 A clearing in the forest where sages meditate and establish their *āśrama*s to teach the methods of meditation to their pupils.

21. Raghunātha laughed aloud at this and said: "it seems you will never be able to overcome your desire for the forest!

22. "Who can ever attain the fulfilment of all the wishes in a dream? Pray do not speak about this to others and make yourself the common laughing stock!"

23. Time passed in this manner until Rāma heard one day the loose gossip adrift in his kingdom.

24. Some wicked tongues were casting doubts on the purity of Sītā, who had been abducted by the *rākṣasa* Rāvaṇa.

25. They questioned Rāma's belief that Sītā had remained faithful to him all the time that she was in Laṅkā.

26. Hearing such scurrilous gossip, Rāma became most sad.

27. He was in a great quandary, as he realised that it was impossible to suppress such evil gossip.

28. "The *sūryavaṃśa*[49] to which I belong," he thought, "never did have any stain. So there is no other way to escape from this calumny except by discarding Sītā."

29. When Rāma took his decision to abandon Sītā, his mind was assailed by grief and concern for her. He saw only darkness all around him.

30. After much reflection and hesitation, he called aside his brother Lakṣmaṇa and said:

---

49 The sun's clan, to which Rāma was born.

31. "Save me from this dilemma, o my brother! Send Jānakī into exile in a deceptive manner.[50]

32. "May I never see her face again, although I will always suffer because of the calumnies spread by the people."

33. Hearing this cruel order of Rāma, Lakṣmaṇa wept aloud in grief, but knowing the state of his brother's mind, he did not reply.

34. Then Rāma spoke again to his brother with an anguished heart: "If you prefer to save Sītā after this, then kill me first."

35. Fearful of hurting his brother's feelings, Lakṣmaṇa sped away on his chariot to Sītā's palace and spoke to her thus:

36. "O chaste one! Rāma has bid you farewell to go to the *tapovana.* So prepare yourself to leave instantly on my chariot."

37. Sītā failed to comprehend the hidden intent behind Rāma's command and dressed herself in all her finery for the journey.

38. She stepped on to the chariot brought by Lakṣmaṇa, and disastrous fate drove her away from thence speedily.

39. After some time, when they reached the forest, Lakṣmaṇa stopped the chariot and, blinded by his tears, he addressed Sītā thus:

---

50 There are two versions of this verse. In the Harinarayan Dattabarua edition (1952, 1968), the word "*chalabād'* (deception) has been used here, while in the Kanak Chandra Sarma edition (1941), "*janabād*" (people's opinion) has been used instead of "*chalabād*". "*Chalabād,*" appears to be more appropriate here.

40. "Alight from the chariot, o mother, and abandon all hopes of returning to Ayodhyā! For you have been exiled by Rāghava."

41. He cried uncontrollably while giving this news and Sītā collapsed on the ground in shock and disbelief.

42. But soon the chaste mother recovered her senses. Then, turning to Lakṣmaṇa, she said:

43. "Return to your brother Rāma in Ayodhyā and do not shed useless tears for me.

44. "When Rāma himself has turned me out of his house, what authority do you have to speak on my behalf?

45. "I have no regrets in accepting my own death, but by destroying my womb, Rāma is killing his own offspring.

46. "Let Rāma enjoy a long and happy reign after abandoning a hapless one like me to die in the forest."

47. She could speak no further after this and Sumitrā's son wept silently while he made his journey back to Ayodhyā.

48. How would he ever be able to narrate to Rāma the sufferings of Sītā, the chaste one?

49. After Lakṣmaṇa had left, Sītā saw only darkness all around. Pierced by the poisonous shaft of grief, she could not decide which way to go.

50. Just as a soft plantain tree is tossed around by the wild winds, so Sītā in her extreme misery trembled and fell down senseless on the forest floor.

51. All the birds and animals surrounded her and lamented aloud. Some spread their wings and gave her shade and some gently fanned her head.

52. Regaining her senses at last, she cried out in pain: "I can live no longer, now that I have nothing more to expect from Rāma."

53. She collapsed again and again in despair every time she tried to rise and sit up. The sight would have engulfed every beholder in the fiery net of grief.

Adhyāya 2

(Sītā brought to Vālmīki's āśrama and the birth of Lava and Kuśa.)

1. While Sītā the chaste one was lamenting aloud at her fate, the sage Vālmīki arrived there with his pupils.
2. They could not withhold their tears when they saw the condition of Sītā and they silently censured Rāghava for this misdeed.
3. "Rāma's mind must be under some evil spell to subject his chaste wife to such pain", they said.
4. The sage and his disciples then spoke words of consolation and persuaded Jānakī to seek refuge in Vālmīki's *āśrama.*
5. Though every moment she was assailed by anger against Rāma, Vālmīki provided her with succour to help her regain her composure.
6. She grew healthy eating fruits and wild roots while the mud floor became her dusty bed.
7. Dressed in the modest attire of an *āśrama*-dweller, Sītā prepared for her painful life in exile.
8. Though her days were drowned in tears of misery, she learnt to accept as her own father the sage Vālmīki.
9. In this way, ten months of her pregnancy passed, measured by her sighs of constant grief.
10. Then one day, surrounded by the wives of the sages, to a pair of twin boys she gave birth.

11. Both the boys were endowed with angelic beauty and the shape of their noses resembled that of Rāma.

12. Their eyes were also as wide as his and their complexion, like Rāma's, was of a lovely dark hue.

13. The elder was named Lava and the younger called Kuśa. They grew up in the abode of the sages and the great sage Vālmīki performed their appropriate *jātakarma.*[51]

14. He taught them in great detail the philosophy of governance and also the seven books of the *Rāmāyaṇa.*

15. When they were given knowledge about war-craft, the two sons of Sītā felt greatly empowered.

16. The two brothers, in voices as sweet as that of the *koyel*, learnt to render the song about Rāma's life and deeds.

17. When they attained perfect mastery over the musical instruments which accompanied their song, the sage Vālmīki blessed them with these words:

18. "May you both attain immortality by singing the song of Rāma in all the lands far and wide!

19. "With your performance may you win the hearts of every dweller in cities and villages. Then may you proceed to Rāma's court and present before him your song.

20. "Rāghava will be greatly pleased with your performance and will offer you many generous rewards.

---

51 *Jātakarma* is a ritual performed for a male child soon after birth in which, accompanied by the chanting of Vedic hymns, the infant's tongue is touched thrice with clarified butter.

21. "But my advice to you is, do not accept any of them. Sing the song about Rāma's life and deeds with selfless devotion."

22. Accepting the sage's orders with reverence, the two brothers travelled across countries with their instruments, singing the song of Rāma.

23. Listening to their nectar-like voice, people were delighted beyond measure.

24. The story of Rāma transported them into such a state of meditation that they even forgot about their hunger and thirst.

25. Overwhelmed by the beauty and talents of the twins, people crowded around them and praised them again and again.

26. People offered them gifts and prizes, but they accepted nothing except fruits and roots and wore only garments made of tree-bark.

27. Let me leave aside for now the story of Lava and Kuśa and narrate what had been happening to Rāma all this while.

28. Ever since he sent Sītā into exile, the bewildered Rāma had lost all interest in food and drink.

29. His eyes had become weary of weeping and the constant refrain on his lips was: "I have committed a grave sin by banishing a pregnant woman".

30. He often cried out aloud: "I am a sinner who has committed this heartless deed of abandoning Sītā. How would a fragile being like her survive in the forest alone?

31. "Lions and tigers must have consumed her in the lonely forest. Alas, by sending her away I have murdered her with my own hands!"

32. Seeing their brother in such a state, Bharata and Śatrughna also became dejected with grief.

33. Sītā's absence had so deeply affected Rāma's heart that he lost his sleep and shed tears each night.

34. He sighed incessantly for days and nights and thus passed several years in sighs and sorrow.

35. But, let me leave aside this story for a while, and narrate how Rāma was preparing to hold the great sacrifice of *aśvamedha.*[52]

52 *Aśvamedha*: A ceremony which culminates in the sacrifice of a horse, performed by powerful kings.

Adhyāya 3

(Rāma performs the aśvamedha *sacrifice)*

1. One day, while Rāghava was holding court, he called for the sage Vasiṣṭha and sought his counsel:
2. "Pray tell me, great sage, which sacrifice is considered the greatest of all?
3. "Which sacrifice has the greatest efficacy in granting all the wishes of he who performs it?"
4. The sage replied, "The *aśvamedha* sacrifice is the supreme sacrifice which can bring greater blessings than all others to him who performs it.
5. "Long ago, there lived a powerful king named Ilā who was transformed into a woman by the curse of Śiva.
6. "He regained his manhood after he offered the *aśvamedha* sacrifice to Lord Govinda."
7. When Rāma heard that there was no sacrifice greater than *aśvamedha,* he became eager to perform it at once.
8. "Let us perform this great sacrifice", said Rāma, as he called Lakṣmaṇa to his side and entrusted him with the duty of making all the arrangements.
9. "Let kings from the seven worlds assemble here and bring the best amongst the Brāhmaṇas without any delay.
10. "Lakṣmaṇa, my companion who shares my sorrow, do not delay in arranging for everything that is necessary for the sacrifice."

11. Obedient to Rāma's command, Lakṣmaṇa at once sent messengers to muster a congregation of ten thousand kings.

12. Many powerful rulers came loaded with gold and silver which they offered humbly at the feet of Rāma.

13. And many monkeys came along joyfully, led by Sugrīva, Aṅgada, Nīla, Nala, and Hanumanta.

14. The king of the bears came with his numerous companions, and the *rākṣasas* were led by their king Vibhīṣaṇa.

15. The three rulers of the bear, monkey, and *rākṣasa* kingdoms came with their various gifts and bowed reverentially before Rāma.

16. Gold and silver was offered in plenty, and Rāghava extended to them his generous hospitality.

17. When they heard about the grand sacrifice organised by Rāma, all the great sages made their way joyfully to Ayodhyā.

18. Viśvāmitra, Atri, Trita, Gautama, Gālava, Pulastya, Pulaha, Bhṛgu, Bhārgurī, and Bhārgava,

19. Marīci, Cyavana, Candrabindu, Vedasāra, Agastya, Astika, Śruta, and Kapilakumāra,

20. Sumanta, Sanaka, Sanātana, Siddheśvara, and many more sages poured into Ayodhyā in an unending stream.

21. Hordes of beggars and destitutes came from marketplaces and riverbanks, and migrants from foreign lands made their way along country roads to Ayodhyā town.

22. All the denizens of the heavenly sphere and the *nāgas*[53] from the netherworld rushed to Ayodhyā in joy to witness the sacrifice.

23. O listen carefully to this story of Rāma's life, because in this Kaliyuga no other religion is more suitable for man than chanting Rāma's praises.

24. People are by nature foolish in this Kaliyuga. So how can any other religion bring them their salvation?

25. All religions flee in fear of the evil Kali. Therefore, the only option is to seek shelter at the feet of Hari.

26. Śaṅkara writes these lines because devotion to Hari is your only path to salvation. So raise your voices and sing in praise of Rāma!

53 *Nāgas*: mythical creatures/demigods with human face and bodies of serpents; denizens of the nether world.

Adhyāya 4

Chabi[54]

1. Soon afterwards, Rāma called Lakṣmaṇa to his side and said: "My wise brother, proceed immediately to the banks of the holy river Gomatī and set up the sacrificial altar there."

2. In obedience to Rāma's command, the brave Lakṣmaṇa proceeded instantly towards the Gomatī bank. The earth vibrated as he sped. Soldiers carrying all the precious material for the altar went ahead, followed by the numerous kings.

3. The brave Lakṣmaṇa first constructed a temple with precious stones of all kinds. Its whole frame[55] was made with gold and the pillars were covered with gems and jewels.

4. The walls were made of rock crystal, the doors studded with diamonds, and the eaves bound with golden strips. Seats made entirely of gold were arranged in rows and the whole sacrificial ground glittered with silver.

5. After thus preparing a huge sacrificial ground resembling a township, Lakṣmaṇa bowed at the feet of

---

54 Stanzas of four lines, with the second and fourth lines rhyming, are used by Śaṅkaradeva here to enable him to digress from the main narrative and embellish a particular moment with his own creative fancy to heighten its significance or to afford an alternate view of the event.

55 The poet lists all the local names for the various fine bamboo pieces cut into flat or round shapes, to be used while constructing a typical bamboo-hut.

Rāma. Rāma then happily proceeded towards the place with Vasiṣṭha and all the sages walking before him.

6. The immortal Hanumanta went, with a white umbrella held over his head. The new king of Laṅkā and Sugrīva walked on either side of Rāma, fanning his head with yak-tail whisks.

7. And the countless kings assembled there surrounded Rāma, raising their voices in his praise. They bowed before him humbly to show their respect. Then the *bhāṭas* recited *capaya*, and the *vidyādharas*[56] enacted plays while the heavenly musicians provided the songs of praise.

8. Surrounded by hundreds of beautiful women, all the queen-mothers of Ayodhyā, led by Kauśalyā, proceeded joyfully towards the sacrificial ground. Hundreds of men and women came along singing and dancing in auspicious formations as they heralded the commencement of the holy event.

9. In this way, the pride of the Raghu clan, the very incarnation of Lord Viṣṇu, entered the holy grounds. He led the great sages to their seats, which had been arranged in uniform rows in an appropriate show of reverence.

10. Brahmā, Viṣṇu, Maheśvara, and all the numerous other divinities who arrived to participate in Rāma's holy assembly were also ushered in by Rāma most respectfully and conducted to their seats.

---

56 *Vidyādharas:* heavenly creatures who have mastered the art of dance, music and drama.

11. And all the serpents from the netherworld, with Vāsukī[57] in the lead, merrily entered the sacrificial ground. They coiled up and sat together, exulting in the glory of Rāma.

12. Then Rāma gave orders for the commencement of the ceremonies, and people took their seats, spreading across the ground in a formation appropriate for a royal assembly. Calling upon the priest Vasiṣṭha respectfully, Rāma then announced: "Let the sacrificial ceremony begin."

57 *Vāsukī*: the son of Vasuka and the king of the *nāgas*.

Adhyāya 5

Dularī

1. Then spoke Vasiṣṭha to Raghupati: "Deeply concerned am I about the propriety of your entering the sacrificial area without your wife Sītā by your side.

2. "I am helpless because the *śāstras* have decreed it so. It is now for the assembly to take an appropriate decision on this matter." Unable to find a solution to the problem, Rāma beat his breast in dismay.

3. Aware of his brother's state of mind, the faithful Bharata immediately decided on a course of action. He ordered an image of Sītā to be carved in gold and brought to the place of sacrifice.

4. Appreciating his brother's presence of mind, Rāma then turned his eyes to the golden image. It was a faithful image of the lovely Sītā, except for the silent lips.

5. The image brought back memories that were most distressing for Rāma. He sighed in pain and shed tears of grief. But when Vasiṣṭha spoke words of consolation, he regained his composure and picked up the sacred *kuśa* grass to begin the holy ceremony.

6. Then Rāma entered the sacred ground accompanied by the golden image of Sītā and, with the sage Vasiṣṭha's permission, began the rituals at the appropriate auspicious moment.

7. The sages began to recite incessantly from the Vedas, the divine *apsarās* danced in rhythm, and all the musical instruments of the three worlds played their unending music near the sacred grounds.

8. And the bustling crowds raised their voices in unison, producing a thunderous roar which filled the earth, the sky, and even crossed the limits of the heavens.

9. I, Śaṅkara, the slave of Kṛṣṇa, offering my complete devotion at the feet of Raghupati, have composed these verses containing the story of *Uttarakāṇḍa.*

10. Listen, o ye wise ones, this life is ephemeral and hideous death awaits you at its end. Yet, if you have failed to see the truth even now, then there is no escape for you except to submit yourself to the will of Rāma.

11. After knowing all this, why do you wish to waste this human life which is precious even to the gods? Only the foolish make the wrong judgement of choosing ordinary glass for the price of the ruby.

12. It is time now to stop and think how you will face the dreadful afterlife. For what you do now will determine your path to salvation. So raise your voice and sing the praises of Rāma.

Adhyāya 6

Pada

1. Listen now to the description of the grand sacrifice performed by Rāma. Gold and silver vessels were there in plenty.

2. Rāma began the holy ceremony accompanied by Vasiṣṭha and all the other sages reciting constantly from the Vedas.

3. Every god that Rāma invoked by uttering the holy incantation appeared before him in person to accept his offerings.

4. He worshipped Brahmā and Maheśvara according to the appropriate customs, and both the divine ones were mightily satisfied with his respectful offerings.

5. The four-armed Nārāyaṇa was present there with his retinue of attendants.

6. He held in his four hands the conch shell, the *chakra*, the mace, and the lotus. As he entered, Prajāpati[58] the creator saluted him with due respect.

7. Rāma worshipped Nārāyaṇa in a befitting manner with offerings of *pādya-arghya*, *āsamani*, and *madhuparka.*[59]

---

58 Another name for Brahmā.

59 *Pādya-arghya*: water for washing the feet with.
Āsamani: water used by worshipper for self-purification.
Madhuparka: a mixture of curd, ghee, and honey offered to honoured guests on arrival.

8. He offered to the divine guests a variety of fruits and juices in innumerable vessels, and with his four hands Mādhava accepted them all.

9. Thousands made offerings to the holy fire and thirty demigods accepted and enjoyed the food which was being offered.

10. Vāsukī and all the serpents from the netherworld received due shares of all the sacrifices which were being made.

11. All the sages who were present in the assembly were adequately satisfied with the clothes and ornaments offered to them.

12. Each was offered gifts in plenty according to his wishes —horses, elephants, chariots, litters, slave-girls, or villages.

13. Then, turning to Bharata, Rāma said: "Let not my munificence be measured only with money.

14. "Even if you have to empty the treasury, give the Brāhmaṇas whatever they ask for instantly. Let there not be anything left half-done."

15. Rāma then entrusted all his courtiers and ministers with assisting Bharata in the task of distributing his generous bounty.

16. Ornaments, clothes, and golden vessels big and small were distributed openhandedly to satisfy each Brahmana.

17. The brave Bharata showered precious jewels on all who asked for them and all the struggle of the poor and the needy to acquire wealth ended satisfactorily here.

18. Some could not lift all the offerings showered on them, so overloaded were they with the king's munificence.

19. Rāghava's treasury was stocked with untold riches and his numerous granaries were overflowing with crops.

20. All this, he instructed, was to be distributed generously; but not even a millionth part could be carried away by the people.

21. All the immortals and the wise men showered their praises on Rāma's ceremonial sacrifice.

22. And all the great sages remarked to each other that never had they heard of sacrifice on such a grand scale.

23. "Indra and all the rulers of the ten directions of the universe have performed numerous grand sacrificial ceremonies," they observed,

24. "But none can compare with the sacrifices made by Rāma. Praise be to the *aśvamedha* and praise to Rāma!"

25. All the inhabitants of the three worlds and all the courtiers of Rāma remained enthralled by the glorious spectacle of the sacrifice.

26. Thus receiving unending praise from all quarters, Rāma was satisfied and happy.

27. Let me leave aside the story of sacrifice here and go back to the songs of Kuśa and Lava.

Adhyāya 7

(Lava and *Kuśa perform the* Rāmāyaṇa *song in different lands and arrive at the sacrificial ceremony of Rāma)*

Pada

1. The twins, in respectful obedience to Vālmīki's wishes, travelled all over the country singing the song of the *Rāmāyaṇa.*
2. The story of Rāma's life and deeds was like divine nectar to the ears of the audience. Joyfully the twins sang the song, bringing happiness to the hearts of the people.
3. Profoundly wise, steady, and deep in perception were they. In the course of their wandering, they arrived on the banks of the Gomatī one day.
4. They entered the precincts of Rāma's capital and began rendering their wonderful song to the accompaniment of the rhythmic beating of the small cymbals held in their hands.
5. Enchanted by the music, people left their food and drink and listened spellbound to the recital of the twins.
6. They were held spellbound in amazement when they heard the story, from the birth of Rāma to the killing of Rāvaṇa.

7. Men and women surrounded the twins and marveled at this miraculous song pouring out like divine nectar in voices as sweet as that of the *koyel.*

8. Their beauty, talent, and music enthralled the audience, and some of the city women even offered them their laps to sit on.

9. Listening to their nectar-sweet music, which was rendered in a smooth and graceful manner, people momentarily forgot even to blink their eyes.

10. So entranced were they by the song of Kuśa and Lava that they were prepared to give away to the brothers everything that they possessed.

11. Some offered clothes, others brought out precious ornaments, and still others cooked a twenty-five-course meal for them.

12. But the twins smilingly refused all the offerings. Clothes made of tree-bark and meals consisting of fruits and roots would suffice for them, they said.

13. "We are forest-dwellers, what use are riches to us?" they asked. And all the people were struck with wonderment at their moral strength.

14. With their hearts filled with joy and their inner beings with supreme pleasure, the courtiers communicated the news to Rāma:

15. "Two beautiful children have arrived from we know not where, and they are singing the story of your life from the beginning to the end.

16. "We have seen in your palace many singers from heaven, earth, and the netherworld,

17. "But never have we heard music like this before. It seems as if divine nectar is raining down from the *koyel*'s throat."

18. Rāma then asked Lakṣmaṇa to send messengers to bring the two boys to his presence.

19. "Who may these boys be and where have they learnt to sing? Let us hear them sing about my life," said he.

20. On hearing his words, Lakṣmaṇa at once selected four trusted messengers and entrusted them with the task of carrying out Rāma's orders.

21. The two brothers were happily singing their song when the messengers arrived and delivered Rāma's orders to them:

22. "Proceed immediately to Rāma's presence in compliance with his orders, and sing your song in front of the king and his court."

23. Kuśa and Lava were overjoyed to hear that Rāghava was keen to see them. They arose at once and proceeded eagerly towards Rāma's royal court.

24. The sons of Sītā were beautiful to behold. Steady in intellect and serious in demeanour, they walked with the dignified gait of the king elephant.

25. As they walked towards Rāma, men and women surrounded the boys in order to get a better view of the two.

26. Rāma was seated on his golden throne, with the adoring Lakṣmaṇa, Bharata, and Śatrughna waiting on him.

27. A grand white umbrella was held over his head and he was being fanned with a white yak-hair whisk.

Hundreds of kings stood humbly, saluting him with reverence.

28. On one side of the court sat happily all the great sages—Gālava, Gautama, Śānta, Sumanta, and Kārtika,

29. Atri, Viśvāmitra, Trita, Agastya, Astika, Pulastya, Pulaha, Basu, and Vasiṣṭha, together with

30. Vibhīṣaṇa, Sugrīva, Jambawanta, Hanumanta, Nala, Nīla, Suṣeṇa, and many other monkey leaders.

31. And millions of monkeys and bears from all around offered their obeisance to Rāma by prostrating themselves on the ground.

32. *Vidyādharas* played on their instruments while the *apsarās* danced, the roaming minstrels recited verses while the *gandharvas* sang songs.

33. While Rāmacandra sat on the throne in all his glory, sages endowed with superhuman powers acquired through meditation strewed flowers on him.

34. His beautiful dark form was attired in luminous yellow garments as, seated on a golden throne, he gave audience.

35. His shapely oval head was covered with dark well-combed hair and on his smooth forehead shone a beautiful *tilaka*,[60]

36. His royal crown shone bright with precious jewels, his shapely ears were decorated with jewelled *makara-kuṇḍalas.*[61]

---

60 *Tilaka*: a small, round mark on the forehead which is considered to be an auspicious sign.

61 *Makara-kuṇḍala*: earrings in the shape of crocodiles.

37. His eyebrows were curved beautifully, his eyes were like lotuses. His nose, lips, neck, waist, and whole body were all pleasingly shaped.

38. His teeth were like closely set delicate rows of pearls, and his arms and wrists were made even more lovely by precious armlets and bracelets.

39. His hands looked most pleasing, with jewelled rings decorating his shapely, long fingers.

40. His beautiful chest was covered with a garland of precious stones and jewels. The robe tied around his waist shone bright with many a glittering gem.

41. His thighs were well-shaped and the soles of his feet were pink. The beauty of his feet was enhanced by anklets set with gems.

42. All gods and *asuras* offered their obeisance to Rāma who appeared like Kāmadeva in his unmatched beauty.

43. While he was seated thus in the court in all his magnificent glory, flanked by rows of standard-bearers,

44. Lava and Kuśa entered his royal presence.

45. The citizens, who had followed them to the venue, stared in amazement at the scene before them.

46. On the king's order, the twins stood up before the royal court. It seemed as if two moons had risen together and were shining at the two poles.

47. They had the same lovely dark complexion as Rāma's and their faces were similar to his, with well-shaped noses and even rows of close-set teeth.

48. Their eyes shaped like lotus-petals were wide like his, and their beautiful ears and sweet voices resembled his.

49. Their sphere-shaped heads, smoothly combed hair, arms reaching down to the knees, their long and slender fingers;

50. Their conch-like necks marked with triple creases were like tender buds, and like Rāma's were their arms, chests, and pink palms.

51. The beholders were enchanted by the shape of their powerful lion-like shoulders, waists, thighs.

52. Their resemblance to Rāma was so stunning that the onlookers took turns to stare silently at Rāma and the two boys.

53. So alike were the twins to Rāma in appearance that it seemed as if they were his mirror-images.

54. Some whispered, "The two lovely boys resemble Rāma both in appearance and bearing.

55. "Their faces and forms are as beautiful as his. Which mother's golden womb could have produced twins like these?

56. "Had it not been for their clothes of tree-bark and their knotted hair, we could have mistaken them for Rāma's own sons!"

57. Even Hanumanta, Śatrughna, and Bharata whispered amongst themselves in amazement:

58. "Sītā was sent to exile in the forest when she was pregnant. Could these boys be hers, the progeny of Rāma?

59. "How can these boys resemble Rāma so much when Rāma has no other wife but Sītā?"

60. In this way, the courtiers whispered amongst themselves in wonderment while Rāma, the glory of the Raghukula, looked upon the two boys with infinite joy.

61. His heart was filled with such great happiness that he trembled as tears of infinite affection flowed from his eyes.

62. In his heart of hearts he wondered why he was so moved by the sight of the two boys.

63. He could not believe that such handsome boys who were so talented at this young age, could be the sons of a sage.

64. Then Rāma thus began speaking to the two: "I have heard that both of you are very good singers,

65. "And that you are well-trained to sing songs. So, let us now hear how you sing the story the *Rāmāyaṇa*."

Adhyāya 8

(Lava and Kuśa's Rāmāyaṇa *song at the court of Śrī Rāmacandra)*

1. On receiving Rāma's orders, the two brothers joyfully commenced with a *rāga,* raising their voices first to the pitch of the fifth note in the scale.
2. Then they commenced their recital after descending into a deeper and lower note of the *rāga*. As they sang, one brother played the instrument while the other kept time with the cymbal.
3. They began with the *Ādikāṇḍa* of the *Rāmāyaṇa*, giving an account of the kings belonging to the Sūrya-vaṃśa.[62]
4. Ikṣvāku, Kakutstha, Raghu, and other great kings of the sun-clan were followed by the story of the arrival of King Daśaratha.
5. He was equal to Viṣṇu in valour and virility. In action he was like Maheśvara. In his capacity for forgiveness he was like the earth, in his patience he was like the deep ocean.
6. In power like the sun, in anger like the god of death, there had never been born a king like Daśaratha.
7. His three queens Kauśalyā, Kaikeyī, and Sumitrāsurpassed in beauty the majesty of Śacī.
8. The three queens gave birth to his four sons. Rāma, the eldest, was born of Kauśalyā.

---

62 *Sūrya-vaṃśa*: Rāma was believed to have been born into the ancient sun-clan.

9. Kaikeyī's son was Bharata and Sumitrā was the mother of Lakṣmaṇa and the youngest son Śatrughna.

10. Rāma's greatness of character was beyond comparison to anyone else on this earth. He was the true master of the universe.

11. His brothers Bharata, Lakṣmaṇa, and Śatrughna offered their humble obeisance at the feet of their elder brother.

12. He resembled Nārāyaṇa in his ocean-like demeanour. He was the light of the family of Kakutstha.

13. With his saintly and gentle behaviour, this supreme human being became the delight and protector of his people.

14. Who can ever fathom the depth of his greatness? Thus sang Lava-Kuśa in their rendering of the essence of the first book of the *Rāmāyaṇa.*

15. As they sang on in their sweet voices, maintaining the proper rhythm and pitch, the audience listened with rapt attention.

16. The song of Rāma's life was like nectar divine. The audience listened silently as it filled their ears.

17. They were not aware whether it was a dream or reality, whether they were on earth or in heaven;

18. They forgot their hunger and thirst and seemed to lose all consciousness as though the song of the two boys had transported them to a state of meditation.

19. Listen intently, all ye people, to the verses of the *Rāmāyaṇa*. If you sing these verses with devotion, you can be saved from all your misfortunes.

20. Since, in this Kaliyuga, chanting the name of Rāma is the only path to salvation, so Śaṅkara has composed these verses. O raise your voices and chant the name of Rāma!

Adhyāya 9

Dularī

1. Rāma was overwhelmed with happiness after listening to the twins' song sung in their nectar-sweet voices. He was keen to reward the boys in the best possible manner for their performance.
2. With a feeling of infinite satisfaction, he called his brother Bharata and instructed him to give instantly to the boys six hundred million rupees in gold.
3. He further ordered his brother to give to the boys slaves, both male and female, land, clothes, precious ornaments, and bamboo mats in plenty.
4. On hearing this, Bharata at once sent for plenty of gold from the treasury and gave it all to the boys, adding some more for Rāma's pleasure.
5. The twins then smiled politely and said, "We have no need for such gifts. We are ascetics who live in the forest. We feed on fruits and wear clothes made of tree-bark.
6. "For such as we, what use are all these servants, land, and treasure?" The audience heard these words and was overwhelmed with admiration.
7. Observing their conduct and inclination, Rāma then spoke to them with great affection: "Who may be the author of these verses you sing, and who is your teacher?

8. "You are both beautiful to behold. Pray, where do you come from and whose sons are you?" To this Lava and Kuśa replied politely, "We are the disciples of Vālmīki.

9. "We learnt this *Rāmāyaṇa* song composed by him from the *śāstras* and by the permission of the sage we travel round the world disseminating the verses in bliss."

10. Rāma then welcomed the two with words of praise and requested them to remain where they were and continue their *Rāmāyaṇa* song.

11. The twins then picked up their musical instruments and joyfully began singing their song about Rāma's life and deeds to the audience which was eager to listen.

12. Now listen to the rest of the story. When King Daśaratha's reign was securely established, the sage Viśvāmitra came to him one day to seek Rāma's help in performing his sacrificial rites safely in the *āśrama.*

13. The king was unwilling to give his permission, but with the sage being persistent in his demand, he reluctantly agreed in the end. The sage gave lessons to Rāma and Lakṣmaṇa on wielding the bow and arrow and the two happily mastered the art.

14. At first, they destroyed the *rākṣasī* called Tāḍakā, and this was followed by the killing of Subāhu. Mārīca, a courageous *rākṣasa*, was also dispatched by them with a single arrow.

15. Overjoyed by these victories, the sage Viśvāmitra then proceeded towards Mithilā with Rāma by his side to attend the *svayaṃvara* of Jānakī which was to be held there.

16. King Janaka welcomed them with great reverence and showed them due honour. Rama then went forward with alacrity to lift the great bow which, as he lifted, broke into two.

17. Sītā accepted him as her husband and Rāma fought with his rival kings and defeated them. He then departed from the Mithilā royal court with Sītā and sped joyfully on his chariot towards Ayodhyā.

18. But, on the way, Rāma was accosted by Paraśurāma, who was enraged at Rāma for having had the audacity to break the great bow of Śiva. Armed with his axe on his shoulder, he forbade Rāma from proceeding further.

19. Though King Daśaratha fell at his feet and begged him to relent, he refused to do so. At this, Rāma at once lifted his bow and sent off an arrow to close Paraśurāma's path to heaven.

20. Rāma then entered Ayodhyā with great merriment and fanfare. He lived there happily in the company of Sītā, enjoying unending happiness.

Adhyāya 10

Chabi

1. The twins thus gave a brief summary of the essence of the *Ādikāṇḍa* and then proceeded to sing the story of the *Ayodhyākāṇḍa*: when King Daśaratha observed that his son Rāma had acquired all the qualities necessary for kingship, he expressed his desire to reorganise the governance of his kingdom.

2. When auspicious music announced the imminent coronation of Rāma as the heir-apparent, people came flocking to the royal assembly to witness the event. But Queen Kaikeyī raised objections to the proceedings by claiming her son Bharata's rights to the throne.

3. She held the king at ransom by reminding him of his own promise and compelled him to uphold the truth by sending Rāma to exile. Then Rāma, in obedience to his father's word, left for the forest with Jānakī and Lakṣmaṇa.

4. The old king Daśaratha was so stricken by grief for his son that he lost his consciousness soon afterwards. So deep and unbearable was his suffering at the departure of Rāma that he soon succumbed to his grief, as his body was unable to withstand the sorrow.

5. Bharata refused to accept the throne and, after performing the last rites of his father, went in search of his elder brother. But Rāma earnestly pleaded with him and persuaded him to go back to his kingdom.

6. Listen, all ye people, to the holy story of the *Rāmāyaṇa* and sing repeatedly the praises of Rāma. Life is short and yet you are unaware of it. So, do not waste your time on useless pursuits.

Adhyāya 11

Pada

1. So the twins sang the *Rāmāyaṇa* song in perfect rhythm and harmony. Their rendition was such that it was like a visual recreation of the whole Rāma story.

2. When they related the reasons for the death of the old monarch, all the members of the assembly cried afresh to express their grief for the deceased one.

3. The courtiers and ministers wept anew for the departed soul of Daśaratha. It seemed as though the death of the old king had taken place at that very moment.

4. Listening to the recital of the song, Rāma, Lakṣmaṇa, Bharata, and Śatrughna grieved aloud for their father.

5. Kauśalyā and all the queen-mothers beat their breasts with clenched fists and wailed again over the death of their husband.

6. Some rolled on the ground and wept, crying, "Where have you gone, o master, so dear to our hearts?

7. "No woman can be as heartless as us, because we are still alive after having listened to the story of your demise!"

8. Thus mourned many others in the crowd, and waves of loud lamentation rose from the throng.

9. Sugrīva and Vibhīṣaṇa consoled Rāma and begged him to compose himself and listen to the rest of the song.

10. At these words of his two friends, Rāghava regained his calm, and the royal mothers were consoled adequately by Lakṣmaṇa.

11. When everyone at last wiped their tears, Bharata then brought back to the assembly some order and composure.

12. There was silence all around as Rāma gave orders to the two boys to sing the rest of the song.

13. Then the twins concluded the story of the *Ayodhyākāṇḍa* and in appropriate measure began the recital of the *Araṇyakāṇḍa*.

14. They sang on as before about the fourteen years spent in the forest by the exiled Rāma.

15. How, deprived of all cereals, he had to consume only the flesh of animals and how he suffered immensely when he saw the plight of Sītā.

16. In the forest of Daṇḍaka, when Rāma encountered grave danger, he had no one to help except his brother Lakṣmaṇa.

17. Then appeared Śūparnakhā, who tried to seduce him with her carnal desires. But Lakṣmaṇa punished her by cutting off her nose and ears.

18. Fourteen thousand *rākṣasas* together with Khar and Duṣaṇa were killed in the forest by Rāma.

19. Then came Rāvaṇa to threaten him with dire consequences and Mārīca assumed the form of a golden deer.

20. When Rāma and Lakṣmaṇa went in pursuit of the golden deer, the ten-headed Rāvaṇa abducted Sītā from the forest.

21. Sītā the divine one was so terrified by Rāvaṇa that she tried at first to hide within her own self.

22. Then, seeing some monkeys in the forest below, she took off her golden ornaments and threw them from above.

23. The powerful Rāvaṇa kept her in the Aśoka garden and employed some female *rākṣasis* to guard her.

24. For long days and nights, Sītā shed unending tears and dwelt upon the memory of her Rāma. Each fraction of an hour seemed to stretch into an era for her.

25. When Rāma returned home after killing the golden deer, he called out to Sītā loud and long.

26. The two brothers then roamed all over the Daṇḍaka forest looking for Sītā and sighing constantly for her.

27. Wandering far and wide in the forest in search of Sītā, Rāma and Lakṣmaṇa killed the two demons Virādha and Kavandha.

28. They met the gigantic bird Jaṭāyu, who had given up his life trying to save Sītā from Rāvaṇa's grip. When Jaṭāyu at last embraced his death, the two brothers performed his last rites.

29. The twins then concluded the story of the *Araṇyakāṇḍa* and proceeded joyfully with the tale of the *Kiṣkindhākāṇḍa.*

30. Rāma and Lakṣmaṇa continued their search for Sītā and from Daṇḍaka forest arrived at Ṛṣyamukha.

31. There they killed Vāli and handed over his kingdom to his brother Sugrīva and Prince Aṅgada was anointed the would-be heir to the throne.

32. But the taste of royal pleasures turned Sugrīva into a lustful monkey. He neglected his pledge to Rāma and delayed his assured help.

33. Then Lakṣmaṇa threatened Sugrīva with dire consequences and showed him the same weapon with which his brother had been killed by Rāma.

34. At this, Sugrīva trembled in fear and ordered a large army of monkeys to be raised at once for Rāma's mission.

35. Then monkeys and bears arrived there from all over the world and went in search of Sītā to distant islands and beyond.

36. Concluding thus the story of the *Kiṣkindhākāṇḍa*, the twins then began to sing the tale of the *Sundarakāṇḍa*.

37. They sang how, after discovering that Sītā was in Laṅkā, it became impossible to find a warrior who was brave enough to visit her there.

38. Then Jambawanta narrated the story of the birth of the brave Māruti and he was chosen to cross the great ocean in search of Jānakī.

39. Hanumanta leapt over the ocean and, finding Sītā in the Aśoka garden, gave her the message of Rāma.

40. He showed her Rāma's ring as proof of his identity and when she saw it she beat her breast in agony and shed many a tear for her husband.

41. Then Hanumanta reassured her most sincerely and solemnly promised her

42. That Rāma would come to her very soon and the ten-headed Rāvaṇa together with all his allies would be decapitated.

43. These words of the monkey adequately consoled Sītā the pure one. Then Hanumanta bowed to her in deep reverence and departed from thence.

44. After thus completing his duty towards Rāma, Hanumanta entered Laṅkā and merrily gorged on all the delicious fruits in Rāvaṇa's orchard. Then he uprooted all the trees and stuck them upside down.

45. With his magic he then destroyed Akṣayakumāra; but soon came Indrajit and tied him up with a snake-like rope.

46. The brave Hanumanta lay prostrate on the ground and in that state he was presented before Rāvaṇa.

47. On the king's orders, his tail was wrapped up in rags and set on fire, but, slipping out of the snake-like noose, the brave monkey merrily jumped out of reach.

48. He leapt up gleefully and let out a loud cry as he began to set the city of Laṅkā on fire.

49. All the *rākṣasas* stared in disbelief and fear as Hanumanta struck terror by setting the whole city ablaze.

50. Then across the sea he leapt again and came back to this earth to convey Sītā's tidings to Rāma.

51. He narrated how the chaste Sītā had been confined in Laṅkā and how she was spending her days in abject sorrow.

52. Rāma wept anew at the thought of Sītā as Hanumanta narrated the whole story in brief.

53. He rolled on the ground in uncontrollable grief, but Sugrīva and Lakṣmaṇa revived and consoled him.

54. "If you doubt even now that you will be able to bring back Sītā," they said, "then piece by piece we will bring you the whole of Laṅkā."

55. "We will feed the vultures and crows with the blood of the *rākṣasas*. So, let each shoulder his responsibility forthwith and strive for the success of our expedition."

56. Hearing these wise words of Sugrīva, Rāma's mind at last recovered from its despondency.

57. He then begged Sindhurāja[63] to make way for him through the sea. But the conceited god refused to grant him audience.

58. Incensed by this behaviour, Rāma threatened to tear open the ocean's heart, and all the sea-creatures fled in panic.

59. The ocean then trembled in great fear and came up to offer his respectful homage to Rāma.

60. "I offer you passage right through the ocean," he said. "Build your bridge which will never sink and march across to Laṅkā without any fear."

---

63 Sindhurāja: the sea-god.

61. Then the monkey king ordered his forces to build a bridge across the ocean. They lifted great mountains on their shoulders and carried them to the sea.

62. In no time, a mighty bridge, ninety miles long and ten across, was erected over the ocean and across it marched all the soldiers of Rāma.

63. In Laṅkā, Vibhīṣaṇa advised the king to hand over Sītā to Rāma. But the quarrelsome Rāvaṇa assaulted him with kicks and blows.

64. Then Vibhīṣaṇa sought the protection of Rāma, who promised him the throne of Laṅkā.

65. Lava and Kuśa thus sang their song, dramatising every scene. It seemed to the spectators as if those moments had come alive before their eyes instantly.

66. Concluding the recital of the *Sundarakāṇḍa* here, the two singers began to narrate the tale of the *Laṅkākāṇḍa*.

67. Rāma rested for some time with all his troops on the Subela mountain, and the next morning he laid siege to Laṅkā from all sides.

68. The *rākṣasas* defended the fort of Laṅkā, but the first to fall in the battle was the *rākṣasa* named Prahasta.

69. When Rāvaṇa heard that Devāntaka and Narāntaka had also fallen in the battle, he rushed forward with all his forces.

70. Roaring like thunder and shaking his ten heads, the king of Laṅkā rushed forward to destroy the monkey forces.

71. Rāma, resolving to preserve his dignity, pursued Rāvaṇa in great anger and Hanumanta lifted him high on his shoulders.

72. Then Rāma shot his arrows in all directions and pierced the heart of the cruel Rāvaṇa.

73. He destroyed Rāvaṇa's chariot and killed the four horses and inflicted three deadly blows on the proud head of the enemy.

74. "This is the angry face which you show to the monkey forces," said Rāma while he held Rāvaṇa by his hair and cut off his royal crown.

75. But, seeing that his enemy was unarmed and without a chariot, he spared him his life and allowed him to go back to Laṅkā.

76. Then the ten-headed Rāvaṇa called upon Kumbhakarṇa to rise from sleep and go to the battlefield. But Rāma's frightful arrows instantly destroyed Kumbhakarṇa.

77. Kumbha, Nikumbha, Mahāpārśva, Brajadaṃṣtra, and numerous other *rākṣasa* fighters fell before the might of Rāma's forces.

78. Seeing the plight of the *rākṣasa* troops, Indrajit too rushed into the battle in great rage.

79. In the company of his *rākṣasas,* the arrogant Indrajit thundered in anger and proceeded towards the banyan tree in the Nikumbhilā temple to perform a sacrifice of great efficacy.

80. Vibhīṣaṇa informed everyone that Lakṣmaṇa had succeeded in killing Indrajit at last.

81. Rāvaṇa mourned long for his dead son and at last rose and dressed for the battle. He shook his head menacingly and sounded the battle call.

82. He shot hundreds of arrows in all directions and for seven days and seven nights the battle waged on.

83. But his arrows could not touch the body of Rāma and neither could Rāma kill him by cutting off his heads.

84. At last, realising that the ten-headed one could not be killed by any other weapons, Rāma used the Brahmāstra[64] to destroy him.

85. The three worlds—heaven, earth, and the netherworld— rang out with the sound of victory as Rāma sent to Death's abode the comet-like *rākṣasa.*

86. Thus Rāma completed his duty with his own masculine power and he entrusted to Vibhīṣaṇa the throne of Laṅkā.

87. Then Sītā was brought before him and he made her go through the ordeal by fire.

88. Brahmā came down and prayed to Rāma and King Daśaratha arrived from heaven to embrace his two sons.

89. Praising Rāma and blaming Kaikeyī, he said, "My son, you had to fight this battle only for my sake.

90. "The world knows that Sītā is a pure and faithful wife. Then why do you mistrust her, my son?"

---

64 A weapon created by Brahma which was said to have been infallible in power.

91. "Why do you want to send her away when there is not a shred of doubt about her purity?" At this, in obedience to his father's wishes, Rāma agreed to take Sītā back.

92. Accompanied by his brother and wife, Rāma then joyfully proceeded towards Ayodhyā on his aerial chariot.

93. To witness Rāma's coronation ceremony, many monkeys, bears, and *rākṣasas* too came along joyfully.

94. By listening to the story of the *Rāmāyaṇa* may all you people attain peace and calmness, and let the whole assembly chant the name of Rāma in harmonious unison.

Adhyāya 12

Chabi

1. Now listen to the story hereafter. Bharata's saddened heart was at last freed of its load by the sight of his brother Rāma. The four brothers then went to the village of Nandigrāma where they shaved off the knots of hair on their heads.

2. The two queens Kauśalyā and Sumitrā hugged their sons and shed many a tear. Sītā too narrated tearfully her tale of woe and touched the feet of the queen-mothers respectfully.

3. Then Rāma was carried to Ayodhyā in a ceremonial procession accompanied by drums and other musical instruments. The earth swayed in rhythm with the joyful celebration of *rākṣasas*, bears, monkeys, and men.

4. All along the way, welcome arches were erected and every doorway was decorated with lamps, plantain saplings, pitchers topped with flowers and fruits. Rows of men and women lined the path, praising Rāma and bowing at his feet.

5. At an auspicious moment, Rāma assumed his place on his throne and people chanted words of benediction. With waters brought from the four seas by the monkey forces, the sage Vasiṣṭha performed the coronation rituals.

6. While Bharata held the royal umbrella over Rāma's head, the other brothers gently fanned him with yak-

tail whisks. People raised their voices in praise of King Rāma, and loud and deafening was the cheer.

7. Elephants in heat roared like thunder and the gigantic bells around their necks rang out. Then Rāma distributed rewards amongst all his monkey and bear soldiers who had suffered grievously in the battle.

8. Satisfied by the royal favours showered on them, on Rāma's orders they left cheerfully for home. With his brothers by his side, Rāma then reigned in Ayodhyā for ten thousand happy years.

9. Sītā enjoyed her position as the great queen who was always faithful and devoted to her husband. Their mutual love increased day by day as they enjoyed the divine pleasures of Ayodhyā.

10. Thus listening to the recital of the story of his life, Rāma was pleased beyond measure. The spectators listened with rapt attention as the song of the *Laṅkākāṇḍa* was concluded by Lava and Kuśa.

Adhyāya 15

Pada

[This section begins with verse number 40 of the original]

1. After they completed narrating the dialogue between Agastya and Rāma, the twins then began the sad tale of Sītā's exile.
2. Addressing the assembly they sang on thus: "Listen, o ye people, to the story as it unfolded after Rāma bade farewell to the sage Agastya.
3. "For ten thousand years Rāma reigned happily in Ayodhyā, facing no obstacles on his way.
4. "But then a great misfortune fell on Ayodhyā and Rāma with his beloved wife suffered its consequences together.
5. "The chaste Sītā, who was ever devoted to her husband, became pregnant with his child after sharing conjugal bliss with him.
6. "In her company, Rāma was immersed in bliss and day by day, her beauteous presence continued to increase his love for her.
7. "But then fell a great catastrophe on them. In response to some scurrilous gossip which was spread about her, Rāma decided to abandon Sītā.
8. "Lakṣmaṇa took Sītā to the perilous forest and abandoned her there. Sītā fainted in fear and exhaustion.

9. "If anyone were to listen to the description of the misery that befell the divine Sītā in the forest, the listener would be overwhelmed by the same pain that she suffered.

10. "It must have been because of some transgression committed in her previous life that Sītā was fated to suffer in this manner.

11. "Or else, how could Rāma, the divinity incarnate, full of mercy, whose excellent virtues have no equal, who does not even hurt an ant unnecessarily, subject her to such suffering?

12. "What could have impelled Rāghava's mind to send to death a woman totally devoted to her husband and pregnant with his own child?

13. "O that fate should ordain thus that for Jānakī her own husband would transform into Death incarnate!"

14. Thus Lava and Kuśa laid bare the details of all the misfortunes that befell the chaste Sītā, and the audience wept aloud in grief.

15. The song of the twins so agonized the listeners that they responded as though at that very moment they were witnessing the exile of Sītā.

16. The whole assembly cried inconsolably in sorrow when they heard the story of Sītā's woe.

17. As the sound of loud lamentation rose from the audience, Rāma's whole being seemed to be seared with agony.

18. Poison-like flames of grief pierced his heart as the memory of Sītā overpowered Rāghava.

19. As though the fire that had once been extinguished had lit up again, it seemed as if his heart would burst with exceeding pain.

20. Bharata and Lakṣmaṇa held him tight as he fell from the throne unconscious on the ground.

21. They sprinkled water on his head and fanned him with the whisk as all the three brothers joined him in his grief.

22. Even the sages, led by Vasiṣṭha, could not control their grief for Sītā as they covered their faces and wept for her.

23. The monkeys too shed their tears while Vibhīṣaṇa, Sugrīva, Jambawanta, and Hanumāna wept in distress.

24. Regaining his consciousness at last, Rāma recounted his wife's virtues and lamented thus:

25. "Alas for the unblemished Sītā, my beloved wedded wife, who was my well-wisher, ever faithful to me and morally upright.

26. "It was my good fortune that I had won a wife for whom one needs to perform prolonged sacrifice. But Fate has snatched her away from me.

27. "Now in this life she is lost to me forever. Alas, that I am the sinful one who is responsible for taking her life.

28. "Even during the terrible days in the forest, she survived the hardship of exile. She continued to live even after Rāvaṇa abducted her.

29. "Now I have proved to be worse than the *rākṣasas* by killing with my own hands the pure and good daughter of Janaka.

30. "O Sītā! While in the forest of Daṇḍaka, you as a chaste wife served my needs faithfully without thinking of your own.

31. "O how could I, like a husband most cruel and merciless, have forgotten all your good qualities?

32. "She for whom I built a bridge of stone over the deep ocean and for whom I destroyed Rāvaṇa and all his companions,

33. "How heartless was I to have abandoned such a beloved! I would certainly be condemned as a *caṇḍāla* by anyone who hears of this tale."

34. Thus lamented aloud Rāma while his brothers Lakṣmaṇa, Bharata, and Śatrughna shared his sorrow.

35. They surrounded him and offered consolation thus: "Come back to your senses, dear brother, and abandon your sorrow,

36. "Better it is for you to realise that no amount of weeping will bring Sītā back.

37. "You who are all-knowing, know in your wisdom that everything in this life is but an illusion.

38. "Son, wife, wealth, and attendants, all are nothing but the abode of grief and sorrow.

39. "These are false and temporal things which are ephemeral in nature and cannot give true contentment.

40. "Just as the foam gathered on top of water proves to be of little worth when it is carried away by the speeding currents below,

41. "So the company of all your friends cannot give you stability. Patience is the only remedy in moments of crisis."

42. Listening to these reassuring words, Rāma regained his calm for a while, but the thought of Sītā brought back his sorrow once more.

43. As tears streamed down his cheeks, his brothers tried to console him again and again

44. Sighing deeply, thus he lamented: "O Sītā, through my action I have brought about my own destruction.

45. "Where should I go now and what should I do? In Sītā's absence, this domestic life now seems worse than a life in the forest.

46. "Take over the reins of the kingdom, o my brother Bharata. I have lost all desire to rule my kingdom and prefer to go into exile."

47. Thus Rāma expressed his boundless sorrow. He saw only darkness all around without Sītā by his side.

48. All the queen-mothers wept for Sītā, their heads bowed in distress.

49. And innumerable other women surrounded them and cried, as though the assembly would be drowned by waves of tears.

50. Just as the leaves and branches toss about in distress when a big tree is uprooted, so Rāma's sorrow drowned everyone in misery.

51. Then the sage Vasiṣṭha stood up and spoke words of consolation and thus he put to an end this loud lamentation.

52. He asked Rāma to give up his grief because none has the power to escape the laws of destiny.

53. "You being the all-knowing master of the universe know that the sorrow of great saints goes against this truth.

54. "Whatever is destined to happen will happen without a doubt. So listen now carefully to the rest of the story of the *Uttarakāṇḍa*."

Adhyāya 16

(The identities of Lava and Kuśa are revealed)

1. Then spoke the sage Vasiṣṭha thus: "Let the two children sing their song and the future will then gradually unfold itself before your eyes."
2. At these words of the sage, Rāma sighed again and, banishing his sorrow, at last sat down to listen to the song once more.
3. Wiping his face and eyes, he calmly ordered the twins to continue with their recital:
4. "Let us hear how you tell the rest of the story. Your recital may perchance bring some solace to my heart".
5. Then Lava and Kuśa took up their tale and began their recital once again: "Listen to the story of what befell Sītā after this.
6. "When Lakṣmaṇa left her alone in the forest, Sītā wept in utter despair, overcome by fear and distress.
7. "Perhaps she had earned some good fortune in some previous life, for just then the sage Vālmīki arrived there in search of fruits and wild roots.
8. "He offered her words of solace and assurance and, adopting her as his daughter, gave her shelter in his hermitage.
9. "In sorrow and distress, she spent her days in that forest home and in due time gave birth to a pair of twins.

10. "The sage named them Lava and Kuśa and gladly taught them to sing the song of the *Rāmāyaṇa*.

11. "We are those two sons of Sītā and we have been singing the song of the *Rāmāyaṇa* ever since our birth.

12. "My name is Lava and my brother here is Kuśa. Know us to be beyond any doubt the sons of Sītā.

13. "We are the disciples of the great sage Vālmīki." Thus they spoke and the assembly responded with joy.

14. By their visage and song, they recognised them to be Sītā's sons and their features left no doubt that they were Rāma's sons.

15. Everyone was happy that Destiny had granted them all their wishes and continuity had been ensured to Rāghava's line.

16. When they heard that Sītā was alive and well in the forest, they raised their voices in benediction.

17. Elated by the glad tidings that Sītā was safe, they called out to each other and shared their joy.

18. Shouts of happiness celebrating the victory of Rāma reverberated through the assembly.

19. When he came to know that the twins were his own offspring, Rāma was immersed in a sea of happiness.

20. His whole body trembled and his heart melted in joy when he realised that the two boys were Sītā's sons.

21. His speech obstructed by tears, his voice hoarse and muffled, he looked upon them with wonderment and affection.

22. His heart in turmoil with excessive love, from his throne he jumped up at last.

23. Pressing the twins to his heart, Rāghava then affectionately breathed into their hair.

24. Tears flowing incessantly from his eyes drenched their heads.

25. He held his sons close for a while and then returned to his throne.

26. Then Bharata and Lakṣmaṇa came and hugged the boys with affection and removed the tree-bark which covered their bodies.

27. They dressed the boys in celestial clothes and ornaments and then the sons of Rāma reverently saluted their father.

28. Rāma once more bestowed fond kisses on them and said: "you have lived in the forest like poor children

29. "And have lived the life of ascetic sages. You have suffered the travails of such a life and I, a sinner, have been the cause of your plight.

30. "I had come to believe that my beloved wife was dead. But today I know that she is alive and well.

31. "I, the sinful one, have caused her so much pain that she has nothing more to suffer in the remaining days of her life."

32. In this manner, Rāma lamented and cried for Sītā and the two sons joined their father in shedding tears for their mother.

33. The spectators wept again in grief when they saw the father and sons sharing their anguish.

34. Kauśalyā embraced her grandsons and cried: "My dear ones, you have lived in the forest for so long!

35. "Alas, alas! My chaste daughter, Sītā! You were born on this earth only to bear sorrow!

36. "All your suffering could not wipe out the stain which evil people have heaped on your name.

37. "O which Creator could have ordained such a fate for you that you have been thus compelled to spend your days in the forest?

38. "Sacrificing your rightful place in the kingdom, you have made at last your truce with death!"Thus spoke Kauśalyā and wailed for Sītā.

39. Lakṣmaṇa and Bharata wept at her distress, but then the sages intervened and forbade further lamentations.

40. They said, "Knowing that Sītā is alive and well, why do you shed tears vainly for her sake?"

41. Then spoke the wise Vasiṣṭha: "This is a moment of joy for us all and not for mournful tears." Rāma heard and at once banished his sorrow.

42. Though his heart was full with sad memories of Sītā, he sighed deeply and wiped off his tears.

43. "I shall bring her back myself," he said, as he rose instantly to bring Jānakī back.

44. Many others from the royal assembly and all the women from the king's inner chambers came out at once to accompany him to the forest.

45. Eager to see Sītā at once, Rāma set out with the monkey and bear soldiers by his side.

46. The earth trembled as they advanced; but at that moment Vasiṣṭha stepped forward. Facing Rāma he reasoned with him thus:

Adhyāya 17

(Hanumanta is dispatched to bring back Sītā)

1. "If you go to her now, Sītā will refuse to meet you because she is now an ascetic and has turned indifferent towards you.
2. It would be better by far if you selected some other virtuous person who can plead with Sītā and persuade her to return."
3. Heeding this counsel of Vasiṣṭha, Rāma retreated from his path, though with concern for Sītā and with a heavy heart.
4. He called Māruti, Vibhīṣaṇa, Suṣeṇa, and Śatrughna, and beseeched them thus to go on his behalf:
5. "Go, you four brave ones, to Vālmīki's hermitage. Touch his feet respectfully as you would touch mine.
6. "Tell him that I have become his son-in-law because Sītā is now his daughter. Reassure her and plead with her to return and give me back my life.
7. "Or else, ask him to give me some space in his hermitage so that I may live on fruits and roots and stay with Sītā there.
8. "My heart seems to burst and I can no longer control it. Only the sight of Sītā can give me back my life once more.
9. "I know that by touching Jānakī I can be cleansed of all sins. Yet, the evil people do not cease to slander her name.

10. "I am much concerned about the calumny spread by people. So I can take back Sītā only after I have put her through a test.

11. "Ask Jānakī to forget all her discontent now and forgive me my grievous offence.

12. "Who can escape what the divine lawmaker ordains? So, for my sake, entreat Sītā to be compassionate.

13. "Listen to me, my dear Hanumanta! It was because of you that I got Sītā back the last time.

14. "Now go, my friend, what more can I say except to persuade Sītā to give me back my life again."

15. Rāma's earnest entreaty brought tears to the monkey king's eyes. All four then bowed to the assembly and set out.

16. Hanumanta was bursting with eagerness to see Sītā once again, and the four soon sped towards Vālmīki's hermitage.

17. The mother of the universe was sitting dejectedly alone, thinking of her husband at whose feet she had always bowed.

18. She resembled an ascetic with her pain-stricken face and her emaciated and dust-covered body clad in faded garments.

19. The four brave heroes stared at her in distress when they observed that her body had been laid waste by her ascetic diet of fruits and wild roots.

20. They prostrated themselves before her and showed their respect; but the chaste lady looked hesitant and shrunk away.

21. She turned aside her face, shielding it with her garment, and sat silently with her hand on her cheek.

22. Śatrughna, Vibhīṣaṇa, Suṣeṇa, Hanumanta, the heroes four, could not hold back their tears on seeing her thus.

23. "Alas, great mother, beloved queen of Rāma, that it should be so! That the divine lawmaker should have brought on you this sorrow!

24. "Our hearts are pained that you who were once richer than Śacī in your garments and ornaments are now thus clad in ascetic raiment.

25. "You who were the wife of Rāma the master of the universe had numerous servants once to serve your needs.

26. "In the king's inner quarters, you walked on silken mattresses, but now you sleep on the hard floor and sit on weeds and grasses.

27. "Your beauty once shone forth as brilliantly as molten gold and you were known as the supremely pure one all over the world.

28. "But such is the quirk of fate that Rāma, who loved you more than his own life, banished you and sent you away here."

29. Thus Māruti spoke and, unable to bear the plight of Sītā, he rolled on the ground and cried out in pain thus:

30. "Alas, alas, the chaste mother of the universe! How can I still be alive when I see you suffering thus?

31. "I crossed the ocean and set ablaze the whole of Laṅkā and after that the ten-headed one was annihilated with all his forces.

32. "But now I feel like giving up my life when I see the misfortunes that have befallen the queen of Rāma and the goddess of the universe.

33. "You who were once served by all the royal queens, whom even the heavenly dancers were ready to worship and serve;

34. "Such a one has now become a companion of the hermit's wife! O what ill fortune could have designed a calamity like this?"

35. Thus Hanumanta wept and then spoke in earnest supplication: "Mother, please forgive Rāghava for his offence.

36. "Rāma's heart is ever remorseful when he thinks of you and he sheds unending tears night and day.

37. "He laments aloud, repeating your name constantly. Worse than a life in the forest is this domestic life of his.

38. "He was under the impression that you were long dead and gone. So he was weeping all the time and cursing himself for your fate.

39. "Then your two sons Lava and Kuśa delighted the world with their recital of the *Rāmāyaṇa* song.

40. "Rāma then recognised them to be his own sons. Holding them to his heart, he has wept for long.

41. "When he heard from them that you are here in this hermitage, he was ready to come at once and take you back.

42. "But the sage Vasiṣṭha told him that it may not be advisable for him to meet you. That is why we have been sent here to bring you back.

43. "Rāma has implored you to be compassionate. So pardon him all his faults, o you chaste one!

44. "We beseech you most humbly to be kind to Rāma. For, despite all that has happened, he is after all your godlike husband.

45. "Rāma has sent this palanquin for you with affection and respect. So, leave your unhappiness and return to your husband.

46. "Adorn your body, o mother, and shine forth in all your glory. Let this day see the end of all the misfortunes of you and Rāma."

47. In this way the four pleaded before her at length; but when she heard them speak, Sītā's agony burst into flames.

48. Recounting before them all her travails in the forest, Sītā cried inconsolably in front of the four brave heroes.

49. Controlling her sorrow after a while, thus answered Sītā the chaste one:

50. "Listen, o Suṣeṇa, Hanumanta, and the king of Laṅkā! Listen, o Śatrughna, my husband's youngest brother!

51. "I have been living here all this while trying to forget my misfortunes. Why do you come now to disturb me by reminding me of my agony?

52. "If I still cherish the desire to return to Ayodhyā and partake of all the royal pleasures there, if I wish to behold the face of Rāma once more,

53. "If I still yearn to live in Rāma's house as his wife, then there never will be a woman more bereft of shame than me!

54. "I beg of you not to speak any more on this. Rāma has done me all the harm that is possible. Now nothing more remains for him to do.

55. "He who arranged to kill me with two infants in my womb, what does he intend to do now by taking me back again?

56. "I am living now only for the sake of my sons because they would be orphaned if I died.

57. "Listen, o Hanumanta, friend of the distressed! Banish all sorrow from your heart for my sake.

58. "Perform your own duties without any regret. But know that Rāma and I are now finally separated.

59. "He banished me because of the calumnies spread by evil men. So, I believe in my heart of hearts that my husband for me is Death incarnate.

60. "Now that he knows that I did not die in the forest, he will surely put me to death this time with his open sword in hand.

61. "Had I known earlier that Rāma was so hard-hearted, I would certainly have given up my life in Laṅkā.

62. "Only because of your assurance have I continued to live my miserable life there, or else would Rāma have found me alive to abuse me thus?

63. "Let any shameless woman have faith in Rāma after all this. But, I beg you brothers not to tell me more about him.

64. "The whole world now knows about my plight. So on my oath I bid you not to speak about this any more."

65. When the four heard these words of despair from Jānakī, they fell silent and none could muster the courage to speak to her again.

66. Māruti, Vibhīṣaṇa, Suṣeṇa, and Śatrughna sighed deeply and seemed to be at their wits' end.

67. So listen, all ye people, to this story of the *Rāmāyaṇa* and reflect on the shortness of human life.

68. Since unending suffering awaits us hereafter in the kingdom of Death, so the only panacea is to chant Rāma's name to save us from that fate.

69. *Dharma* has been robbed of all its support in this epoch of Kali. So *dharma* now finds shelter only at the feet of Hari.

70. Those who constantly chant the name of Rāma and Hari achieve in this earth all the virtue and merit.

71. Know this for certain that this is the essence of all the religious texts. Chanting Hari's name is the supreme faith to which all other religions are subservient.

72. Search all the old and new religious texts and you will find that only the virtues attained through chanting Hari's name can save you from the assault of Kali.

73. Under the influence of Kali, all the purity of body, soul, and wealth is lost. Even wisdom remains clouded.

74. Know that the chanting of Hari's name is the only appropriate dharma in the era of Kali. So Śaṅkara writes these verses. Raise your voices now and chant the praises of Rāma!

Adhyāya **18**

Dularī

1. When, dejected by Sītā's reply, the four brave heroes stood hanging down their heads in sorrow, the sage Vālmīki arrived there carrying fruits and wild roots.

2. With great respect and humility, they told the sage, "We have been sent hither by Rāghava to make earnest supplication on his behalf. He seeks your permission to allow us to take Sītā back to him.

3. "Rāma believes that he has become your son-in-law by virtue of being the husband of your daughter Sītā. You may if you please bring her over and get her married to him once again, thus giving him back his life.

4. "We cannot recount what suffering Rāma has undergone. So, put an end to his anxiety and restore Sītā to him. He will take her back after testing her chastity once again.

5. "We have failed to make the goddess Sītā respond to our plea. So, for Rāma's sake, persuade her to return in any manner you may deem fit."

6. Hearing this humble request from Rāma, Vālmīki spoke thus to Sītā: "O daughter of Janaka! Why should you reject the offer of Rāghava?

7. "Being a devoted wife, you know too well that your husband continues to be your god. So forgive him now for all his past errors. Whatever has befallen you two is according to the designs of destiny.

8. "So give your consent, I entreat you, and end your excessive resentment." So said the sage while Sītā stood apart and silently wept.

9. She continued to scratch the ground with her toe and made no reply. But Vālmīki understood that her mind was slowly regaining its composure.

10. Then to the four brave heroes Vālmīki spoke: "As desired by Rāma, I shall convince Sītā and bring her tomorrow morning before the congregation in Ayodhyā.

11. "When I bring her before Rāma, let the whole world witness how she goes through the test by fire. I too will take my oath there for Sītā's sake and the world will then know the truth."

12. Reassured by these words of the sage, the four brave heroes departed happily from thence. They faithfully narrated the whole story to Rāma when they bowed before him at Ayodhyā.

13. Then thus spoke Rāma to the assembled congregation "Hear me, o sages and all others present here! Vālmīki will bring Sītā tomorrow morning before this audience.

14. "She shall then go through the test by fire in full view of the assembly." With these words he dismissed the congregation. Then holding the hands of his two sons, he rose from his royal throne.

15. That night was for Rāma prolonged to an era. Waking or asleep, he could dream of none other than Sītā.

16. Waiting impatiently for the dawn, he got up several times to search the night sky for the sun. He would lie

down and then sit up again or would stretch out his arms to hug his sleeping sons.

17. Sighing constantly for Sītā, Rāma at last saw the night come to an end. At dawn he bathed and prayed and then at the assembly hastily assumed his place.

18. Anxious about their duties, Bharata, Lakṣmaṇa, and Śatrughna took their seats. All the great sages and the courtiers, led by the sage Vasiṣṭha, assumed their designated places.

19. And all the *rākṣasas*, bears, and monkeys surrounded Rāma to show their love for him. And a multitude of kings encircled him, bearing their precious offerings.

20. While Rāma was seated in that divine court, illuminating it with his presence, the great sage Vālmīki with Sītā by his side was hastening with quick steps towards the site.

21. Hearing that Sītā would go through the test by fire, all the gods and goddesses, led by Brahmā, were waiting eagerly on their aerial chariots, enveloping the whole sky.

22. And all the men and women stood in rows, eagerly awaiting the arrival of Sītā. They were all bursting with impatience to get a glimpse of their beloved mother Sītā.

Adhyāya 19

Chabi

1. The village of Bardovā, situated favourably on the banks of the Lauhitya,[65] was blessed with an abundance of fish and crops. In that village dwelt a headman by the name of Rājadhara who was the lotus of the Kāyastha clan.

2. His son Sūryavara, who was known for his charitable and courteous nature, was a much respected ruler of the place. He was the best amongst all the Barās[66] and his fame burns bright to this day. His two younger brothers bore the names Jayanta and Mādhava Doloi.

3. Sūryavara's son bore the fair name of Kusuma[vara],[67] and he was renowned and respected far and wide for excelling in charity and all other virtues. He was the best amongst all the Bhoumikas and none could be his equal.

4. His son Śaṅkara, the servant of Keśava,[68] who is childish in nature and bereft of wisdom, has composed in verse this *Uttarakāṇḍa*, which is the concluding part of the Rāmāyaṇa, in a variety of metrical forms, condensing and elaborating as required.

---

65 The ancient name of the Brahmaputra river.

66 Śaṅkaradeva's ancestors were from the powerful family of Bāra-Bhuñās. It is not clear whether "mahābarā" here refers to that family. [for details see Maheswar Neog, pp.48-58]

67 Śaṅkaradeva's father is better known as Kusumavara, though the name occurs as "Kusum" in this verse.

68 Keśava is another name for the supreme god Kṛṣṇa, Viṣṇu, or Hari.

5. Most humbly do I pray to the wise to pardon me for shouldering a task for which I am not competent. For it goes against the *dharma* of those who should bestow forgiveness on others to look for flaws in my composition and censure me.

6. My predecessor Mādhava Kandalī, a poet who is without a flaw, had rendered the story of Rāma into verse. In comparison, my effort is as futile as that of a rabbit desperately trying to produce the dung of an elephant.

7. You, who possess superior talents, learn how to derive infinite pleasure from listening to the story of Rāma. In this era of Kali, those who do not chant the name of Hari vainly search for paths which can only lead downwards.

8. Those who worship other gods and abandon Hari the supreme one, whose name alone can lead to salvation, are like the blind who abandon the boat and drown for a million births in the deep currents of this life.

9. Foolish are those who, born in the Kali age, abandon the supreme one's name and seek shelter in other religions. They are deceived by the divine lawmaker because they fail to realise that the ultimate panacea for all maladies is single-minded devotion to Hari.

10. Unable to grasp the counsel given in the ancient religious texts, they immerse themselves in other futile efforts and forsake the true path of chanting the name of Rāma. But know this that only by raising your voices and singing aloud the praises of Rāma can you achieve ultimate bliss and salvation.

Adhyāya 20

(*Sītā in Rāma's royal court*)

Pada

1. Immerse yourself in contemplation of the infinite and listen intently to the story of the *Rāmāyaṇa*.
2. Rāghava sat in his divine court awaiting the arrival of Sītā escorted by Vālmīki.
3. Meanwhile, unable to turn down the *ṛṣi*'s request, Jānakī at last agreed to follow him to the court.
4. So mortified was she by shame and indignity that she withdrew within herself and followed slowly in the footsteps of the sage.
5. Her garments, which were dyed in myrobalan juice, bore an ascetic saffron hue. They seemed to burden and encumber her reluctant steps.
6. Resenting the *ṛṣi*'s advice to appear before the assembly, Sītā seemed to retreat within her own body.
7. Her tender form, dear to behold, was so pierced by grief that, as she walked, her steps seemed to be covered in blood.
8. Thus Sītā the pure, the ever faithful wife, walked along with downcast eyes.

9. Unwilling to face the curious eyes of the beholders, she shrank in shame as the crowds followed her.

10. To get a glimpse of her whose memory they cherished, people ran out from homes with joyous hearts.

11. From the king's inner courtyard emerged Kauśalyā, accompanied by all the women who were eager to greet Sītā.

12. And all the maids of Sītā joyously cried out, "Our day has dawned at last, now that our goddess is here."

13. With great eagerness they ran towards her, but their joy withered away when they reached her side.

14. All the men and women wept and cried out in grief when they saw the plight of Jānakī.

15. "Alas, that destiny should have treated you thus, you who are so pure, the mother of the universe!

16. "How can we live when you suffer so?" cried the people, hanging their heads in sorrow.

17. Thus they followed her silently through the streets of the town, walking in twin rows, their voices choked in pain.

18. One could only hear sounds of lamentation all around as they followed in the footsteps of the goddess in anguish and pain.

19. She neither lifted her head nor looked up at the crowd; but, with her heart pounding wildly, she continued to walk forward in silence.

20. Not a word did she speak in response to the anxious queries, but, with her eyes fixed on the ground, walked along resolutely.

21. As, when the great seas were churned for the celestial nectar, the goddess Lakṣmī emerged from the waters and walked behind her divine father in order to wed Viṣṇu,

22. So did Sītā, the wedded wife of Rāma, follow Vālmīki with dignity and grace.

23. The crowds accompanied her all the way and at last they reached the sacrificial place.

24. As she climbed up slowly to the sacrificial ground with Vālmīki by her side, it seemed as though the moon's luminous orb had risen in the horizon.

25. Beholding the sage Vālmīki enter his presence, Rāma arose and knelt before him in reverence.

26. Holding the sacred *tulsi* leaves in his hand, the sage blessed him, chanting appropriate Vedic hymns.

27. Rāma accepted the sage's benedictions humbly, while Sītā stood apart silently.

28. Her head covered in modesty and her eyes downcast, she waited patiently while Vālmīki spoke:

29. "Listen, Rāma, Vasiṣṭha, and all ye illustrious ones assembled here! By bringing Sītā to Rāma, I have fulfilled my duty.

30. "Much have I striven to console and persuade the reluctant Sītā. Now let Rāma take the decision and put her to test as he desires.

31. "I assure you that Janaka's daughter is so faithful in her devotion to her husband that, even if you were to search, you would not be able to find a single flaw in her.

32. "So pure is her body that it can cleanse the mind of the beholder. Yet her heart has been wounded sorely by slander most unkind.

33. "In all the three realms you will not find a woman so pure who dreams of no other but her husband Rāghava.

34. "Hence, in front of the august audience today, I raise my arm to take a solemn oath on Jānakī's behalf:

35. "All the good deeds I performed in previous lives and all my meditations in this present life,

36. "All the severe ascetic vows that I have undertaken will prove to be naught if Sītā is found guilty.

37. "All the good deeds performed by my forefathers and all the merit I earned by pleasing my revered father will be in vain if Sītā is proven guilty.

38. "I have acquired knowledge of the past and the future through my meditation. No one in this world can hide anything from me.

39. "On the basis of that knowledge I have spoken the truth. Now judge her, o Rāma, as you may deem fit."

40. The assembly heard him and sang in unison Sītā's praises. Celestial music from above proclaimed her innocence.

41. As the heavens showered petals on Sītā's head, Rāma, with folded hands, addressed the sage:

42. "I know Sītā to be pure and sinless. Yet I have made her suffer because of the slanderous comments made by evil men.

43. "Now, if the court desires, I shall take her back because the oath uttered by the sage is more potent than a million tests.

44. "Now, since her innocence is established before the three worlds, may the faces of her detractors be forever smeared with soot."

45. Thus spoke Rāma and with his own hands he rolled out for the *ṛṣi* an appropriate mat amongst the sages.

46. Then he turned and beheld the sorrowful form of Jānakī. Clad in saffron raiment dyed in myrobalan juice, her appearance was like that of an ascetic.

47. Grief and austerity had so shrunk her lovely form that Rāma stared at her in disbelief and amazement.

48. Seeing her thus, tears seemed to well up in his eyes; but the son of Kauśalyā at once controlled himself and wiped them off.

49. All the people assembled there wept at the sight of Sītā's suffering. Sages, and celestials men cried out in anguish:

50. "See how our mother Sītā has escaped from the clutches of death! Now surely the misfortunes of Rāma and Sītā have come to an end!"

51. Thus whispered all the people, as the jewel of the Raghu clan gradually regained his composure.

Adhyāya 21

(*Sītā's anger and her entry into the netherworld*)

1. Showing loving concern for Sītā, Rāma then looked towards his brother, and Bharata at once offered her a golden chair.

2. All the three brothers then implored her to accept the seat; but the heartbroken Sītā, with her eyes cast down, stood apart in grief.

3. When Kauśalyā and the other elder ladies tried to reason with her, she neither looked up nor responded to anyone.

4. Anger, insult, and shame had so wounded Jānakī's heart that, as she stood, uncontrolled tears streamed down her cheeks.

5. Her anguished and storm-tossed soul seethed with rage, as she cast angry sidelong glances at her husband.

6. His loving gaze rebuffed by Sītā's angry looks, Raghunātha lowered his head and stood.

7. Afraid and ashamed to face Jānakī's wrath, Rāghava the destroyer of foes diffidently stood apart.

8. Remembering all her sorrows, Sītā burnt anew in rage and Rāma had no strength left to return her gaze.

9. Like a luminous flame of burning fire, Sītā's body trembled in grief and anger.

10. Seeing her thus, Rāma's heart was seized with great fear, and people stared at him in amazement.

11. So overcome was Sītā by her rage that the audience feared that she might reduce her husband to ashes with her curses.

12. Anticipating that a great catastrophe was about to strike the world, the sages and divines trembled in apprehension.

13. Silently she stood for a while with eyes cast down, sorrow and anger shaking her tender frame.

14. Then, turning her back upon Rāma in her anger, Sītā faced the audience without any fear.

15. She spoke thus to the assembly from the depths of her unhappy soul: "I know you will censure me when you hear my words.

16. "Everybody knows that Rāma is my husband and I am his wedded wife, faithful and obedient.

17. "He went to the forest when he was banished by his father and I too spent fourteen years by his side in exile.

18. "I am a woman who is not a free being because I am subjected to the will of a single master. Therefore, when Rāvaṇa abducted me, I could not protect myself.

19. "In Laṅkā, I wanted to put an end to this life of mine, but Hanumanta prevented me from doing so.

20. “So I lived and waited patiently for my Rāma. Then Rāma destroyed Rāvaṇa and brought me back.

21. “Then he tested my chastity by throwing me into the fire; but even that could not satisfy Rāghava’s suspicious mind.

22. “Only when the departed elders intervened on my behalf, was he persuaded to take me back with a clear heart.

23. “I have served Rāma with complete sincerity and devotion, knowing him to be my only lord and master.

24. “My husband is at the centre of all my yoga and meditations, all my sacrifices and prayers. Not even in my dreams have I ever thought of another.

25. “But, despite all this, his heart has turned against me. His kisses inflict wounds and his caresses are like blows.

26. “Fearing the calumnies spread against me by evil men, in a deceitful manner he sent me to exile again.

27. “Judge, o ye people, whether such deceitful conduct is appropriate for a husband. Why did he adopt such treacherous means in order to get rid of me?

28. “Instead of plotting to destroy my two babes in the womb, why did he not banish me before I had conceived them?

29. "My whole body burns in anger when I recount his deeds. He tried to take three livcs, minc and those of and my two unborn babes.

30. "After showing such disrespect for our lives, what more is left for Rāma to achieve now?

31. "Others may praise him for all his deeds. But Death incarnate is Rāma for me.

32. "I have never heard of a husband more unkind than he. O how can I again look upon him again with love and pride?"

33. Thus she spoke and shed bitter tears, as though with sorrow and pain her heart was seared.

34. She stood silently for a while, her face lowered in grief, while tears continued to stream down her cheeks.

35. The audience watched speechless as Sītā struggled to control the storm that raged within her.

36. When they saw the rising tide of anger in Sītā, the people feared that a great calamity was surely near at hand.

37. In unbearable pain, Sītā raved on thus: "If you place some grains of paddy on Rāma's treacherous tongue, they will instantly puff up and crackle in the heat!"[69]

38. Then, throwing an angry glance at Rāma, she enquired, "Why did you take me back only to discard me again?

---

69 This is a common Assamese proverb that indicates a false tongue.

39. "Alas! Had I known earlier about your cruel intentions I would have happily accepted death as my salvation.

40. "O most heartless of men whom I call my husband, you never could remember even a single virtue of mine.

41. "Evil tongues had slandered me and so you bound your hard heart with a thunderbolt and banished me.

42. "Am I your enemy who has caused you great harm that you could decree for me a punishment so harsh?

43. "Just like an ordinary man who suddenly discards his wife, you sent me to exile by sheer deception.

44. "Your evil behaviour is even worse than that of the *rākṣasas* because you tried to kill a woman defying all righteous codes of behaviour.

45. "Can you recall from amongst all your illustrious ancestors one instance of someone committing a sin so grave?

46. "By punishing me unjustly for a crime that I know not of, you have spread my infamy all through the world.

47. "Never will my name be cleared of such infamy as Rāma's unfair judgment has heaped upon me.

48. "Now what more pain do you wish to inflict on me by raking up my wounds and bringing me here?

49. "Am I a savage specimen for public display that you wish to subject thus to cruel banter someone who is already dead?

50. "Are you not satisfied yet to see me burn in the fire of agony that you wish to sprinkle pepper on my wounds again?

51. "If I now agree to live with you once again as your wedded wife, there never will be born a woman more devoid of shame than me.

52. "I am Sītā, the beloved daughter of King Janaka and the wife of the eldest son of King Daśaratha.

53. "My status was once that of King Rāma's queen; but it is you who have reduced me thus to ruin."

54. Thus spoke Jānakī as she sought her mother's lap. Lying on the ground, she moaned aloud and wept.

55. Sītā's sorrow moved the hearts of all the beholders. They cried out in grief, sharing her great sorrow.

56. Nothing could expel the shaft that pierced her heart, as slighted by Rāma, she writhed in agony and insult.

57. She spoke again in a voice that was choked with pain: "Never again will I set my eyes on the face of this Rāghava."

58. Then, turning to the Earth, with palms joined she prayed, "You who had brought me to this world, o my mother,

59. "Grant me this wish that I may never again hear the name of this Rāma. So, open your door, mother, and shelter me below.

60. "May the sun, moon, earth, and air bear witness, that, if I have truly preserved my purity and merit,

61. "If my soul has remained ever faithful to my husband, then open the door, mother, and shelter me below.

62. "If my devotion to my husband is beyond any doubt, if I have never known any other man but Rāma,

63. "Then let me be free from all infamy forever and let me enter your world, o my mother!

64. "If I have worshipped Rāma with my speech, mind, and body; if even in my dreams I have thought of none but he,

65. "Then shelter me in your bosom, o my mother, because I do not wish to behold a human face ever.

66. "With a firm mind have I worshipped Rāma as my lord and never accepted anyone else as my god,

67. "Yet my fate has rewarded me in this cruel manner. I do not wish to see his face again; open your door, o my mother.

68. "Let Rāma hark after me again and again but I will not wait any longer here on this earth.

69. "Totally withdrawn am I from the pleasures of thc world; open your door, mother, and shelter me below."

70. Thrice did Rāma's beloved cry out to her mother in distress, and the earth in response began to tremble and shake.

71. With a deafening sound the ground split open and from the deep crevice ascended a glittering throne.

72. Borne aloft on the shoulders of four *nāgakanyās*,[70] the earth had sent the splendid golden throne to bring home her beloved daughter.

73. The audience watched in silent wonder, and the divine spectacle struck fear in the hearts of all the forces of the valiant Hanumanta.

74. Rāma lost his senses, while Lakṣmaṇa, Bharata, and Śatrughna stood speechless with wonder.

75. Therefore, all ye people, learn from this story that life is brief, so crave not wealth or glory.

76. Seeing the mighty sorrow of Rāma and Sītā, lesser mortals should not seek salvation in domestic pleasure.

77. If you wish to escape from all the temptations of the world, seek your eternal salvation at the feet of the Lord.

78. Since none can foretell when death will come, so seek Kṛṣṇa's feet and sing the praises of Rāma.

---

70 *Nāgakanyā:* a daughter of the mythical Nāga-devatā, a serpent-god who rules in the netherworld. The *nāgakanyās* are said to be half-human and half-serpent.

Adhyāya 22

Dularī

1. Then, moved by the earth's affection, Sītā rose at once to her feet and bowed respectfully to Brahmā and all the gods.

2. Then she knelt down and, with her palms pressed together in supplication, she bowed respectfully to Vasiṣṭha and all the sages. Then, lifting her eyes, she began to speak again thus:

3. "May King Janaka be my father forever and may King Daśaratha be my *śvaśura*.[71] May Kauśalyā be my *śvāśu*[72] in all my lives to come.

4. "May all the bears and monkeys who have been my friends in need be like my sons in my future life, and may the three brave heroes Bharata, Lakṣmaṇa, and Śatrughna for ever be my *devara*.[73]

5. "In my dreams and in my senses I have never wished for any other husband except Rāma. So, may his two feet be my destination in every life to come.

6. "May these two lovely boys Lava and Kuśa always be my sons; but may such infamy and abuse as I have suffered never again be my lot."

---

71 *Śvaśura*: father-in-law

72 *Śvāśu*: mother-in-law

73 *Devara*: brother-in-law

7. Then addressing Kauśalyā respectfully, thus she made her entreaty for compassion: "Whatever has happened is my fate. Now I offer my two sons to you, mother, for their protection and care.

8. "Rāma has no faith in me, so what use does he have of these sons? Far from taking care of them, he would be ashamed to call them his own."

9. Then, hugging her two sons Kuśa and Lava, she cried her heart out and said: "sons, I could not look after you until you were older because Fate has punished me thus.

10. "I am so unfortunate that I had to desert you at this early age and this is the last time in this life that the three of us will be seeing each other. O that it should be so!

11. "Live together in harmony and do not quarrel amongst yourselves, my sons. Do not worry about me, because whatever has happened is my destined lot.

12. "With my life added to yours, may your lives be long. Let me depart from this world, carrying with me all your pain and sorrow. Sītā who bears the unlucky sign now takes leave from you to make her journey to the world below."

13. With these words she wept uncontrollably, holding the boys to her heart. But then she wiped her tears and once again regained her serenity.

14. Banishing her sorrow and worldly desires, the goddess Jānakī then steeled her heart and reverentially circumambulated Rāma thrice.

15. Then, touching her hair with the dust on his feet, she bowed to him and said: "My lord, may you now reign over your kingdom happily while I depart for the world below.[74]

16. "Forgive me for all that I said to you out of pain in my heart. It is because of my own deeds in the past that I am deprived of the chance to serve you in this life.

17. "Some sin committed by me in my past life must have deprived me of a husband like you." Then, with tears blinding her vision, she could speak no more.

18. Thus, with the words of farewell on her lips, she tearfully took her seat on the throne of resplendent beauty.

19. Mother Earth came up from below and, uttering sweet words of consolation to her daughter, she embraced her with affection. Legions of Nāga women worshipped Sītā with fragrant flowers, incense, and earthen lamps.

20. As Sītā entered the netherworld, sweet-smelling flowers were strewn on her head and victory music resounded from the kingdom of the Nāgas.

21. At that moment, when she abandoned her husband, sons, and all the well-wishers, her heart was filled with great apathy for the world. Sītā, the chaste one, thus vanished from sight as the moon disappears behind clouds.

22. When Sītā left for the netherworld, leaving Rāma to suffer his agonised heart, the distraught Rāma seemed to have lost all his senses as he looked up at the sky with bewilderment.

---

74 *Pātāla* or the world below the earth.

23. In his grief he saw darkness all around and, as the two sons of Sītā clung to him and wept, he collapsed unconscious on the ground.

24. Witnessing this amazing sight, all the assembled people were dumbstruck with fright. The sound of helpless lamentation reverberated from every direction as people saw the plight of Rāma and the two children.

25. All the gods and the sages could not control their sorrow. Rolling on the ground, they cried inconsolably, the bear and monkey legions.

26. The brave Bharata, Lakṣmaṇa, and Śatrughna fell on the ground and wept. Beating their chests with clenched fists, Kauśalyā and all the women cried out to Sītā:

27. "How could you bind your heart in steel to abandon sons like these? Where have you gone, o mother, setting our bodies on fire? Appear before us once again," they cried.

28. And all the maids leaned on each other and wailed in sorrow. The sound of their tumultuous cries reached the very vault of the heavens.

29. Listen, all ye courtiers, to the *Rāmāyaṇa* verses and observe how painful domestic life is. If Rāma and Sītā are fated to suffer like this, what pain could be in store for the common men like ye?

30. Time, like a serpent, swallows everyone and none can tell when death will come. So in this dark Kaliyuga, the only path to salvation is the chanting of the name of Rāma.

31. Being born a human being in the land of Bharata, why do you wish to waste it? Why sell a precious jewel foolishly at the price of mere glass?

32. Knowing this, abandon all other occupations and meditate on the glory of Viṣṇu. Thus writes Śaṅkara, the servant of Kṛṣṇa. Chant aloud the praises of Rāma.

Adhyāya 23

(Rāma's anger against the earth)

Pada

1. Here ends the story of Jānakī; but listen now to all the misfortune that befell Rāma hereafter.

2. Rāma regained his consciousness after a while and, like a madman, he cried out, "Sītā, where are you?"

3. He searched for her frantically amidst the courtiers in the assembly, crying out ,"Where are you my chaste, beloved Sītā?"

4. Like a crazy person lost in a maze, he called out to Lakṣmaṇa in desperation, "Run after her quickly, my beloved brother, and bring her back at once."

5. "O where has she gone, my friend, I cannot find her anywhere. Rāvaṇa must have abducted Sītā from here.

6. "O dear Hanumanta, go and search for her in Laṅkā. For I have lost my Sītā who is dearer to me than my life.

7. "Dear friend, Sugrīva, help me in this time of distress. Tell me truthfully who has taken away my Sītā.

8. "Build a bridge of stone, all my bear and monkey soldiers! I will not survive this time the loss of Sītā.

9. "My friend Vibhīṣaṇa, I got Sītā back the last time because of your help. Be my well-wisher now and tell me the truth again."

10. In grief and pain he wept and rolled on the ground, crying "O my heart will burst now and I will die of grief for the loss of my beloved friend."

11. In loud lamentation, he called upon Sītā again and again, "You have forsaken me, my beloved, to drown in this ocean of pain.

12. "Before I could look at you properly you have disappeared from my sight. O it is my own misfortune that now you are hidden from me for ever.

13. "My heart will burst, my beloved, I burn in the fire of grief. Return and speak to me just once, I entreat you most desperately.

14. "Now I know that you have left me forever," he said, and lost his consciousness once again.

15. Seeing Rāma's plight, people stopped grieving for Sītā and turned their attention to Rāma, thinking that he would die mourning for Sītā.

16. As they surrounded him and lamented over his condition, Rāma slowly sat up for a while, responding to their concern.

17. His heart pounding in distress, he said, "I know now for certain that she is hiding beneath the earth."

18. In agony over separation from his love, he knelt before Mother Earth with folded palms:

19. "O Mother Earth, since Sītā is your own beloved daughter, consider me your own son because of her.

20. "Sītā has gone to your house because she was angry with me. Please persuade her now and send her back to me.

21. "Or else, give me a little space in the netherworld so that my burning soul may find some solace.

22. "So that I may become worthy of Sītā and reunite with her, open your door to the netherworld, o mother!

23. "My whole body burns with the agony of separation. Do not try to rebuild a temple that is broken.

24. "It will behove a sage to take away life and then give it back. Such is not the appropriate action according to *dharma.*

25. "Longing for Sītā, my soul is burning in agony. How can you take away my life if you are my wife's mother?

26. "It seems you will not bring out Sītā so easily because I have indulged you too long by kneeling at your door!

27. "You have failed to gauge my power, o evil Earth-goddess! It appears that if I address you as kin you will not bow to my wishes!

28. "You are responsible for compelling me to abandon all my hesitation now! To which kingdom will you fly from my wrath if you do not give back Sītā?"

29. His whole body trembling with extreme distress, he picked up his bow and arrow and aimed his weapon at the earth's bosom.

30. Shaking his head in rage, he roared: "Wait, you goddess of the earth! A low-born can be taught to think clearly only by applying force.

31. "You may beg to be forgiven because I am your kin. But, after you have taken Sītā away from me, why should I accept you as my kin?

32. "You may forbid me to aim my arrow at a woman. But you should remember that it was I who killed the female *rākṣasa* named Tāḍakā.

33. "How can a kinsman be responsible if someone seeks her own death? Why have you dared to play with my feelings, wicked earth?

34. "If you wish to live, bring out Jānakī at once! Or else, o Earth-goddess, I shall tear your heart apart!

35. "I shall cut you up in pieces and send you to hell! I shall shoot my arrow to suck up all the waters from the seven seas!

36. "With my powerful arrow, this very instant I shall penetrate the seven layers of the netherworld and bring up Sītā to my side!

37. "Who can keep away my wife from me when I am dying of grief for her?

38. "The Digpālas of the universe be my witness now! It is not my fault that I am shooting this arrow to split open the earth and the netherworld."

39. With these words Rāma aimed his arrow at the earth while all the courtiers trembled in apprehension.

40. All the divines, *asuras*, and the Nāga inhabitants of the netherworld trembled in alarm. Then Brahmā came down seated on his swan and stood before Rāma.

41. "Abandon your anger, Rāma, and listen to my words. Learn to let your own genius recognise who you are.

42. "Know that this whole universe emanates from you. Yet you do not seem to know your own real self.

43. "What use is there in venting your anger on the earth? The *Rāmāyaṇa* was written even before your birth.

44. "What has been ordained by God is bound to take place. So your fame will inevitably spread over the entire universe.

45. "Devotion to you will increase in those who sing or listen to the recital of the *Rāmāyaṇa.*

46. "The future will at once unravel in front of you when Lava and Kuśa sing the concluding verses of their *Rāmāyaṇa* song.

47. "Things will come to pass as they are destined to. So does not befit your divinity to be angry with the earth.

48. "Abandon your grief for Sītā because you must not forget that Rāma is the lord of the universe.

49. "Remember that you attained this incarnation in order to lessen the burden of this earth. So control your anger, my dear Rāma."

50. In response to these reassuring words of Brahmā, Rāma then bowed before him respectfully.

51. Hearing Brahmā's comforting words, he set aside his bow and arrow and regained his composure.

52. Thus calming Rāma's anguished heart with his soothing words, Brahmā departed on his swan-chariot for his heavenly abode.

53. With tearful eyes, holding his two sons to his heart, Rāma then sat down again on his throne.

54. But the memory of Sītā still made him sigh and, in constant pain, he bent down his head.

55. Then a voice suddenly spoke out from the world below to console Rāma's heart, which was distraught with sorrow.

Adhyāya **24**

(Voice from the Pātāla speaks to Śrī Rāma)

1. "Compose yourself, dear Rāma, and give up your sorrow. For it is no longer possible for you to see Sītā again.

2. "She has sought refuge in this netherworld out of extreme despair. So, of her two sons only you can now take good care.

3. "Do not fret about Jānakī, dear Rāma. For you will not get her again in your present incarnation.

4. "The chaste Sītā is being worshipped with great reverence by the inhabitants of the world below and she will be safe there in their constant care.

5. "The divines from heaven too come here with incense and fragrant flowers to offer their appropriate prayers to Sītā.

6. "Sītā has become the principal goddess of the seven worlds below and all the devotees beg for divine blessings from her now.

7. "So do not grieve for her any more, but show your concern for her two sons now.

8. "The *Rāmāyaṇa* composed by Vālmīki is like a Veda. If you listen to it attentively you can attain great solace.

9. "This scriptural text was composed even before you were born. So events will unfold as they have been ordained to."

10. Thus spoke the voice from the world below and Rāma heard and grasped the truth of those words.

11. Bowing respectfully to Vālmīki he said: " To the rest of the story let us listen tomorrow."

12. Then he dismissed the court and rose from his throne. But when he beheld the faces of his two sons, sorrow once again wrenched at his heart.

13. Holding the two sons to his heart, he lay down to sleep; but the memory of Sītā brought back uncontrollable tears that drenched his chest.

14. Unable to calm his agitated mind, he sighed aloud and called out to Sītā even in his dream.

15. Thus tossing and turning on his bed, he awaited the morn and at the crack of dawn he was ready to assume his place in the court.

16. There he sat and listened to the last part of the story of the *Uttarakāṇḍa* until the moment when Sītā entered the world below.

17. He heard them when they narrated how Rāma became distraught with anger and grief and how Brahmā appeared to soothe his rage.

18. Then he heard how the voice of the earth-goddess emanated from the world below and how she consoled him with her soothing words.

19. When he heard them sing about all these events, Rāma's soul at last attained some serenity and peace.

20. But when the twins took up the tale again, Vālmīki stopped them, saying that the rest of the story would cause the people great pain.

21. "So, enough for now because Rāma need not hear any more." Thus forbidden by the sage, the twins stopped their song.

22. The assembly was wonderstruck by the story of the *Rāmāyaṇa* which was written even before the birth of Rāma.

23. Loudly they raised their voices with joy in their hearts: "We praise you o great Vālmīki, long may your fame last!"

24. Though Rāma was surrounded by all his courtiers and brothers, yet their assurance was not enough to remove his sorrow.

25. Thinking of Jānakī, he lived with a broken heart and lost all interest in food and drink.

26. He lived thus with his mournful thoughts, never regaining his happiness and peace of mind.

27. As misfortune came to him one after another, let us end this section of the Pātālīkhaṇḍa.[75]

28. All ye people who are listening to the verses of the *Rāmāyaṇa* realise how full of hazards is this domestic life of man.

29. If such was the tragic fate of Rāma and Sītā, judge how difficult it is for others to attain happiness here.

30. Life on this earth is illusory. All wealth and friends are ephemeral.

---

75 *Pātālīkhaṇḍa*: refers to the first half of the *Uttarakāṇḍa* which deals with Sītā's entry into the world below. The second half of this *kāṇḍa* is called the *Svargakhaṇḍa*, from *Adhyāya* 25.

31. Although you have seen how your friends have preceded you to death's abode, yet you do not fear for your own impending fate.

32. Stop and think now of how you may escape from the grip of Time. Devotion to Viṣṇu is the only path to salvation.

33. His supreme name is the only friend you will have in the life after death. So abandon all other thought and chant incessasantly His name.

BIBLIOGRAPHY

Aklujkar, Vidyut 'Crying Dogs and Laughing Trees in Rama's Kingdom: Self-reflexivity in *Ananda Ramayana*,' in Paula Richman (ed.) 2000 (reprint 2012). *Questioning Ramayana: A South Asian Tradition*, New Delhi: Oxford University Press.

Altekar, A.S. 1938. 'The Position of Women in Hindu Civilization: Retrospect and Prospect.' in Kumkum Roy (ed.) 1999. *Women in Early Indian Societies*, New Delhi: Manohar.

Barua, Kanaklal. 1933. *Early History of Kamarupa*, published by the author, Shillong.

Bhattacharya, Debendranath. 2008. (translator) *Kalikapurana* Guwahati: Banimandir.

Bhavabhuti. 1962. *Uttararamacarita*, translated by P.V. Kane and C.N. Joshi, Delhi: Motilal Banarasidass.

Bhuyan, Surya Kumar. 1984, (ed.) *Kachari Buranji*, DHAS: Guwahati.

Bora, Lilavati Saikia. 1993. *Madhava Kandalir Ramayanar Bhasha*, Jorhat: Asam Sahitya Sabha.

—. (ed). 2007. *Badu Candidasar Srikrishnakirtan*, Guwahati: Asam Prakashan Parishad, Guwahati.

Brown, Nathan. (ed.) 1983. *The Orunodoi* 1846-1854. (Compiled and re-edited by Maheshwar Neog) Guwahati: Publication Board Assam.

Chakravarti, Uma. 1999. 'Beyond the Altekarian Paradigm: Towards a New Understanding of Gender Relations in Early Indian History,' in Kumkum Roy (ed.) *Women in Early Indian Societies.*

Chakravarty, Ajaykumar. 1996. (ed.) Hem Saraswati's *Pracin Puthi*, New Delhi: Sahitya Akademi.

Chattopadhyaya, B.D. 2017. *The Concept of Bharatavarsha and Other Essays*. Ranikhet: Permanent Black.

Chatterji, Suniti Kumar. 1966. Artavallabha Mahanti Memorial Lectures, First Series, Orissa Sahitya Akademi: Bhubaneswar.

Endle, Rev. Sidney. 1911. *The Kacharis*, London: Macmillan and Co.

Gait, Edward. 1933. *History of Assam*, Calcutta: Thacker Spink and Co.

Goldman, Sally J. Sutherland. 2000. 'The Voice of Sita in Valmiki's Sundarakanda,' in Paula Richman (ed.) 2000 (reprinted 2012) *Questioning Ramayanas: A South Asian Tradition*. New Delhi: Oxford University Press.

Goswami, Dev and Basanta Kumar. 1994. *A Critical Study of the Ramayana Tradition of Assam*. Punthi Pustak: Calcutta.

Goswami, Hemchandra. 1930. *Descriptive Catalogue of Assamese Manuscripts*, University of Calcutta.

Goswami, Indira. 1996. *Ramayana, from Ganga to Brahmaputra*. Delhi: B.R. Publishing Corporation.

Kakati, Banikanta. 1941. *Assamese, its Formation and Development*. Guwahati: DHAS.

—. (ed.) 1953. *Aspects of Early Assamese Literature*, Gauhati University.

Khan, Ahmed and Amanatulla Choudhury. 1910. 'Koch Biharar Prachin Bhasha,' *Paricharika*, Sravan-Bhadra, 1326 (1910), translated from Bangla by Anjan Sarma, in B. Mahanta (ed.) 2015. *Shukladhwaja*, Guwahati: Bhabani Books.

—. 1936. *Kochbiharar Itihas*, translated from Bangla by Anjan Sarma, 2014. Guwahati: Bhabani Books.

Lekharu, Upendrachandra. (ed.) 2006. *Katha Guru Carita*, Guwahati: Dattabarua,

Macfie, John Mandeville. 1930. *The Ramayana of Tulsidas or the Bible of Northern India*, Edinburgh: T&T Clark.

Mahanta, Bapchandra. 1987. *Aitihasik Patabhumit Mahapurush Sankaradeva*, Guwahati.

Misra, Tilottoma. 2004. 'Marriage, Conjugal Norms and the Reformist Agenda in Nineteenth Century Assam, in *Man and Society: A Journal of North East Studies*, Volume 1, Number 1, Spring 2004, ICSSR-NERC, Shillong.

—. 2007. (translator and editor) *Ramnabami-Natak: The Story of Ram and Nabami*, New Delhi: Oxford University Press.

—. 2015. 'Sita's Voice in the Assamese Ramayana', *Jadavpur Journal of Comparative Literature*, Volume 51, 2015, Department of Comparative Literature, Kolkata: Jadavpur University.

—. 2016. 'Literary Cultures in North-East India: Shrinking Frontiers', [special article], *Economic and Political Weekly*, 51:38.

Nath Gogoi, Jahnabi. 2009-2010. 'Women, Religion and Society in Assam: Reflections from a Medieval Biographical Work', in Proceedings of the Indian History Congress, 2009-2010, Vol. 70 (2009-2010), pp. 329-337, Indian History Congress.

Neog, Maheswar. 1959. 'Assamese Literature before Sankaradeva,' in Banikanta Kakati (ed.) *Aspects of Early Assamese Literature*, Guwahati University.

—. 1963. *Sri Sri Sankaradeva*. Guwahati: Lawyers' Book Stall.

—. 1965. *Early History of the Vaisnava Faith and Movement in Assam*, Guwahati: Lawyers' Book Stall.

—. 1974. *Prachya Shasanavali*. Guwahati: Assam Publication Board.

Pollock, Sheldon. 2006. *The Language of the Gods in the World of Men: Sanskrit, Culture and Power in Premodern India*. Berkeley: University of California Press.

Roy, Kumkum. 1999. (ed.) *Women in Early Indian Societies*. Delhi: Manohar.

Sabin Alun. 1986. *The Karbi Ramayana* (collected, translated and printed by Samsingh Hanse) Assam Sahitya Sabha.

Sarma, Dimbeswar. 1981. (ed.) *Kamarupasasanavali*, Guwahati: Publication Board.

Sarma, Nabin Chandra. 1991. *The Vaisnavite Poets of North-Eastern India: Ananta Kandali*, Calcutta: Punthi-Pustak.

Sarma, Satyendranath. 1972. *Epics and Puranas in Early Assamese Literature*, Guwahati: Baniprakash.

——. 1981 (1986). *Asamiya Sahityar Samikshatmak Itibritta* Guwahati: Saumar Printing and Publishing.

——. 1984. *Ramayanar Itibritta*. Dibrugarh University.

Shastri, Biswanarayan. 1980 (reprint 2009). 'The Ramayana in Assamese Literature.' in V. Raghavan (ed.) *The Ramayana Tradition in Asia*, New Delhi: Sahitya Akademi.

Smith, William L. 'The Wrath of Sita: Sankaradeva's Uttarakanda,' www.atributetosankaradeva.org (accessed on 10.6.2017)

Thakuria, Ramcharan. 1983. 'The Ramayana of Madhava Kandali: A Text-critical and Historical Study of Four Kandas of Ramayana, viz., Ayodhya, Aranya, Kiskindhya, and Sundara Kandas,' unpublished thesis, Gauhati University.

Ramayana Texts

Bardalai, Madhavchandra. (ed.) 1899. *Sampurna Asamiya Sat-kanda Ramayana*, Barpeta.

Chaudhury, Prasannalal. 1941. *Asamiya Sat-kanda Ramayana*, Barpeta.

Datta Barua, Harinarayan. (ed.) 1952, 1968. *Sapta-kanda Ramayana*, Nalbari.

Goldman Robert, P. and Sally J.S. Goldman. (transl.) 2007. *The Ramayana of Valmiki, Vol. V; Sundarakanda*, Delhi: Motilal Banarasidass.

——.and Barend A. van Nooten. 2010. *The Ramayana of Valmiki, Vol VI: Yuddhakanda*, Sarga 104, Delhi: Motilal Banarasidass.

Nagar, Shanti Lal. (transl.) 2000. *Madhava Kandali Ramayana*, in two volumes, New Delhi: Munshiram Manoharlal.

Pollock, Sheldon. (transl.) 2008. *Ramayana of Valmiki, Vol II, Ayodhyakanda*, New York: New York University Press.

——. 1984. 2007.*The Ramayana of Valmiki, Vol.III, Aranyakanda*, New Jersey: Princeton University Press; Delhi: Motilal Banarsidass.

Sarma, Kanakchandra. (ed.) 1941. *Kabiraj Madhavakandali Biracita Ramayana*, Bebejia, (reprinted Guwahati: Lawyers' Book Stall, Guwahati, 1998).

Srimad Valmikiya Ramayana, Vol. 2, (Sanskrit with Hindi translations), Gita Press, Gorakhpur, 47th edition.

Varma, Navarun. (transl). 1979. *Madhava Kandali Ramayana* (in Assamese and Hindi), Lucknow: Bhuvan Vani Trust.